An AMERICAN BIBLE

AN

AMERICAN BIBLE

A History of the Good Book in the United States,

1777-1880

PAUL C. GUTJAHR

STANFORD UNIVERSITY PRESS

STANFORD, CALIFORNIA

Stanford University Press
Stanford, California
© 1999 by the Board of Trustees of the
Leland Stanford Junior University
Printed in the United States of America
CIP data appear at the end of the book

For Cathy

Yet Be most proud of that which I compile,
Whose influence is thine and born of thee.
In others' works thou dost but mend the style,
And arts with thy sweet graces graced be;
But thou art all my art and dost advance
As high as learning my rude ignorance.

—William Shakespeare

Acknowledgments

Every book has a history, and this one is no exception. Here, history begins with two of my junior high school teachers: Walter Newcomb who taught me that there is something sacred about literature, and Giles Florence Jr. who taught me something about sacred literature. My college career is also marked by professors who took a deep personal interest in my education. Jay Fliegelman has had such a profound influence on my scholarly career that I find it impossible to encapsulate. Suffice it to say, Jay has been an incredible mentor and friend for nearly twenty years.

I owe an equally unpayable debt to Wayne Franklin, who sponsored me in myriad ways through my doctoral studies and ultimately directed the dissertation behind this book. Wayne believed in me, and this project, to a degree I never seemed able to muster within myself. I only hope I might be able to offer the same kind of dedicated friendship to my own students and colleagues.

The members of my doctoral committee were also exemplary. No person could hope for a better committee member than Ken Cmiel whose humor, practical savvy, and command of American history and historiography pushed this project to become more ambitious, more interesting, and ultimately a lot more fun than I could have ever envisioned on my own. Bob Sayre, John Peters, and Dwight Bozeman gave of themselves in ways that made me truly glad I chose to pursue a degree in American Studies, where dissertation committee members from five different departments could sponsor a project that never fit neatly into disciplinary categories.

Other scholars have been stunningly generous with their time and insight. As readers for the press, Lawrence Buell and David Hall provided wonderful criticisms and new avenues of inquiry. Mark Noll, who I believe to be the great modern-day pioneer of studies of the bible in American culture, never failed to give both his encouragement and his expertise. Steve Stein offered not only timely and sound advice, but his friendship. David Morgan, Richard Hutson, and Terry Belanger were all of immeasurable help in refining my ideas on how visual and verbal texts interact. Ed Mc-Clellan and Milton Gaither opened whole new worlds to me in the area of American moral education. Michael Zinman and Keith Arbour were of immense help with the subscription sales aspect of American Bible production. Leon Jackson continually gave me insights and tidbits on early American bible production, including the Duganne poem which prefaces the volume. David Nord, Shirley Wajda, Michael Winship, and David Nordloh never tired of answering a ceaseless stream of questions about everything from patent rights on American photo albums to the evolution of a particular printer's watermark.

Then there are the countless friends who cheered me on as I stumbled through the seemingly Bataan-Death-March-like dissertation process. Bob Brown sat through many a dinner listening to, and helping me refine, almost every idea contained in this book. For their wisdom, support, and laughter, I will also be forever grateful to Alex Van Riesen, Matt and Christina Johnson, Grant Smith, Pete Simonson, Catherine Lewis, Marnie Schroer, Matt Pustz, John Gregg, Dan Nathan, Scott (the Bear) Juengel, and Jon Olesberg.

Aside from the endless generosity of my parents and my wife (who put me through graduate school), a number of sources have provided funding for this project. Under the direction of Skip Stout and Jon Butler, the Yale Program in Religion and American History endowed by the Pew Foundation believed enough in this project to give me both summer dissertation and first book grants. The Beinecke Rare Book and Manuscript Library, as well as the Yale Divinity School Library, then helped me make good use of these fellowships. The Massachusetts Historical Society awarded me a Mellon Fellowship to plumb the depths of its magnificent collections. The University of Iowa awarded me a one-year Seashore Dissertation Fellowship, and the English Department at Indiana University has helped fund both permissions and research trips to complete this manuscript. Certain lines of inquiry on *The Book of Mormon* in the last chapter first appeared in the journal *ATQ*, while the journal *Mosaic* printed my earliest examination of *Ben-Hur*. Small sections of these early works are revised here and are reprinted by permission.

I have also experienced tremendous generosity from various institutions and their staffs. Helen Tartar at Stanford Press pursued this manuscript with an aggressiveness at which I can only marvel. I, for one, hope she bet on a winner. Stacey Lynn and Karen Lamoreux carried on their editorial duties with such enthusiasm, kindness, and professionalism that this book is infinitely better because of their dedication and expertise.

The American Bible Society has been so kind that I want to do another project that uses its collections simply to spend more time with its staff. It is no exaggeration to say that without the help of Peter Wosh, Mary Ellen Gleason, Mary Cordato, Maria Deptula, and Liana Lupas this book would not exist. Warren Platt of the New York Public Library also went far beyond the call of duty in helping me research various lines of inquiry.

Other libraries whose wonderful staffs helped make this project possible include the Lilly Library, the Newberry Library, the Library Company of Philadelphia, the American Antiquarian Society, the John Pierpont Morgan Library, and the main libraries at Indiana University, Stanford University, and the University of Iowa.

Finally, I would like to thank my family. With their inexhaustible love, my parents and my sister, Karen, have helped me battle myriad academic dragons on the way to completing this book. My most sincere gratitude, however, is reserved for my wife. Our sons, Isaac and Jeremiah, are fortunate enough to be too young to remember the labor pains that birthed this book; but my wife, Cathy, is not. More than any other person, she has sweated and sacrificed to see this project come to completion. In her love for me and my dreams, she constantly and patiently embodies the words we sing to our sons each night as we put them to bed:

'Tis grace that brought me safe thus far, and grace will lead me home.

P.C.G.

Contents

Figures

'Tis no man's fault—(I clear friend Harper of it),
That foreign books are cheap, and pay a profit;
He did not hire Dumas, or Paul de Kock,
To jest at truth—at decency to mock;
A publisher who'd mend his country's morals,
With his own bread and butter madly quarrels.
He's not to know if books work ill or well—
The question he must ask, is—"will it sell?"
And if today he prints a moral libel,
Tomorrow squares the account—he prints a bible!

—A. J. H. Duganne, 1851

Note: The Bible is a unique book in Western culture, reflected by the frequent capitalization of the word *Bible* in general usage. I differ slightly from this practice—by capitalizing the word *Bible* only when I refer to the work itself, but not when I speak of bibles collectively.

An AMERICAN BIBLE

PREFACE

In the beginning was the Word. So begins the Gospel of John, and so could begin any description of early American print culture. Dating back to the Puritans, Americans have long enjoyed the nickname "A People of the Book."[1] A religiously bent printing industry coupled with a Protestant penchant for teaching literacy made the Bible the most imported, most printed, most distributed, and most read written text in North America up through the nineteenth century. For well over two hundred years, if any book touched the lives of Americans, odds are it was a bible. When it came to the printed word, early Americans often gloried in the fact that they were a people who "knew much of their bible" and "little besides."[2]

One wonders what happened. Where once the Bible's language, stories, and physical production dominated the world of American print—creating countless idioms, metaphors, narrative themes, and publishing innovations—today it appears that Americans need to be reminded of the Bible's importance.[3] While Edward Everett began his famous oration on the Bible in 1850 freely admitting that it was "hopeless" and "unprofitable" to say anything new on the topic of the Bible's centrality in American thought and life, E. D. Hirsch, Jr., in his 1988 best-selling tome on what constitutes cultural literacy in America, felt it necessary to point out the importance of the Bible in the country's literary and cultural traditions.[4] When formerly bibles were regularly read in school classrooms and treated as the urtext of all important knowledge, now teachers are forbidden to even display a bible on their desks.[5] And the invincibility of bible sales also seems to be changing. Recently, bible publishers have had to face the return of hundreds of thousands of bibles as American demand wavers.[6]

Providing answers for the drift of the Bible from the center of America's print culture has proved a difficult task, made all the more vexatious by what Mark Noll has called the "shocking" lack of scholarly work done "describing the Bible in America."[7] The reasons for such a drift are incredibly complex. Within this complexity, however, certain central threads can be traced to help explain how a book that was absolutely foundational in our country's early written and oral cultures slid from its elemental role. In a rare analytical attempt to explain the decline of the Bible's influence in the United States, the religious historian Grant Wacker has argued that, for the ordinary American, "the 1920s and 1930s seem to have been the decisive years" that marked a transition from an American ethos based on the Bible's teaching to a culture less aware of, less interested in, and less convinced by the Sacred Scriptures.[8] Wacker claims that this transition actually had its roots in the educated theological elite of the late nineteenth century who, influenced by German biblical criticism, began to view and teach the Bible as "a mixture of Scripture and literature." Or, put another way, they held the Bible to be "a human as well as a divine document."[9] The following generation of ordinary Americans bore the fruit of the seed sown by these intellectuals, and America's belief in, and use for, the Sacred Scriptures seemed to recede. While Wacker's essay makes a convincing case for the importance of considering the late nineteenth century as a watershed period in American biblicism, the roots of the Bible's deteriorating presence in the United States are found much earlier.

The absolute dominance the Bible enjoyed in American print culture began to slip in the opening decades of the nineteenth century. While the Bible was once regarded as "the book;—the book of books," as early as 1817 one writer bemoaned the fact that the "prodigious multiplication of books" in the United States had already "jostled the Bible from its place, or buried it from notice; so that those who formerly read it because it was the only volume they possessed, might be surprised to find, if they were now alive, with how many [people] it is the only volume which is not worth possessing."[10] Not everyone was so pessimistic about the place of the Bible in American print culture, but a comment, no matter how accurate, about the "jostled" position of the Bible is telling.

As the nineteenth century unfolded, radical changes in printing technology, educational practices, reading tastes, transportation networks, labor relations, demographics, political institutions, and religious traditions combined to erode the Bible's "classic preeminence."[11] Whereas printed material had been relatively scarce at the time of the American Revolution, a century later American publishers were producing, and Americans were reading, hundreds of thousands of books, journals, newspapers, magazines, and tracts. Such explosive growth in the area of print threatened the position of the Bible as America's most read and revered written text. While many still believed it to be "the book of books," it was equally true that the Bible was increasingly a book among books.

In considering the Bible amid the increasingly plentiful and complex print culture of nineteenth-century America one discovers both a profound shift and a profound paradox. On the one hand, the heady years of the Second Great Awakening, the meteoric rise of local and national bible societies, the emergence of powerful publishing enterprises, and the widespread use of bibles as school texts gave the Bible an unprecedentedly large readership and influence. More bibles were distributed to Americans in the first three quarters of the nineteenth century than ever before. On the other hand, by the 1880s it was already an oft-repeated lamentation that "the Bible does not now hold that place . . . which it formerly held. . . . It no longer commands the reverence or the faith which it once inspired as *The* Book, the Word of God, the sun of the moral and intellectual world, 'the fountain light of all our day, the master light of all our seeing.'"[12] Although the Bible remained the country's most-produced and most-distributed text even in the closing decades of the nineteenth century, it had lost its undisputed command as America's chief written text. Sheer numbers had not insured its ascendancy. In fact, the paradox deepens as one discovers that these prodigious numbers may well have contributed to the Bible's shifting role in American culture.

It is my contention that in order to discover the roots of the Bible's move from the center of the United States' print culture, one must begin with the book—or more accurately, the books themselves. Scholars have paid stunningly little attention to "the book" when considering "the Book." The little scholarship that has been done on the Bible's role in the United States has explored the Bible in terms of American theology, genteel society, economics, politics, and educational practices.[13] The vast majority of such scholarship ignores a key fact, namely that the English Bible in America was never a simple, uniform entity. When scholars have noted the presence of the Bible in American culture, they have treated it as a volume containing a kind of mythic core text, entirely overlooking the reality that the different English translations, commentaries, illustrations, and bindings significantly complicate any understanding of the Bible's influence in American society.[14] Once it began to be printed in the United States, it soon underwent a great many textual revisions and changes in format, as different editors and publishers appropriated it to meet a wide range of changing ideologic and economic demands. By 1880, nearly two thousand different editions of the Bible were available to Americans.[15]

This study argues that the reasons for the diminishing role of the Bible in American print culture are largely founded and revealed in the evolving content and packaging of the Holy Scriptures. The Bible's myriad mutations played an enormous, and hitherto almost entirely ignored, role in determining the Bible's place in American hearts and minds.

Needless to say, the development of so many different versions of the Scriptures is a matter of considerable complexity. At its core, however, one finds—pounding like a heartbeat—a fervent longing to keep the Bible the country's most physically and intellectually accessible text. This book examines the principal strategies that various, often antagonistic, con-

3

stituencies used in their attempts to maintain the Bible's "preeminence" in the country's print culture.[16] Those involved in these struggles for preeminence came from a wide range of backgrounds, vocations, and economic levels. Ministers, politicians, businessmen, reformers, educators, and housewives, as well as publishers, artists, and booksellers dedicated themselves to seeing the Bible remain the country's most read and revered text. In exploring their pursuit of biblical preeminence, one uncovers vital insights to the changing role of the Bible in the United States.

This study analyzes this quest for preeminence by considering five different aspects of bible production, distribution, and reception, each aspect being set forth in one of the book's five chapters.

Enforcing the belief that one must attempt to understand the Bible as a physical artifact in its own commercial milieu to grasp its role in the larger culture, Chapter 1 examines various ways of producing and distributing the Bible in the United States, ultimately focusing on the attempts by the American Bible Society to provide a Bible for every household in America. The Society sought preeminence for the Bible through a brute force approach, believing that by making the Bible the most accessible text in the United States, they would make it the country's most influential text. This strategy led to the production and circulation of hundreds of thousands of bibles, but it also created a massive diversification of bible editions as publishers sought to compete with the ever cheaper editions of Scripture offered by the mammoth American Bible Society. In attempting to woo buyers and readers to their bible editions, American publishers helped erode the timeless, changeless aura surrounding "the Book" by making it "the books."

Competition among bible publishers created an ever-expanding array of bible packaging. Bindings became more elaborate, page formatting diversified, and bible illustrations multiplied. Chapter 2 examines how different "readings" of bible bindings and bible illustrations changed both why people bought bibles and how they interpreted the bibles they bought. Expensive materials could make bibles markers of gentility rather than a book to be read, and illustrations could subvert or obscure the meanings of the passages they were supposed to illuminate. Consequently, publishers' battles to foreground different bible editions in the marketplace created books in which the meaning of the Word was radically altered by its very presentation.

While bindings, illustrations, and the vast array of tables, marginal commentaries, and extended introductory material helped guide one's interpretation of the scriptural text, a new wave of work revising the Bible's central text began. Chapter 3 looks at the new English translations that appeared throughout the nineteenth century fostered by debates over manuscript accuracy, as well as by differing opinions on how the meaning of the original text might be conveyed to contemporary readers. As Unitarians, Baptists, Disciples of Christ, and others argued over the trustworthiness of the Bible's central text and the limits of language translation, Americans became painfully aware that what they had hitherto viewed as a divinely unmediated text was, in fact, heavily influenced by the fallible nature of human intervention.

As debates raged over the purity of the Protestant bible's core text, new concerns arose over the relationship of that purity to the nation's public institutions. Chapter 4 examines the diminishing role of the Bible in the nation's schools. The once largely homogenous composition of the United States began to change in the early years of the nineteenth century as wave after wave of immigrants flooded into the country. Looming large among these numbers were Catholic immigrants from Ireland, Germany, and Italy who helped make Roman Catholicism the largest single denomination by the end of the nineteenth century.[17] No longer was the United States a clearly Protestant country, and the nation's public institutions had to deal with this fact. The controversies that emerged in the midst of the rise of American Catholicism found one of their bloodiest battlegrounds in American public education, where hundreds of Americans would die, be injured, or lose property as various educational reformers, government officials, and religious factions attempted to redefine the role of the Bible in American culture.

Not everyone attempted to determine the place of the Bible in American culture by addressing institutional concerns; some approached the topic of winning attention to the Bible through new rhetorical strategies. Chapter 5, the final chapter, looks at how a number of authors, publishers, and clergymen began transforming the Bible's story into less sacred forms of print to turn American readers once again to the Bible. As narrative forms such as the novel became more popular with the American reading public, American Protestants decided to commingle scriptural truth and fictional fancy in order to attract their countrymen to the Bible's message. Perhaps the most popular manifestation of this mixture was the nineteenth-century genre of the lives of Christ. Increasingly fictionalized lives of Christ offered Americans both a new way to imagine themselves as characters in the Bible's story, as well as a means to avoid the density and complexity of that story. Consequently, an attempt to emphasize the Bible's story resulted in de-emphasizing the Bible itself.

Because the Bible "has been nearly omnipresent in the nation's past," any study of it in American culture demands certain parameters to confine the enormity of the topic.[18] Even with my aforementioned focus on the evolution of the actual book itself, I have imposed chronological, lingual, and geographic boundaries upon this study. One will quickly discover that in many ways this book is a treatise painted in broad strokes. So little work has been done on the Bible's place in American print culture, I thought it best to concentrate on large central issues. Certainly, more work on the Bible under rubrics such as race, gender, class, regionalism, and religious tradition needs to be done. This study is simply an attempt to further the nascent discussion of the immense, and immensely important, place of the Bible in various segments of early American culture.

The study's temporal boundary begins in 1777, while its lingual boundary is confined to English bible editions. I begin in 1777 because it marks the appearance of the first American edition of an English New Testament. Before the American Revolution, the British Crown held a royal copyright on the Scriptures that forbade their publication in America.[19] I conclude with the advent of the first widely produced and accepted textual revision of the Scriptures in 1881, the Revised Version. The Revised Version was the first "authorized" revision of the King James Version, and its appearance was both the publishing event of the century and a moment of pivotal transition when no one version of the Scriptures could any longer claim near universal American Protestant allegiance. Within this time frame, I concern myself solely with English versions of the Scriptures. I make this choice because English was the country's most prevalent language, and American bible production through 1880 overwhelmingly reflects this linguistic preference. Yet, it is vitally important to remember that beginning with John Eliot's famous Indian Bible in 1663, scores of foreign and Native American language editions of the Bible were produced in the United States.[20] Such translation work raises its own unique and complicated issues, making it too large a topic to be dealt with meaningfully here.

Finally, the geographic center of gravity for this study is the Northeastern United States. This region takes center stage because only a little more than three percent of the nearly two thousand editions of the English Bible published in the United States by 1880 were published outside the Northeast.[21] It was not that Southerners, and later pioneering Westerners, did not own or read the Bible. A combination of factors (including literacy rates, availability of printed material, and regionally differentiated religious practices) worked together to make the cultures of the South and the West less biblically centered and biblically literate. Through 1880, bible production remained almost entirely a Northeastern endeavor, although as transportation networks improved and the enterprise of publishing spread, so would the geographic locations of bible producers. Imported versions of the English Scriptures do not play any significant role in my analysis. The reason for this is the absolute poverty of sources on importation of English

Scriptures. While bibles were most certainly imported from Europe in this period, there is good reason to believe that such imports were not nearly as substantial in quantity as the volume of bibles produced in America.[22] With the emergence of the American Bible Society in 1816, the United States had come into its own in the area of bible production, making it far more difficult for foreign publishers to make a profit by importing and selling their bibles in America.

While the first verse of the Gospel of John may aptly describe early American print culture, the Gospel writer's last verse gives an equal measure of insight. In writing that "there are also many other things which Jesus did, the which if they should be written every one, I suppose that even the world itself could not contain the books that should be written," John hints at the possibility of scriptural multiplication, a strikingly appropriate image of the myriad American biblical and quasi-biblical texts available by 1880. What so many scholars have considered to be the story of a single book and its far-reaching influence in American society has really been the influence of many editions and permutations of a book. This is a story not so much about a people of the Book, but a people of the books.

Chapter One

PRODUCTION

1 Let us talk of fear: fear born of despair, disgust, and a deep sense of urgency. In 1816 at the age of 75, the long officially retired Elias Boudinot—baptized by George Whitefield, onetime neighbor of Benjamin Franklin, fellow patriot of George Washington at Valley Forge, mentor of Alexander Hamilton, first president of the Continental Congress, delegate to the Constitutional Convention, and decade-long director of the United States Mint—accepted the position of president of the American Bible Society. He considered this appointment to be "the greatest honor that could have been conferred on me this side of the grave."[1] This was no small statement considering his pedigree, and were heartfelt words for a man who desperately feared that the country he had given the better part of his life to birthing and nurturing might collapse in his lifetime.

When Boudinot retired from directing the Mint in 1805, he left his last government post deeply disillusioned. Demoralized by how he and like-minded Federalist friends were increasingly marginalized in the United States' nascent government, Boudinot was particularly depressed by the election of Thomas Jefferson to the presidency in 1800. There could be no clearer sign to Boudinot that his dream of the new republic being led by an elite-centered government comprising "men who possess most wisdom . . . and most virtue" was quickly dying.[2]

Jefferson was doubly a devil in Boudinot's estimation. Boudinot viewed Jefferson as a proponent of dangerous democratic leanings—the results of which could be seen in the bloodletting and chaos of the French Revolution—and as an open skeptic of many traditional Christian beliefs. Boudinot believed that the rise of Jefferson, with his heretical religious views and ill-advised optimism in the abilities of the common man, could only mean the decline of the United States.

As Boudinot and his fellow Federalists found themselves excluded from official government posts, many turned to voluntary organizations or other civic-minded humanitarian institutions as a means of countering the Jeffersonian menace.[3] Boudinot decided to pour his energy and resources into the area of print, first publishing his own writing and then working to establish a voluntary organization based on publishing. What is fascinating in this strategy is that Boudinot chose the same weapon that he claimed "Thomas Paine, Ethan Allen & other infidels in America" had chosen to influence the American people so insidiously.[4]

In choosing to pursue publishing as a means of influence, Boudinot showed his hand and revealed one of his central beliefs, namely, that if people would not defer to the leadership of those in the society who enjoyed greater privilege due to talent, birth, and education, then the masses would have to be educated so that they might be able to supply their own, sound leadership. Boudinot decided to appeal directly to the American people through the medium of print in a desperate attempt to save his country by molding an inner character within Americans that would help develop the responsible, educated citizenry necessary for the republic to survive.

Michael Warner, Bernard Bailyn, and others have convincingly shown that by the time of the American Revolution, printed material had become an essential medium of mass persuasion in the colonies.[5] Perhaps there is no more vibrant example of this than the writings of Thomas Paine. Paine's *Common Sense* burst like a lightning bolt upon the publishing horizon in April 1776. In an era in which the common press run for books was often less than 2,000 copies and pamphlet press runs half of that, *Common Sense* sold 120,000 copies in its first year. This figure appears all the more astounding when one considers the general estimate that five times as many people actually read the pamphlet.[6] No pamphlet in the Colonies had ever experienced such popularity.

Paine would follow up the success of *Common Sense* with *Rights of Man* (1791) and *The Age of Reason* (1794). Both books sold so well in the United States and Europe that they broke every existing publishing record.[7]

Boudinot was not so much bothered by Paine's popularity as he was by the radical political and religious beliefs in Paine's writings. In *The Age of Reason,* Paine proclaims that the Bible is more "the word of a demon, than the word of God" and "a history of wickedness that has served to corrupt and brutalize mankind."[8] So, when Boudinot heard in the late 1790s that "thousands of copies of the Age of Reason, had been sold at public auction, in this city [Philadelphia], at a cent and an half each" making "so unworthy an object" accessible to children, servants, and the lowest people, he decided to write his own rebuttal to Paine's work.[9]

Boudinot published his extended answer to Paine in 1801 under the title *The Age of Revelation, or The Age of Reason Shewn to Be an Age of Infidelity*. Whereas *The Age of Reason* sold 100,000 copies in 1797 alone, Boudinot's *The Age of Revelation* sold so poorly that it never went beyond an initial press run (probably less than 2,000 copies), further convincing Boudinot that his beloved country was in a severe state of spiritual and moral decay.[10]

Even with the failure of *The Age of Revelation*, Boudinot did not abandon print as a medium through which the country might be saved. Instead of using his own words to defeat the infidels, Boudinot turned his energy toward the development of a national organization to produce and distribute the Bible.[11] Boudinot was convinced that the best way to counteract evil in print was with the most powerful piece of printed material, the Bible. He sensed his rebuttal to Paine may have been a failure partially because it was a work wrought by human hands.

Confident in the ability of the Word to speak for itself, Boudinot spent his remaining years occasionally taking up the pen himself, but predominantly using his considerable energies, finances, and personal connections to bind together disparate local bible societies into one powerful, centralized group. He realized this dream in the spring of 1816, when sixty delegates from thirty-four local societies met in New York and decided to incorporate into one central organization.[12] The American Bible Society was born.

For Boudinot, none of this was happening any too soon. Moved by feelings of disillusionment and disgust, Boudinot was also propelled by a deep sense of urgency. Repeatedly, Boudinot stressed that it was "the eleventh hour"; Christ's Second Coming was imminent.[13] It is one of the ironies of history that Paine's famous line, "These are the times that try men's souls," aptly characterizes Boudinot's feelings as he frantically worked to establish a national Bible society. Boudinot passionately believed that if he and others did not act quickly, God—not the times—would try men's souls, and the outcome of that trial was not blood Boudinot wanted on his doorstep.

The American Bible Society that Boudinot helped create pioneered many aspects of American publishing, including innovations in the areas of centralized production, steam-powered printing, in-house binding, and national distribution. Its fervor to make the Bible the chief text in the United States through sheer numbers led, however, to some unforeseen consequences. The American Bible Society's ability to produce and distribute hundreds of thousands of bibles and New Testaments by the 1830s radically reoriented the bible market in the United States, making both that market and the Bible itself more complex, diverse, and fragmented.

2 The massive popularity and volume of Paine's writings were but a taste of the print explosion that would rock antebellum culture. In the four score years that followed the American Revolution, the United States

experienced what Samuel Goodrich, an antebellum publisher and author, characterized as a "vast development in all branches of the industry connected with the press."[14]

Whereas printed material in the United States was relatively scarce at the close of the eighteenth century, by 1855, book "editions of 100,000 or 75,000, or 30,000" were common. The forty newspapers published during the Revolutionary period had given way by the middle of the nineteenth century to over two thousand weekly and daily papers. Religious periodicals, which had been "virtually nonexistent in 1800," had "become the grand engine of burgeoning evangelical culture," with groups such as William Miller's Adventists producing and distributing four million pieces of literature in the 1840s.[15]

The explosive growth in the American publishing industry was the result of no single cause. Indeed, to understand this growth, one must first appreciate the symbiotic relationship in the period between publishing-related technologies and the societal values that drove Americans to value reading and buy books.[16] The antebellum period experienced the appearance of vastly improved printing technologies, leading to increases in production speed, quality, and diversity.

Such improvements do not necessarily equate to increased consumption. Faster presses, more plentiful paper, and better distribution networks only point to the fact that printed material could be made more available. Social and ideological factors fueled the production because they supplied the demand.

The major changes in printing technologies in the early nineteenth century took many different forms. First, power presses replaced hand presses. Before the 1820s, hand presses dominated the publishing industry. Such presses required at least two, more commonly three, workers to operate them. One person operated a lever that lowered the type platen onto the paper, another inked the type, and a third worker was often added to feed and extract the paper from the press. Hand presses could produce 200 to 250 printed pages an hour. In 1821, David Treadwell introduced the first practical power press to America. Treadwell created a press whose type platen mechanism could be harnessed to a horse; overnight, the output from a single press was doubled. Treadwell continued to refine his ideas, and by 1823 had a working steam-powered press.

Steam power found its most efficient and popular model in presses designed by Isaac and Seth Adams in the 1830s. The Adams presses required less laborers to operate them and could produce up to 1,000 impressions per hour. Gradual refinements over the next fifty years would make power presses faster and capable of ever higher levels of production, but no design innovation until the introduction of economic cylinder presses in the 1880s would have such a profound influence on printing as the advent of steam-powered presses.[17]

Coupled with power presses introduced in the 1820s was a revolutionary change in how type was set. Type had long been a source of extreme expense, and thus severe limitation, in print shops.[18] Having to hand-set type for each page was a time-consuming enterprise and the expense of type fonts meant that printers were ingenious in how they stretched their type resources. Frequently, printers would produce sermons and other pamphlets at night so that they might be able to use the same type during the day to set newspaper articles.[19] As the nineteenth century progressed, type became more accessible in the United States. Type foundries were established, and technology to produce type improved so that more letters could be manufactured in less time with less expense.[20]

The most radical shift in typesetting to occur in the early nineteenth century was the process of stereotyping. Stereotype plates of type were made from plaster of paris forms that allowed printers to print certain works without having to reset the type every time or keep large volumes of loose type set standing in molds. Stereotyping had been preceded by the idea of buying enough type to keep type standing in molds ready for use. However, the standing type process was expensive, and it required a great deal of storage room. For example, the Philadelphia publisher Mathew Carey kept certain editions of the Bible in standing type in the early 1800s. The cost was immense, and it required an entire room to hold the preset blocks for a single bible edition.

Stereotyping, which arrived in the United States in 1812, offered publishers a way to set type for large-volume sellers at less cost than the practices of standing type or resetting the type for each printing. Not having to constantly reset type also decreased the number of textual errors. In the early days of stereotyping, publishers stereotyped books that were guaranteed best-sellers, such as school and religious texts. The first book to be printed from stereotype plates in the United States was a bible, and other early stereotyped books included catechisms and school spellers. As time passed, stereotyping became cheaper and thus more widely used. Consequently, money that had been tied up in standing type or in the wages for type composition was freed up to allow publishers to produce a greater variety of printed material.[21]

Changes in printing presses and printing type were joined in the early nineteenth century by the advent of machine-made paper. The Fourdrinier machine, which came to prominence in England in the first decade of the century under the direction of Henry and Sealy Fourdrinier, revolutionized the speed and cost of making paper. "In 1806 the machine with nine

13

hands did the work of seven vats with forty-one hands"—costing one-third of the price in terms of material and labor. By 1813, the quantity of paper the machine could produce per hour was doubled.[22] In the late 1820s, Americans imported several Fourdrinier machines, and in 1829, they began to manufacture their own improved versions of the machine.

Along with the Fourdrinier machine came another machine invented in 1817 by Thomas Gilpin. Paper made from the cylinder process of this machine was used more widely by newspapers than book publishers, yet publishers such as Mathew Carey did use its paper for their books upon occasion.[23] It was not until the 1830s that machine-made paper came to dominate the book market, but such paper was extensively used by large-volume publishers such as the American Bible Society and American Tract Society beginning in the early 1820s.[24]

How books were bound is the final significant change in book production during the early nineteenth century. As the volume of printed material grew, binding came to be more mechanized also. Whereas professional binders would exist throughout the century, more and more binding work was done by publishers in-house.

In-house binding was part of the new systematic centralization that large publishers underwent in the 1850s. In this decade, both the American Bible Society and the firm of Harper and Brothers brought most of their printing enterprise into single buildings. These buildings held the presses, the compositors, and the binders, who began to bind entire editions—leaving behind the days of selling books in sheets to be bound later by their buyers.[25] The art of individual bookbinding receded as huge press runs were published. Books were still bound in different styles, but without the individual flourishes and nuances with which binders once had the time and skill to mark book covers.[26]

Another major change in bookbinding came with the widespread replacement of leather by cloth bindings, which were cheaper and easier to attach to books.[27] The switch from leather to cloth bindings began in the 1820s but came into prominence in the 1830s.[28] As bindings began to come automatically with books, publishers changed their marketing strategies to accommodate different bindings for different market segments: expensive leather for high-end books and cloth binding for low-cost items.[29]

All these improvements in publishing technology were aided by changes in how publishers distributed their books. Radical advances were made in the area of transportation, as a burgeoning railroad industry accented ever-expanding road and river traffic.

Books are heavy—and in some ways delicate—material objects. Transporting them has always been a challenge; they are vulnerable to water damage if transported by river, lake, or ocean, and to weather and mud if transported by road. The advent and spread of the railroad in the 1830s would greatly ease hardships in the transportation of books, broadening the publishing marketplace and making book production more profitable.[30]

By the 1870s, selling books by subscription only, through the mail, and by using commercial travelers who served as middlemen between retailers and publishers radically increased the scope of book distribution by building upon the nation's ever-improving transportation infrastructure.[31]

One must also consider book prices in examining the growth of America's print marketplace. Although some forms of printed material, such as newspaper and reform tracts, decreased in price during the first three quarters of the nineteenth century, books were still highly priced items to the average worker through the 1870s. With the important exception of certain inexpensive books that, at their cheapest, were priced around twelve cents, most clothbound books still cost around one dollar—the average daily wage of the common laborer.[32]

The increase in the volume of books produced partly explains the increased availability of cheaper editions of books, and helps to account for the growing practice by publishers of producing books targeted for certain institutions, most notably the common schools and libraries.[33] As these institutions grew, so did their demand for books. Firms such as Harper and Brothers made fortunes specifically by publishing book series, such as their *Harper's School District Library* used in educational curricula.[34] The institutions that had acquired these books sometimes resold them at lower prices when newer series appeared or reading tastes changed. Thus, the used book market grew in the United States, providing another avenue for the growth in the consumption of books.

Converging with technological improvements and changes in book distribution improvements were societal values that put an ever-increasing value on the ability to read. Although factors such as access to education, geography, race, gender, and economic status make all-inclusive generalizations about early literacy rate in the United States impossible, historians agree that by the 1860s white male literacy in the Northeast hovered around 95 percent, while the literacy rate for women in this region was slightly lower. The South boasted moderately lower numbers, 85 percent and 75 percent, respectively.[35] The factors that account for such astoundingly high literacy rates were complex, dating back to the American Puritans who passionately believed that the ability to read God's word taught people both the way to heaven and the way to live harmoniously on earth.[36] As early as 1642, the General Court of Massachusetts passed a law to support universal schooling in the colony stating, "It being one chief project of that old deluder, Satan, to keep men from the knowledge of Scriptures" that teachers were to be appointed in townships to train people to read.[37]

Well into the nineteenth century, American Protestants believed that religious reading taught one about the divine and also reinforced a morality that helped the earthly community function with a high degree of cohesion.[38] In the nineteenth century, the religious fervor of the Second Great Awakening added significant fuel to the fire of American Protestantism's voracious appetite for print. As people converted to Christianity, many denominations felt it necessary to teach new converts the rudiments of bible reading. Added to the efforts of individual denominations, the American Sunday School Union emerged in the 1820s. Its curriculum concentrated on reading the Bible and other religious material.[39] Even with the rise of the common school, much of nineteenth-century literacy education remained anchored by the belief that religious texts were the best and highest good to which one could apply one's ability.[40]

While religious motivations undergirded literacy education in the eighteenth and early nineteenth centuries, the American Revolution added a significant political dimension to the role of reading in American culture. The Revolution created within many Americans a desire to be better informed about events that were taking place outside one's immediate proximity. Suddenly, national and international events came to be of great interest to the American rural farmer and city dweller alike. Newspapers grew in importance as they kept an increasingly politically minded public informed.[41]

Political concerns found their way into American schools. Americans began to view education as essential to their republican form of government. In 1826, Governor De Witt Clinton of New York declared: "The first duty of government, and the surest evidence of good government, is the encouragement of education. A general diffusion of knowledge is the precursor and protector of republican institutions; and . . . will watch over our liberties, and guard them against fraud, intrigue, corruption and violence."[42]

In the first half of the nineteenth century, reading—more than any other educational skill—was considered the mark of being educated.[43] Beginning in the 1780s, but hitting stride in the 1820s, common schools began to play a more prominent role in the education of the young republic, emphasizing the belief that an educated American citizenry was essential for the republic's survival.[44]

Economics also began to play a larger role in why people read. Literacy as a tool for upward economic mobility became more important. As William Gilmore has pointed out, even in rural fringe regions such as Windsor, Vermont, in the opening decades of the nineteenth century commercialization was becoming closely tied to literacy: "changes in cultural and social relations as well as in economic exchange—was the most important motive for expanding literacy and maintaining it through lifelong reading. . . . Market transactions were regularly recorded in blotters, day-books, and ledgers of family accounts. The spread of market activity required citizens to be reasonably educated—able to read, to calculate, and to sign their names, if not to write."[45]

As technology changed and cities grew, the rural ethos of limited, casual reading was replaced by a rising importance on being able to compete in a literate marketplace. Stuart Blumin has convincingly argued that while a revolution was occurring in the manual labor sector in the decades before the Civil War, there was a nonmanual labor revolution that was no less important going on at the same time. This nonmanual revolution created a wide range of new occupations. Blumin states, "Where before there were only artisans, there were now manufacturers, contractors, subcontractors, supervisors, retailers, wholesalers—men who withdrew from direct participation in production in order to supervise or coordinate the manual work of others, or to sell or distribute goods they did not make themselves."[46]

This nonmanual work demanded higher levels of literacy and proved to be one of the distinguishing marks of the emerging middle class in America. Professions that demanded high degrees of literacy increasingly became the more lucrative professions. Thus, literacy came to be a prerequisite for many avenues toward economic success.

Economic status was not the only positional concern connected with reading in the early nineteenth century. The elusive goal of social refinement and gentility came to be increasingly associated with reading.[47] Owning books and reading certain kinds of material distinguished one in significant cultural ways. More refined individuals in the colonies, and later in the United States, had long been associated with learning and with books. Doubtless, much of this connection came from the simple fact that certain respected vocations, such as the ministry, required education and were closely associated with reading.[48] Books signified not only learning, but wealth, for only the wealthy could afford to own many books prior to the nineteenth century.

Class distinctions went beyond simply reading and owning books. People who were considered to be higher on the social ladder exhibited preferences for certain kinds of books.[49] Perhaps the clearest example of this can be seen in how the more educated showed a marked preference for Greek and Roman classics. It is noteworthy that these classics were closely associated with both wealth and higher learning.[50] Obviously, the connection stemmed from the fact that to read the classics in the original Latin or Greek required a more advanced level of education. The demand for these works by those unable, or unwilling, to read them in the original created a growing number of editions of the classics translated into English and abridged into more popular paraphrases. Such abridgments and translations point toward a wide demand for seemingly "classic" literature for the masses in the early nineteenth century.

In the pursuit of gentility, reading also became an important means of self-instruction and self-improvement. Emulation of those considered more genteel reached far beyond copying their reading habits. The imitative drive also played a large part in the success of advice manuals and instructional works, which appeared in such numbers after 1830 that the literary historian James Hart called the antebellum years "the age of the etiquette book."[51]

Individuals who wanted to learn "the proper" way to do everything from organizing a pantry to writing personal letters could find the appropriate instructional book or pamphlet. Such knowledge acquisition allowed one to join a larger, ill-defined body of Americans who were also attempting to better their social station.[52] Reading became a means to learning how to maneuver successfully within changing social rules and how to better one's social standing.

Finally, reading increasingly became a means of relaxation and enjoyment during the early nineteenth century. A rise in reading as a leisure activity can be seen as an increasing number of titles blurred the line between edification and entertainment. Genres such as the novel and travel literature are good examples of this blurring.[53] Reading as recreational activity clearly appears in diaries throughout this period. Edward Jenner Carpenter who lived in Greenfield, Massachusetts, kept a diary in the mid-1840s that showed his preference for histories and romances over morality tales.[54] Rebecca Lowell, a member of the distinguished Boston Lowells, kept an extensive reading journal for over two decades beginning in 1813 that clearly showed that she read as much for entertainment as for edification.[55]

While it may be argued that reading always had an entertaining quality, this quality was increasingly foregrounded as fiction came into prominence through reform tracts, books, and newspapers. Reading as recreation would become even more prominent as the nineteenth century progressed and the fissure grew in printed material between edification and entertainment.

3   The explosive growth of antebellum American print culture held great promise and great peril. While Americans could read a greater quantity and greater diversity of printed material as the century progressed, such extensive reading threatened the intensive reading of certain privileged texts, most importantly the Bible. When print had been scarce, bibles were among the few texts that were widely owned and thus widely and constantly read. As other forms of printed material became more ac-

cessible, the Bible's clear role as the centerpiece of American print culture came into question.

Elias Boudinot had caught an early glimpse of the competition to the Bible presented by other mass-produced, readily accessible printed material when he heard of the availability of Thomas Paine's *The Age of Reason* on the streets of Philadelphia. This sense of print competition was a constant refrain among American Protestants of the period, their common sentiment well-captured in a minister's admonishment: "Do not neglect [the] Bible in this age of many books."[56] Into the midst of this "age of many books" sprang Boudinot's American Bible Society, an institution that was bent on using the upsurge in printing technology, book distribution networks, and American love of reading to combat the thousands of books, newspapers, journals, and pamphlets that kept people from reading their bibles. In fact, the very means that created such a plethora of printed material would enable the Bible Society to embark on the most ambitious scheme in the history of American publishing, namely, to provide every household with a copy of the Holy Scriptures. For the Society, the solution to print competition was simple: Make the Bible the most accessible written text in the United States, and you would make it the most important.

With this philosophy firmly planted in their minds, the Board of Managers of the American Bible Society announced in the spring of 1829 that the Society intended to provide a bible to every household in the United States within two years. The Society's Fourteenth Annual Report encapsulated this goal with the words: "A Bible to every household, a Bible to every houshold—must be the motto of each [auxiliary] Society, and must be sounded through all our borders, until every soul in the whole land has access to this fountain of life. And this supply of the Bible is not to be furnished for this year only, but continually."[57] This plan became known as the "General Supply," the first of four such supplies the Society would undertake in the nineteenth century.[58]

This strategy was fueled by the twin beliefs that the widest distribution of the Bible was the best way to insure religious and civil well-being, and that for the first time in history changes in publishing had made it possible to meet the scriptural needs of a nation of twelve million inhabitants.[59] The General Supply of 1829–1831 stands as the most ambitious, and perhaps most successful, attempt at placing the Bible in a preeminent position in the United States print culture through the sheer number of volumes produced and made available.

Although the American Bible Society was not able to achieve its goal of getting a Bible into every household, it did produce over one-half million volumes of scripture for distribution in their first General Supply. To fully appreciate the magnitude of the Society's vision and accomplishment,

19

it is instructive to consider how far bible publishing had come since the first English copy of the Scriptures had been printed in America. Perhaps the best way of doing this is to examine two key figures who preceded the American Bible Society in bible publishing: the colonial printer Robert Aitken and the premier book publisher of the early republic, Mathew Carey.

The story of publishing an English Bible in America finds its roots in the American Revolution. By 1777, bibles for sale in America had become scarce. The war with Britain had stopped much of the colonies' international trade, and among the items temporarily lost to the American marketplace was the English Bible. Because of the royal copyright, American printers had never seriously concerned themselves with producing their own English bibles until political events forced the issue. As the process of seeking to publish bibles in America would soon show, however, it was more than just a copyright that had made printers slow to publish an English bible in the colonies.

To meet an impending bible shortage, a group of Presbyterian clergy offered a petition to the Continental Congress in the summer of 1777 requesting that bibles be procured because of their high price coupled with the "Scarcity and Difficulty in importing them from Europe."[60] Congress replied by calling for bids from various printers for the work. Five Philadelphia printers offered estimates that varied widely in terms of the amount of time, type, and paper that would be required for printing an edition of the Bible. After considering the bids, the Congress decided that it would be much cheaper and more reliable simply to import bibles, and so they decided to attempt to procure 20,000 bibles from Holland. No action was ever taken on this decision, for soon after it was made, the Congress had to flee Philadelphia. This petition for bibles, and the idea of importation of bibles from Holland, faded into the background forever as the Congress found itself with the more pressing concerns of war.[61]

Enter Robert Aitken, one of the five printers who had submitted a bid for an American printing of the English Bible. Having immigrated from Scotland with his family in 1771, he set up his shop on Front Street in Philadelphia and began printing everything from newspapers to books. His contemporaries saw his shop as the largest and best stocked bookstore in Philadelphia.[62] Aitken was an aggressive businessman who used his Philadelphia location to advantage. He often dined with various members of the Congress at the London Coffee House near his shop, and he used these connections to become the Congress's official printer, publishing the *Congressional Journal*.

Aitken did not let the Congress's decision to try to import bibles stop his own entrepreneurial drive. In 1777, he published the first English New

Testament printed in the colonies.[63] A New Testament required substantially less work and resources than an edition of the entire Bible, and it met with such great success that Aitken continued to produce editions in 1778, 1779, 1780, and 1781.[64] Then in 1782, Aitken made the boldest move of his printing career; he set type and printed 10,000 copies of the entire Bible.[65] The magnitude of this accomplishment goes easily unappreciated today, but one should keep in mind just how large and complex the Bible is. Aitken was not setting out to produce the usual newspaper, broadside, or even short collection of sermons. He had committed himself to setting and proofing type for nearly two thousand pages of text. He then had to acquire the necessary amount of paper when such paper had to be made by hand, and better grades of paper usually had to be imported from Europe. Because of limited resources, it is not surprising that the bible Aitken produced is an unobtrusively spartan volume. The fifty extant copies reveal that it was bound both in one and two volumes, most in simple brown calfskin, but some with gold-tooled ornamentation.[66] With slight variations, the book measures five and one-half inches by three and one-eighth inches. Because of the need to use paper sparingly, margins are almost nonexistent in his volume, and the usual marginal notes of the King James Version are absent (see Figure 1). The astronomical expense of such a project led Aitken to apply for help to insure the success of his project. From the General Assembly of the Commonwealth of Pennsylvania he secured a loan, and from the Continental Congress he secured a written endorsement that he placed as a preface to his bible edition.

To sell this amazing feat of colonial printing, Aitken moved beyond the common subscription sales strategy to a method that involved other booksellers selling his wares. The subscription tactic involved getting people to subscribe for an as-yet-unpublished book with a small fee up front. The subscription was a good-faith contract stating that the purchaser would pay the balance when the book was published. The arrangement had the dual benefit of helping insure book buyers and giving printers a rough idea of how many copies of the book they should print. With an edition of 10,000 volumes, Aitken was aiming much higher than a market dictated by a subscription list. His success with the New Testament encouraged him to think of a strikingly large press run, but to sell so many copies, Aitken had to resort to another method of book distribution common in the period. He sold or traded copies of his bible to other printers and store owners who might in turn sell these copies in their shops.[67]

Aitken's timing proved tragic. With the end of the American Revolution, imported bibles again flowed into the United States. As it turned out, English publishers could undersell the price of Aitken's bible and better it in terms of quality because of the long practice of English publishers and

21

their access to better raw materials. His account book for this period shows that many of the bibles he had consigned to fellow booksellers were returned to him unsold.[68] Thus, Aitken's audacity ironically distinguished him as not only printing the first English bible in America, but also printing one of the few unprofitable early editions of the Bible in America. Aitken's failure also shows why publishers through the 1830s often worked together to produce a single bible edition; the resources and risk of such a project were just too much for a single publisher.[69]

As it became clear that Aitken was going to lose a fortune on his bible

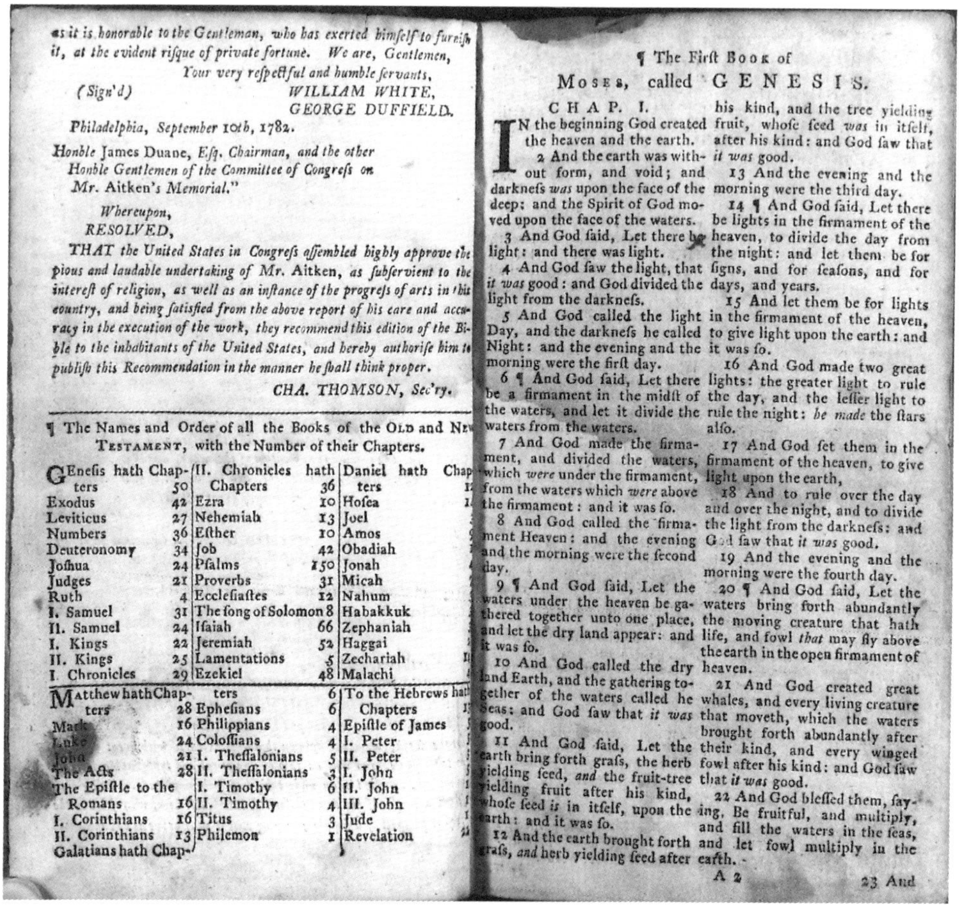

as it is honorable to the Gentleman, who has exerted himſelf to furniſh it, at the evident riſque of private fortune. We are, Gentlemen,
Your very reſpectful and humble ſervants,
(Sign'd) WILLIAM WHITE,
GEORGE DUFFIELD.
Philadelphia, September 10th, 1782.
Honble James Duane, *Eſq. Chairman, and the other Honble Gentlemen of the Committee of Congreſs on* Mr. Aitken's *Memorial.*"

Whereupon,
RESOLVED,
THAT the United States in Congreſs aſſembled highly approve the pious and laudable undertaking of Mr. Aitken, *as ſubſervient to the intereſt of religion, as well as an inſtance of the progreſs of arts in this country, and being ſatisfied from the above report of his care and accuracy in the execution of the work, they recommend this edition of the Bible to the inhabitants of the United States, and hereby authoriſe him to publiſh this Recommendation in the manner he ſhall think proper.*
CHA. THOMSON, Sec'ry.

¶ The Names and Order of all the Books of the OLD and NEW TESTAMENT, with the Number of their Chapters.

GEneſis hath Chapters	50	II. Chronicles hath Chapters	36	Daniel hath Chapters	[illegible]
Exodus	42	Ezra	10	Hoſea	[illegible]
Leviticus	27	Nehemiah	13	Joel	[illegible]
Numbers	36	Eſther	10	Amos	[illegible]
Deuteronomy	34	Job	42	Obadiah	[illegible]
Joſhua	24	Pſalms	150	Jonah	[illegible]
Judges	21	Proverbs	31	Micah	[illegible]
Ruth	4	Eccleſiaſtes	12	Nahum	[illegible]
I. Samuel	31	The ſong of Solomon	8	Habakkuk	[illegible]
II. Samuel	24	Iſaiah	66	Zephaniah	[illegible]
I. Kings	22	Jeremiah	52	Haggai	[illegible]
II. Kings	25	Lamentations	5	Zechariah	[illegible]
I. Chronicles	29	Ezekiel	48	Malachi	[illegible]

MAtthew hath Chapters	28	Galatians hath Chapters	6	To the Hebrews hath Chapters	[illegible]
Mark	16	Epheſians	6	Epiſtle of James	[illegible]
Luke	24	Philippians	4	I. Peter	[illegible]
John	21	Coloſſians	4	II. Peter	[illegible]
The Acts	28	I. Theſſalonians	5	I. John	[illegible]
The Epiſtle to the Romans	16	II. Theſſalonians	3	II. John	[illegible]
I. Corinthians	16	I. Timothy	6	III. John	[illegible]
II. Corinthians	13	II. Timothy	4	Jude	[illegible]
		Titus	3	Revelation	[illegible]
		Philemon	1		

¶ The Firſt BOOK of
MOSES, called GENESIS.

CHAP. I.

IN the beginning God created
the heaven and the earth.
2 And the earth was without form, and void; and
darkneſs *was* upon the face of the
deep: and the Spirit of God moved upon the face of the waters.
3 And God ſaid, Let there be
light: and there was light.
4 And God ſaw the light, that
it was good: and God divided the
light from the darkneſs.
5 And God called the light
Day, and the darkneſs he called
Night: and the evening and the
morning were the firſt day.
6 ¶ And God ſaid, Let there
be a firmament in the midſt of
the waters, and let it divide the
waters from the waters.
7 And God made the firmament, and divided the waters,
which *were* under the firmament,
from the waters which *were* above
the firmament: and it was ſo.
8 And God called the firmament Heaven: and the evening
and the morning were the ſecond
day.
9 ¶ And God ſaid, Let the
waters under the heaven be gathered together unto one place,
and let the dry land appear: and
it was ſo.
10 And God called the dry
land Earth, and the gathering together of the waters called he
Seas: and God ſaw that *it was*
good.
11 And God ſaid, Let the
earth bring forth graſs, the herb
yielding ſeed, *and* the fruit-tree
yielding fruit after his kind,
whoſe ſeed *is* in itſelf, upon the
earth: and it was ſo.
12 And the earth brought forth
graſs, *and* herb yielding ſeed after
his kind, and the tree yielding
fruit, whoſe ſeed *was* in itſelf,
after his kind: and God ſaw that
it was good.
13 And the evening and the
morning were the third day.
14 ¶ And God ſaid, Let there
be lights in the firmament of the
heaven, to divide the day from
the night: and let them be for
ſigns, and for ſeaſons, and for
days, and years.
15 And let them be for lights
in the firmament of the heaven,
to give light upon the earth: and
it was ſo.
16 And God made two great
lights: the greater light to rule
the day, and the leſſer light to
rule the night: *he made* the ſtars
alſo.
17 And God ſet them in the
firmament of the heaven, to give
light upon the earth,
18 And to rule over the day
and over the night, and to divide
the light from the darkneſs: and
God ſaw that *it was* good.
19 And the evening and the
morning were the fourth day.
20 ¶ And God ſaid, Let the
waters bring forth abundantly
the moving creature that hath
life, and fowl *that* may fly above
the earth in the open firmament of
heaven.
21 And God created great
whales, and every living creature
that moveth, which the waters
brought forth abundantly after
their kind, and every winged
fowl after his kind: and God ſaw
that *it was* good.
22 And God bleſſed them, ſaying, Be fruitful, and multiply,
and fill the waters in the ſeas,
and let fowl multiply in the
earth.

A 2 23 And

FIGURE 1. Sample pages from Robert Aitken's 1782 edition of the Bible. Space-conserving attributes include the closing paragraphs of the Congress's endorsement of the volume on the same page with the edition's table of contents, the lack of margins, and the absence of marginal commentary. (Courtesy of the Lilly Library, Indiana University, Bloomington, Indiana)

venture, he petitioned Congress to purchase a portion of the edition in attempt to reduce his financial losses. He even approached George Washington with the idea of giving one of his bibles to every veteran of the American Revolution. Neither idea was accepted. Eventually, Aitken received
some help from the Philadelphia Synod of the Presbyterian Church, which
agreed to purchase his bibles to distribute among the poor. Even with this
act of charity, Aitken was financially ruined.[70] His star in the printing trade
would never again burn as brightly, even though he would continue in the
profession until his death in 1802.

Three years after Robert Aitken released his unsuccessful bible, a
young Irish-Catholic printer by the name of Mathew Carey opened a
printing shop in Philadelphia. Carey would become a dominant force in
American publishing over the next thirty years.[71] As exhibited in his vitri-
olic confrontations with the British government that eventually forced him
to flee Ireland, Carey was shrewd, ambitious, and a risk taker. He was also
no neophyte to the printing trade; he apprenticed in Ireland and later
worked in Paris with both Benjamin Franklin and the French printer
Didot. That Carey would embark on his first bible publishing venture only
five years after opening a shop bears witness to his daring.

In 1790, Carey printed 471 copies of the Catholic Douay bible.[72] So
much work was involved in producing this edition, and so slight was the
profit margin, that Carey avoided bible publishing for over a decade.
When he did return to it in 1801, it was to produce editions of the Protestant King James bible. Carey's sensitivity to the marketplace, exacting attention to detail, quick adoption of standing type, and aggressive marketing practices made his methods both a model and a harbinger for much of
nineteenth-century scripture production. Carey became the largest American producer of bibles in the first two decades of the nineteenth century.

Although Carey would make himself a small fortune by becoming the
premier bible publisher of his day, he neither originated nor showed much
initial enthusiasm for printing an edition of the King James bible.[73] The
impetus behind the project was Parson Mason Locke Weems, the famous
biographer of Washington who gave the nation the story of George chop-
ping down a cherry tree. Carey had hired Weems in 1796 to serve as a rov-
ing bookseller.[74] Through his sales trips and accompanying correspondence, Weems relayed a wealth of information to Carey on American book
buying tastes.[75] Such data proved critical to Carey's success in the American bible market.

As early as 1798, Weems cried out to Carey to send him bibles.[76]
These pleas eventually led Weems and Carey to seek subscriptions for a
new bible edition. From its inception, this edition proved to be an arduous, on-again, off-again proposition. By 1800, the Bible still had not been

23

published, and the competition from rival printers was increasing daily. Weems complained to Carey that their plans to publish a new bible had "knock'd up just such a dust here among the Printers as woud a stone if thrown smack into the center of a Hornet's nest. The whole swarm is out. You hear of nothing here now but printing the Bible. Collins is going to print a bible—Swords is going to print a bible—Hopkins is for a Bible—and Durell for Folio! Everything that can raise a type is going to work upon the Bible. You'd take New York to be the very town of Man-Soul, and its printeriest saints on earth."[77] Threats of lively competition and his awareness of the public's hunger for bibles gave Weems's entreaties for the quick production of Carey's edition an ever more frantic tone. By August 1800, Weems resorted to military metaphors in an attempt to move Carey to action when he pleaded, "Many things are not worth powder and shot. The Bible is a Galleon! Reserve your ammunition for that."[78]

Rather than bowing to Weems's constant assurances of public demand and certain success, Carey writes Weems, "The Bible is absolutely suspended for the present—perhaps for ever."[79] Carey blames Weems for the imminent death of the bible project saying that he has not received any money from his book sales. Carey is clearly concerned about the financial viability of a bible edition, a project his wife had long argued is full of "dangers . . . far beyond the profits," and demands that Weems should suspend any attempts "at procuring subscribers for the Bible; for I would as soon set my property on fire, as engage in such a work with such remittances as you make."[80] Publishing was always a financially risky venture, and Carey is clearly beginning to lose faith in Weems's ability to help bring him profit through printing a bible.[81]

The desperate tone of the letters between the two escalates. Weems begs for bibles, saying it will make them both rich; Carey rails against Weems's promises and lack of sales receipts. Weems even begins to plead for Carey to employ a printer on his behalf who will produce the bibles he has promised.[82] At this point, Weems gets help from an unexpected quarter. Thomas Jefferson's election to the presidency assuaged some of Carey's financial fears. As a Jefferson loyalist, Carey was confident that he would be able to attain lucrative government printing contracts and credit from the national bank. The bible project began to appear less risky, and after corresponding with other booksellers on an edition's viability, Carey decided to once again proceed with his edition.[83] In mid-May of 1801, Carey put his bible to press; it would take months to finish the printing.[84]

The bible Carey produced in 1801 was substantially different from the one Aitken had printed almost twenty years earlier. While Carey's bible was noticeably larger than Aitken's, the physical size of the two books is only the first clue to the differences (see Figure 2). Carey's Douay bible of 1791 was probably the first bible published in quarto format in the United States, and Carey kept to the quarto format in his first King James Version. This time, however, Carey did not print the bible himself, but hired the work out to Joseph Charless. This practice of giving out one's sizable printing jobs to other printers was largely pioneered by Carey, who would increasingly distribute his book projects to various printers while he focused more on the distribution end of his business.[85] Charless was in charge of the printing, but the binding was handed over to the professional bookbinders of the day.

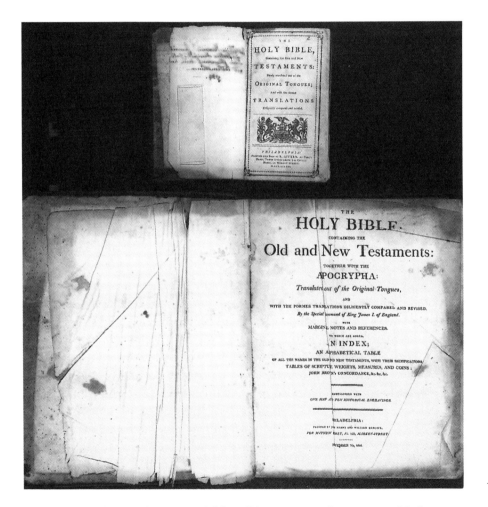

FIGURE 2. Robert Aitken's 1782 bible edition compared to an 1803 Mathew Carey quarto bible edition. With a volume as large and complex as the Bible, such size difference translated into significant production cost differences in regard to ink, type, paper, and binding material. (Courtesy of the Lilly Library, Indiana University, Bloomington, Indiana)

Carey's 1801 edition was usually bound in simple brown calfskin, with the interior contents greatly expanded from Aitken's bible of twenty years prior. Carey included a number of items aside from the actual text of the Bible: multiple engravings; A Table of Officers; Tables of Scripture Measures; Tables of Proper Names; Table of Time; A Clergyman's Address to Married Persons at the Altar; The Old and New Testaments Dissected; Portrait of an Apostolic Preacher from Cowper; A Table of Kindred and Affinity; and a description of the Holy Land. He had loaded his bible with such material in order to make it a more attractive purchase. The problem with such a strategy soon became apparent as customers began to compare Carey's price of six dollars for this bible with Isaac Collins's quarto bible of 1791, which was priced at four dollars. In recounting a typical conversation with a potential bible buyer, Weems writes:

> "What do you have for your Bible?" says the Man to whom I make a leg with Book & hat; "*Only six dollars Sir*" "Hoot, hoot" quoth he, "why Isaac Collins gives us a Bible for 4"!! "But please to observe, Sir, the style in which this is done: Mr Carey has made on this—here, Sir, you see is a fine map on Copper plate of the holy land; here, Sir, is Nazareth where Christ was born, here is Cana of Gallilee [sic], where he wrought his first miracle, *here* is a view of the country immortaliz^d by his travels, labours, &c. &c. &c." . . . "All this is clever, yes, 'tis clever enough indeed, but I w^{d}n't give a fig the more for all that, for it only sarves to make the Children spoil the book, however the Isaac Collins ax^d but 4 dol^s for his'n, here's five doll^s for your'n."[86]

Price is already a key issue in the bible competition, and it would only intensify in the years to come. Although a bible's content could be manipulated to make a bible a more attractive purchase, such manipulations always had to take into account what customers were willing to pay. Many a reader may have thought the Bible to contain priceless content, but publishers were well aware of the price-filled world it was called to inhabit.

Competition not only affected the price, but the product as well. While cheap bibles appealed to a certain constituency who would "never put up with a 5 or 6 Dollar Bible," others planned on buying "but *one bible*, as one *Wife*, in their life time" and so wish "to have *that one* of the best sort."[87] Publishers began to produce bibles in a wide range of sizes and formats.

Carey is a pivotal figure in bible publishing not only for the vast quantities of his production, but also because of his sensitivity to a rapidly diversifying bible marketplace. Between 1801 and 1815, Carey stood on the leading edge of the diversification that the American bible market would experience throughout the nineteenth century. He offered his customers a range of bibles printed on different kinds of paper, bound in different kinds of leathers, set in different sizes of type, and furnished with a wide variety of maps and pictures.

By 1807, Carey was advertising well over twenty versions of the quarto bible under such categories as "Coarse Medium," "Fine Medium," and "Superfine Medium." Their prices ranged from $3.50 for a Coarse Medium Quarto without the Apocrypha to a Superfine Medium with ten maps, Apocrypha, and Scotch Psalms for $8.75. He continually sought to make his editions the most "curious, usurious and wonderful" editions available.[88]

Weems told Carey to make certain his "Bible contains more Curious things than were ever seen in any other bible" and to pay special attention to illustrations, remembering that "Good Engravings are a luxury, a feast to the Soul. . . . The fame of them goes abroad and the Bible sells with Rapidity." By 1816, Carey's initial complement of nine engravings in his 1801 bible had grown to as many as seventy illustrations and maps in his more expensive volumes.[89] While other publishers offered slight variations in the bibles and testaments they produced, Carey offered a spectrum of bibles unheard of in American publishing.[90]

Absolutely central to Carey's ability to diversify and multiply his various quarto bible editions was his quick adoption of standing type. Carey must have smelled the success that would follow the publication of his first quarto bible, because three weeks before this edition appeared, Carey purchased the standing type of Hugh Gaine's duodecimo New Testament. Carey then informed Weems that he would be able to provide all the New Testaments that Weems might need.[91] Two years later, Carey's bible sales continued to go so well that he purchased enough type to keep his quarto edition standing. By 1803, Carey was able to forgo the expense of typesetting and proofreading. By trimming these production costs, Carey was realizing ever-higher profit margins on his bible editions.

Carey had to consider more than just content if he wanted to remain at the forefront of bible publishing. He also needed to figure how best to bind and distribute his volumes. Since some binders did not show up to execute the work, and others were slow to fulfill their obligations, Carey found himself unable to bind the books quickly enough to keep Weems supplied.[92] Bindings proved to be yet one more source of tension between Weems and Carey. Weems raved to Carey: "The Binders! The Binders! The Binders! Ncver did a Wild Asse's Colt so tremble at thought of a Lion as I do at thought of the Binders. Stain^d with paste, the fly leaves look wretchedly patch^d—however let the subject drop. Your Fame and Fortune are at Stake."[93]

Distribution was an even larger problem. Joseph Charless may have finished the printing of the bible in November, but that did not mean that

27

these bibles reached Weems that same month. On top of slow binding processes, the bibles also had to get to Weems as he traveled the country. Carey's bible of 1801 appeared long before railroads and canals had become staples of American transportation. Weems operated in the time of exceedingly poor roads. His mode of transportation was first horse, and then horse and carriage. He traveled with a handful of books, a variety of sample pages, and subscription lists. His sales strategies varied from wooing the most wealthy and influential members in a town, to visiting court-houses during meetings, to attending camp meeting revivals, to appointing various local merchants to act as agents for himself. Through correspondence, Weems kept Carey apprised of his movements and advised Carey where to direct the next shipment of books.

These shipments proved one of the most vexatious links in this distribution chain. Weems had to deal with books that were often sent to the wrong locations, and were often damaged in the course of transit. Weems was forever writing messages on how books should be packed. If packed too loosely, they would rub against one another and the bindings would be ruined.[94] Frequently, nails that were used to seal the crates found their way into the bibles themselves. With typical wit and flourish, Weems writes of one bible's stigmata: "Beg Sylvester to have mercy on the word of God, and not to crucify it afresh thro his miserable Carpentership. I give this hint because one of the Bibles is so crippled by a spike nail, that I must doctor it marvelously indeed if ever to bring it to survive a fair daylight inspection."[95]

Aside from these vicissitudes of travel, there was the problem of getting reliable booksellers in various locations to handle books once their subscriptions had been collected. As mobile as Weems was, he could not be everywhere at once, and he worked hard to establish more permanent depots for Carey's books in various towns. This was a risky proposition. These depots were most often small merchants who had no great feel or aptitude for selling books. They frequently did not know what to do with book stock when they had it or how properly to distribute it to those who had subscriptions for certain books. Finally, such small merchants were forever going out of business, taking whatever books of Carey's they had with them as they sold off their stock to settle debts.[96]

As arduous as the printing and selling of a bible was in the opening years of the nineteenth century, it is clear that the profits of Carey's quarto bible were worth the hardships.[97] The success of his bible ventures is reflected in the number of editions brought out—over sixty between 1801 and 1824—and in his ability to dominate so much of the market. One sign of his dominance is an 1807 pamphlet entitled *Mathew Carey's Plan and Terms of Supplying the Booksellers Throughout the Union, with School and*

Quarto Bibles.[98] In it he states that "M. Carey having now prepared, and intending to keep constantly for sale, a large assortment of quarto & school Bibles, respectfully solicits the patronage of the trade, which he will studiously endeavor to deserve."[99] Carey's plan for such a supply included numerous different bibles exhibiting a range of binding styles and illustrations. Carey also offered discounts for larger purchases and listed possible payment and credit plans. He also states that, because of the continual rise in the cost of paper, purchase prices cannot be guaranteed if orders are not placed promptly. Finally, he lists seventeen booksellers in seven cities who have bible specimens on hand for inspection.[100]

By 1807, Carey's books had perhaps the widest circulation of any bibles produced in America. He was responsible for furnishing bibles to common schools, Sunday schools, and booksellers across the nation, and had also begun to supply bibles for the Philadelphia Bible Society in 1808—the first bible society to be founded in the United States.[101] Carey would supply bibles to the Philadelphia Bible Society through 1812 when the Society decided to take more direct control of its bible production with stereotype plates that had been furnished by the British and Foreign Bible Society.[102]

The fact that Carey would supply not only booksellers and schools, but also benevolent enterprises such as the Philadelphia Bible Society, points to the deep penetration Carey had made into the bible market of the early nineteenth century.[103] Carey is an important figure in American bible publishing because he pioneered mass bible production and distribution in the United States, and because he diversified the Bible as a product that attempted to capture as much of the bible market as possible. His wide range of bibles, along with his ability to produce them in large quantity for low prices, allowed him to become the dominant bible producer in the United States for close to twenty years. It is only with the emergence of the American Bible Society that Carey's role as America's preeminent bible producer would come to an end.

4 Among Parson Weems's many talents was his seeming ability to prophesy. In the winter of 1815, he wrote Carey: "I am afraid the Stereotype Bible will hurt you much."[104] In 1812, the Philadelphia Bible Society acquired stereotyped plates from England for a bible edition and printed the first stereotyped book in America.[105] Three years later, publishers were using American-made stereotype plates to print bibles.[106] By the 1820s, fifty percent of American bible editions proclaimed their stereotyped status on their title pages.[107] Stereotyping revolutionized American book publishing in the first third of the nineteenth century, and no book was so radically touched by this revolution as the Bible.

No publisher more enthusiastically embraced stereotyping than the American Bible Society. Using the British and Foreign Bible Society as its model, the Society adopted a vision of encouraging the widest possible circulation of the "Holy Scriptures without note or comment."[108] So central was stereotyping to this vision that the Society initially advertised a mission of providing "a sufficiency of well printed and accurate editions of the Scriptures; but also to furnish great districts of the American continent with well executed stereotype plates, for their cheap and extensive diffusion throughout regions which are now scantily supplied at discouraging expense."[109]

As it turned out, only once did the Society send stereotype plates to an outlying member society, finding it easier to keep product quality high and expenses low by centralizing all production in New York City.[110] By 1820, the Society had ten different sets of stereotype plates able to produce five different types of bibles and New Testaments.[111]

Stereotyping allowed the American Bible Society to improve on Mathew Carey's cost-saving idea of keeping bible editions in standing type. Stereotype plates were cheaper to produce than several sets of standing type, since separate type did not need to be purchased and set for each set of plates. As the Society was quick to point out, "a number of plates may be formed with the same types; and the greater the number of plates, the less is the average expense; as in the common mode of printing, the larger the edition of a book, the less is the cost of a single copy."[112]

The Society's rapid adoption of stereotyping is all the more amazing because in the second decade of the nineteenth century, stereotyping was still a largely new and untested means of printing. The first large publishing firm to adopt stereotyping was Harper and Brothers, and they did so in the 1830s, more than a decade behind the American Bible Society.[113]

The American Bible Society was quick to adopt other innovations in printing as well. Along with the American Tract Society, the American Bible Society was one of the first publishers to extensively employ power presses. By 1829, Daniel Fanshaw was operating sixteen Treadwell steam-powered presses exclusively for the printing needs of the Society.[114] While press runs for publishers remained around 2,000 copies for a given book through much of the 1820s, the Society printed over 20,000 copies of its stereotyped bible edition in 1816, and by 1830 was producing 300,000 copies of Scripture a year.[115] Once the Society was born, no American bible publisher could match its volume of production.

Printing bibles, however, was only one half of the bible production process. Bibles also needed to be bound. As an 1848 Society report pointed out, "Binding constitutes more than one half of the cost of every book produced, so that 'judicious and economical administration' demands that the processes be carefully considered."[116] Although the American Bible Society in its earliest years distributed bibles in unbound sheets, the Society soon discontinued this practice in order to retain more control over the finished product. One of the major problems for the Society of not binding its bibles was the tendency of others to bind extra material into bibles, such as commentary notes or copies of the apocrypha.[117] To keep its editions "without note or comment," the Society brought binding in-house, making the Society one of the earliest American publishers to sell books already bound.[118]

In addition to securing control over the finished bibles' contents, the change to in-house binding allowed the Society to increase its production efficiency by placing its binding and publishing operations in close proximity. The binding problems that had plagued Mathew Carey and other publishers were significantly lessened by this arrangement. Almost from the outset, the Society led the way in housing binding and printing operations together in order to produce the most economical bible editions possible.[119]

The first bibles issued by the Society stand as vivid examples of the values of economy and efficiency. Printed in 1816, these early bibles were nothing spectacular, having more in common with Aitken's 1782 edition than the more contemporary editions of Mathew Carey.[120] The duodecimo format of the Bible was straightforward: The bible was small, about six by three and one-half inches, printed in a two-column style with chapters preceded by a short heading and a handful of short tables of information. The pages were almost completely devoid of margins, a sign of paper conservation. Finally, the Society bound these bibles in low-cost leather without elaborate spine or cover ornamentation. This small, sturdy bible edition was designed for function; a modest product inexpensively produced. It was this simple bible, and the hundreds of later editions for which it served as a model, that began to reshape significantly America's English bible market.

Producing economical bibles was not the Society's only concern. As one historian of the Society noted, by "1841 it had become a commonplace axiom that though the number [of bibles] printed be enough to bury the Bible House, the books would do no good unless carried forth to the needy."[121] The American Bible Society experienced the same concerns as Mathew Carey had. Once books were produced, reliable means of distributing them had to be found. The American Bible Society, however, had something Carey did not have: namely, more than one hundred local organizations that had formed themselves with the express purpose of supplying bibles to those in need.

The distribution practices of the American Bible Society fall roughly into two periods.[122] The first of these runs from 1816 through the 1830s; it is marked by distribution through local bible organizations known as bible auxiliaries. Having grown out of these local auxiliaries, the American Bible Society originally saw its job as producing bibles and the auxiliaries' job as distributing them. A local bible society could become an auxiliary to the national organization by applying for auxiliary status and agreeing "to place their surplus revenue, after supplying their own districts with Bibles, at the disposal of the national Society."[123] As auxiliaries, the local bible societies were able to buy bibles from the American Bible Society either at the cost of production, or at production cost plus five percent for production expenses and overhead.[124] Before the emergence of the American Bible Society, these auxiliaries were formed and administered by local members. The American Bible Society did employ agents to circulate among the local societies and attempt to organize societies where none existed, but these agents were employed for only short periods, and it was clear that most of the distribution work was to be done through the volunteer leadership and labor of the local societies.

One of the major problems with these auxiliaries was the fact that they often were poorly administered and lacked the means and motivation to adequately collect money and distribute bibles. Put bluntly, more auxiliaries existed on paper than in reality. Beginning in the 1840s, the American Bible Society saw that it would have to make changes in its use of bible agents in order to survive. These agents changed from short-term workers to more permanent administrators.

The change to longer-term agents characterizes the second period of the American Bible Society's distribution practices. The Society began to hire agents for longer periods, assigning them larger territories and greater administrative responsibilities. As a result, agents became more important links between the parent and local societies. No longer were the auxiliaries handled in a strictly volunteer manner. The rise of a more coherent and well-trained agency system meant a more effective auxiliary system.

These two periods are well illustrated in the first and fourth General Supplies, inaugurated in 1829 and 1882, respectively. In both these Supplies, the American Bible Society set forth the goal of distributing a bible to every household in the United States. In 1829, one of the societies moved that the American Bible Society seek to supply every household in the nation with a bible.[125] Local bible societies committed themselves to surveying their regions carefully and systematically to determine who was in need of bibles, and then supply the need. In 1829, ten local societies were already engaged in this process of canvassing and supplying their regions.[126]

It is important to note that only rarely in any of the four General Supplies were bibles simply given away.[127] The American Bible Society held the belief that bibles should be paid for by their new owners wherever possible, convinced that the volumes were valued more if they were not obtained for free. This belief meant even more work for the auxiliaries, for bibles were often bought in payment installments. Bible Society volunteers had to make regular visits to purchasers to collect the money that had been promised when the bible had been distributed.

Money also had to be raised to provide the capital for producing the gigantic number of bibles needed to accomplish the General Supply. The period of 1829–1831 was a time of immense bible production and fundraising for the American Bible Society. So many bibles were produced, in fact, that in 1833 the Society printed no new bibles, but instead worked distributing the volumes they already had stored in their repository.

In contrast to the American Bible Society that carried out the first General Supply, the Society that orchestrated the supply of the 1880s was highly centralized in governance and distribution practices. Instead of local auxiliaries inaugurating this General Supply, the Society's Board of Managers began discussing it as early as 1880. Again, as it had done during the second and third General Supplies, the Board carried out the Society's design to canvass the nation for those destitute of the Bible.[128] The Board of Managers believed that the Society had never been better able to meet the needs of large-scale scripture production and distribution. This belief, coupled with the conviction that the United States had become "eminently missionary ground" through the growing influx of immigrants (by the Society's count, 600,000 in 1881 alone), convinced the Board that the time was ripe for yet another attempt at supplying every household with a bible—in a nation then numbering 53,000,000 inhabitants.[129] Integral to the fourth General Supply was the importance laid on the more professional distribution network that had been formed since the first General Supply. The Board of Managers stated in its resolution, "Highly as the Board prizes the active co-operation of local auxiliaries it no longer relies upon them alone for supplying the people with the Bible." When local auxiliaries could not assume the responsibility, the Society would send its "own colporteurs to visit every family and thus directly [bring] the Scriptures within the reach of those who had hitherto been neglected."[130]

The fourth General Supply began in 1882 and lasted eight years, twice as long as any of the General Supplies that had preceded it. Still, the most optimistic estimates reveal that it got bibles into the hands of only 10 percent of the general population.[131] Even with the longer span of time in the fourth General Supply, the Society simply could not keep up with America's ever-growing, ever-moving, ever-diversifying population.

Judging the Society's General Supplies through a strictly statistical grid undervalues the importance of the attempts. Although the General Supplies failed to place a bible in the hands of every American destitute of the Scriptures, the vision and immense effort involved in door-to-door visiting of millions of families and the production of millions of bibles stand as vibrant testimony to the persevering belief by the American Bible Society in the importance of the Bible in American culture. The continued presence of a mighty publishing organization that enjoyed the luxury of being able to concentrate on a single product and print that product in figures that annually hovered around, or exceeded, a million volumes had profound repercussions in the print culture of the time.[132] While the general culture was touched to differing degrees by the Society's efforts, these same efforts touched every segment of American bible publishing.

With its ability to focus on a single type of book, the American Bible Society developed a production power that made it increasingly difficult for smaller publishers to compete in the production of cheap, durable bibles. The fact that the Bible was a large, complex volume demanding considerable resources from a publisher did not make competing with the Bible Society any easier. Alluding to the dominant role of the American Bible Society in bible production, a Congregational minister by the name of Chauncy Goodrich addressed a meeting of a local bible society in 1830:

> It has been generally understood and believed that the printing of bibles is now confined, in a great measure, to Bible Societies. If this be true in any part of our country—if we have dried up any of the thousand streams which were carrying life and fertility throughout our land, we are doubly bound to make broad and deep the river of the Word of Life, which proceeds from this fountain; or we shall leave the condition of our country incomparably worse than we found it. But it has been said, you are establishing a monopoly for the production of Bibles, and are doing it in opposition to the clearest principles of trade. I am perfectly aware, Sir, that the most effectual mode of circulating any ordinary commodity to the widest extent, is to throw it at once into the hands of individual enterprise. But the Bible is a commodity of a very peculiar kind . . . it is a commodity, which valuable as the world acknowledge it to be, the greater part of mankind do, after all, *exceedingly dislike*. They choose to keep it as far from *their* bosoms as they conveniently can. And all experience has shown that our country will utterly outgrow the knowledge of the Bible, if we leave its circulation to the ordinary channels of trade.[133]

What Goodrich states in this address is as interesting as what he implies. He argues that the Bible is a special book requiring special measures. Free trade is no match for a nation that is teetering on the edge of infidelity. He argues that bible societies must exist along with every other form of bible production and distribution in order to create a society able "to stand forth in the light of Divine approbation."[134] He also makes no apology for the monopolistic tendency of bible societies. He is clearly more interested in getting bibles into circulation than he is in probing the influential role of bible societies in the commercial market.

Not everyone was as unconcerned with the economic ramifications of bible societies as Goodrich. Goodrich's descriptions of the Bible as a commodity and the American Bible Society as potentially monopolistic provide a vivid backdrop for the contents of an anonymous pamphlet that appeared at about the same time called *An Expose of the Rise and Proceedings of the American Bible Society During the Thirteen Years of Its Existence*.[135] This pamphlet offers remarkable insight into the state of the American bible trade. The author writes: "Previous to the formation of this institution, the most lucrative branch of the book trade was that of vending Bibles. Since then, this has been entirely cut off from the regular booksellers. They find that the competition is vain."[136]

The American Bible Society's desire to have "the sole right of furnishing the printed Bible to the inhabitants of this country" had squeezed a host of other bible publishers out of the market. The pamphlet's author rants that booksellers who have invested in bible stereotype plates might as well "melt them up" because the Society's bible editions are making all rival editions worthless.[137]

It is no accident that both *An Expose of the Rise and Proceedings of the American Bible Society* and Chauncy Goodrich's speech came out in 1829 and 1830, respectively. The American Bible Society's first General Supply brought to the forefront much of the tension existing in bible publishing up to that date. From the tone of the *Expose*, one begins to see that the days of printers like Mathew Carey, who were able to make significant sums of money publishing the Bible, were threatened with extinction. Religious publications, so long the mainstay of American printers, were slowly coming under the control of a few large publishing enterprises such as the American Bible Society, the American Sunday School Union, the Methodist Publishing House, and the American Tract Society. The enormous production volume and extensive volunteer distribution network of the American Bible Society brought into bold relief what the emergence of such a powerful publishing enterprise meant for other publishers who had an interest in bible production.

In 1829, the American Bible Society printed 360,000 bibles. By the 1860s, the Society was regularly printing over a million volumes a year. The immensity of these production statistics, coupled with the fact that such high volume allowed the Society to perform at unprecedented economies of scale, highlights just how threatening the Society and its low-cost bibles would be to rival publishers.

The reason behind the *Expose* writer's lament that no "regular trader in books" could hope to compete with the Society is seen in a comparison of the booksellers' prices to those of the newly emergent American Bible Society.[138] Between 1814 and 1844, the Society's cheapest volumes were consistently priced lower than the bibles of its competitors. The Society would actually undersell "regular traders" throughout the century.[139]

With Society prices as low as six cents for testaments and forty-five cents for bibles in the 1840s, it not only becomes clear that the Society was underselling other publishers, but also that its bibles were cheaper than most books of the period. American Bible Society bibles were almost entirely hardbound, and hardbound book prices remained largely constant during the antebellum period, ranging from seventy-five cents to one dollar and twenty-five cents.[140] For publishers, lower prices meant lower profit margins. Profit meant little to the American Bible Society, since its goal was more missionary than economic in nature.

It did not take bible producers long to realize that it was well nigh impossible to compete with the American Bible Society in the area of cheap bibles. Thomas Whitearsh, a Chicago book agent for G. & C. Merriam, captured the futility of such an endeavor when he wrote to his firm in 1844 that "Bibles sell here as cheap as they do at the East. The Bible Society of this city afford them low."[141] This futility, however, did not mean that publishers ceased bible production; they simply decided to produce bibles of a different type than those of the American Bible Society. Parson Weems's strategy of filling bibles with as many curiosities as possible characterized this new type of bible production. The diverse brand of bible publishing Mathew Carey had begun in 1807 would now come to greater and greater prominence as the American Bible Society continued to produce an unprecedented volume of bibles.

Because publishers could not compete with the American Bible Society in terms of price, they chose to approach the bible market through a different door which the American Bible Society had closed to itself. The Society had committed itself to publishing bibles "without note or comment"; other bible publishers felt no such restrictions. To avoid directly competing with the publishing power of the American Bible Society, bible publishers increasingly turned their energies to producing bibles filled with more notes, more tables, more commentaries, more illustrations, and more elaborate bindings. More specialized bibles began to appear, as evidenced by names such as *The Cottage Bible Family Expositor*, *The Devotional Family Bible*, *The Illuminated Bible*, *The English Version of the Polyglott Bible*, and *The Illustrated Domestic Bible*. Although other publishers could not beat the Society's bible prices, they could outdo the Society's bibles in terms of ornamentation and content.

This diversity of bible production and marketing is reflected in Margaret Hills's bibliography of the English Bible in America beginning in the 1830s. Two previously rare elements in bibles—illustrations and commentaries—began appearing in bibles as early as the 1820s due to changes in technology, coupled with the emerging strength of the American Bible Society. The dramatic increase of these elements reveals the changing nature of bibles produced in America following the emergence of the American Bible Society, which did not publish bibles with notes or pictures. Bible editions published with illustrations dramatically increased throughout the nineteenth century, growing from 16 percent of the editions produced in the decade beginning in 1810, to 28 percent in the 1820s, to 38 percent in the decade following the first General Supply.[142] This upward trend rose to 59 percent in the 1870s.

The same growth trend can be detected in the publication of bible editions containing major commentary notes.[143] In the decade before the first General Supply, 27 percent of English Bible editions produced in America included some sort of commentary. This number grew to such an extent that by the 1870s, 60 percent of American bible editions included some sort of extended commentary. By midcentury, editions produced by the American Bible Society—austere in content and often packaging when compared to other bibles of the period—were in a noticeable minority in the bible marketplace.[144]

The emergence of the American Bible Society not only brought forth more English bibles, but also helped significantly reshape the bible market in America. As the Society continued to churn out hundreds of thousands of cheaper bibles and testaments, other book publishers quickly realized that profit and survival in the bible market could more easily be found in areas left alone by the American Bible Society.

In its fervor to flood the United States with bibles, the American Bible Society had laid the groundwork for an American bible marketplace filled with increasingly diverse versions of the Sacred Scripture. The same printing technology that had enabled the Society to entertain the dream of giving the United States a central text also enabled an ever-wider range of publishers to take that text and turn it to their own ends. By the 1830s, it had become strikingly clear that a bible was no longer just a bible; it could be any one of myriad different editions. Although Americans had never enjoyed a total uniformity when it came to the bibles they read, the emergence of the American Bible Society greatly amplified the fragmentation of the American bible market. Rather than helping facilitate Boudinot's dream of national and moral unity by building a city on a hill (of bibles), the Society had helped lay the foundation for a new type of Tower of Babel.

Chapter Two

PACKAGING

1 Among the thousands who flooded New York City in the spring of
1789 to catch a glimpse of George Washington's presidential inauguration was the fifteen-year-old Eliza Morton. A careful diarist, Eliza kept a
meticulous record of the event, describing awe-inspiring military escorts,
fifteen-gun naval salutes, nightly banquets, adoring crowds, and even a
spectacular fireworks display. All this activity was peripheral, however, to
the inauguration's "dignified and solemn" crowning moment when Washington stepped out onto the balcony of New York's Federal Hall to take his
oath of office.[1] Eliza writes: "Chancellor [Robert] Livingston read the
form of oath prescribed by the Constitution; Washington repeated it, rest-
ing his hand upon the Bible. Mr. Otis, the secretary of the Senate, then
took the Bible to raise it to the lips of Washington who stooped to kiss the
book"[2] (see Figure 3). Jacob Morton, an attendant on the balcony, then
stepped forward to mark the place Washington had kissed.

Physically and symbolically at the center of this momentous event
stood "a large and elegant bible" that lay on "a table, with a rich covering
of red velvet; and upon this, on a crimson velvet cushion."[3] The centrality
of the bible is all the more striking when one realizes that the Constitution
does not require a bible for administering the oath of office. Those present, however, clearly felt the need for a copy of the Scriptures, so much so
that they nearly panicked before the ceremony when they realized they
had no available copy of the Bible. They only narrowly averted a disaster
in decorum through a last-minute dash to a local Masonic lodge where
someone had remembered there was a copy of the Holy Scriptures.[4]

The use of a bible at Washington's inauguration testifies to how the
Bible functions as a material entity, not simply a written text. From its role
in the actual ceremony to the red cushion upon which it rested, the use
of the Bible testified to its cultural value. Such venerable usage derived,
of course, from Old World practice. Cushions had long been used to cradle bibles and keep them from touching profane surfaces, and the Bible's
role in oath-taking dates back to St. Augustine.[5] For centuries, kings and

The auspicious 4th of March 1789, when the Father of his Country, as President of United America, gave the first energies to that Federal Compact which has proved the Palladium of the Nation.   *Chap.ᵗ XLII Page 274.*

FIGURE 3. The inauguration of George Washington as depicted in Frederick Butler's *Sketches of Universal History* (1818). Even in this later fictional representation of the event, the Bible plays a central role. (Courtesy of the American Antiquarian Society)

queens—including the British royal family—had adhered to the tradition of taking their coronation oaths upon a bible.[6] As Washington's inauguration shows, the Bible had to be present for the oath; invoking its contents was not enough. The physicality of the Bible is further underscored in how Washington placed his hand upon the book and then leaned down to kiss it. According to the custom exercised in British ecclesiastical courts, kissing the Bible completed the oath ritual.[7]

Jacob Morton's action, however, of noting the pages Washington had kissed points beyond the Bible's role in oath taking. For centuries, men and women had randomly opened revered cultural texts such as the *Iliad* or the *Aeneid* as oracles of wisdom. In many Christian countries, including the United States, this practice of haphazardly opening a book came to center primarily on the Bible, revealing yet again its central importance in early American culture.[8] Such randomly chosen passages were believed to have an almost magical power to reveal the future and answer difficult questions.[9] Washington had kissed Genesis, chapters 49 and 50, passages that include Joseph's dying reminder that God had promised the Israelites a new land.

What is perhaps most striking in considering the Bible at Washington's inauguration is the complete absence of any mention that the volume was actually read. Participants urgently sought it out, had it carefully displayed, touched, opened, and kissed it, but at no point did someone read from its pages. Such ceremonial usage belies the common belief that books essentially communicate meaning via written symbols. Additionally, books are often powerful mediums of communication in and of themselves. The Bible was a text that conveyed meanings on a number of levels. The increasingly diverse bible market of the nineteenth century left no doubt that the Scripture's content *and* covering were both critical elements in how early Americans understood and used the sacred volume.[10]

The publishing competition spawned by the American Bible Society ushered in an era of exceptionally elaborate bibles. These magnificent bibles may have contained the same core text, but they accompanied that text with increasingly complex commentaries, luxurious illustrations, and ornate bindings.

The American Bible Society had attempted to flood the world of print with numberless copies of the Bible to insure the preeminence of the text; other strategies for achieving this same goal involved enhancing the Bible's material and textual content. Striking among such strategies were bindings and illustrations. The physical packaging of the biblical message became a powerful means of accenting both the importance and trustworthiness of the Bible's message. Also, packaging often had the perverse effect of contradicting or de-emphasizing the sacred words it was intended to highlight.

2   While the act of reading is most often associated with interpreting written messages, books can also be "read" in a different way without ever looking at the words they contain.[11] The fact that a book's packaging was "read" in antebellum America can be seen in a number of different ways.[12] Displaying books had long been a sign of learning, but such displays took on new meaning at the beginning of the nineteenth century. The presence of books also came to be regarded as a signal of the cultural refinement of their owner.[13] Bookbinding practices in the early nineteenth century "dictated that the cover reflect the content of the book."[14] Law books, medical books, novels, and bibles all had a particular look that made them easily identifiable from a distance.[15] At midcentury, owners of bookstores displayed bibles randomly throughout their stock because costly bibles were often the most ornate and beautiful books to be found in their stores.[16] The diversity of binding styles also produced an element of product differentiation that encouraged a link between a book's binding and its buyer's social and economic status.[17]

Because of their cultural importance, bibles are particularly revealing examples of how a book's binding can influence the interpretation of a book's content. One is able to see this interpretive significance of a bible's exterior presentation by considering the changing nature of bookbinding in the first half of the nineteenth century. Before 1820, books were most often sold in unbound sheets. The purchaser would then either pay the printer an additional fee to have the sheets bound or go to a bookbinder to have this service rendered. This procedure began to alter in the 1820s with the invention of prefabricated bindings, greater mechanization in the binding process, and the introduction of cloth as binding material.[18] These three factors radically altered the business of bookbinding.

Books began to be distributed in what came to be known as "edition bindings," whereby an entire press run of a given book would be bound in a predetermined range of styles. Cloth, both cheaper and more accessible than leather, quickly became a favorite among publishers who increasingly found it a sales advantage to bind their books in the wide variety of styles and colors available in cloth.

Bibles reflected the shifts in binding practices in the 1830s and 1840s, but only in a strikingly small degree. Long after cloth came to dominate almost every other area of the bookbinding trade, bibles continued to be predominantly bound in various types of leather. Convincing evidence for the slow acceptance of cloth for binding bibles is found in the library of the American Bible Society, the largest collection of bibles in the United States.[19] The holdings of the American Bible Society show that leather bindings dominate American Bible binding throughout the nineteenth century. While cloth binding was quickly being adopted throughout the wider publishing industry for all books except the most expensive editions of certain works, ninety-two percent of the American-produced English bibles in the American Bible Society collection were still bound in leather throughout the 1840s.[20]

It is only in the decade directly preceding the Civil War that the percentage of leather-bound bibles begins a steady decline, dropping into the eightieth percentile in the 1850s and into the seventieth percentile in the next two decades.[21] Thus, the 1850s saw the beginning of a trend toward a more marked acceptance of using cloth to bind bibles. It should be noted, however, that through the 1860s no complete folio or large quarto bible is bound in cloth. Thus, while smaller editions of the Bible slowly adopted the convention of cloth binding, larger bibles continued to be bound almost exclusively in leather.

While the material used for binding bibles was slow to change, bibles produced in this period did not lack diversity. Because of their prized nature, American bibles were often decoratively bound, following an age-old tradition of binding ornamentation that probably originated with bible binding.[22] The type and style of decoration varied greatly, but it most often involved stamping a range of designs into the leather bindings with hand tools. Later, binders embossed leather bibles, a process whereby the cover of volumes was decorated in relief by pressing a metal design block into the leather.[23] Embossed designs usually covered the entire surface of a book, while stamped designs were often limited to decorating a binding's edges or center. The highly personal nature of bible binding is reflected in the common use of decorative monograms, as well as distinctive binding leathers. One bible owner bound his volume with the hide of a favorite dog.[24]

In the midst of diversity, however, one confronts the fact that bibles were predominantly bound in leather long after cloth had gained wide acceptance among book manufacturers.[25] While a number of reasons are responsible for this persistence of leather bindings, it can be seen as an attempt both to maintain an already established cultural association between biblical content and covering, as well as mark the inward value of the book with an expensive exterior.[26] Bibles bound in leather could be distinguished from more "secular" volumes as their more expensive binding materials echoed the book's priceless content.

Leather binding also conveyed another message about the book it covered. The relatively stable nature of bible bindings underlined the timeless, unchanging message of the Bible. In a broad sense, God's word—and the packaging of that word—was the same yesterday, today, and tomorrow.

3   In the early nineteenth century, the easily recognizable physical appearance of bibles played an important role in the creation of material environments intended to foster spiritual growth and moral action. One of the best examples of this trend is the presence—and often ostentatious display—of the Bible in family parlors.[27]

As the cultural historian Karen Halttunen has argued, the parlor was a mediating room in the home between the public space outside the house and the more private interior space inhabited by the family.[28] In many homes affluent enough to enjoy a parlor as a place for entertaining visitors and holding organized social gatherings, there stood on its own table a prominently displayed family bible.[29] In such settings, the mere presence of a bible communicated certain meanings that did not depend on the reading or recitation of biblical texts.

Standing amid the carefully choreographed furnishings of the parlor, a bible became a piece of furniture, a decorative addition to the room.[30] Like all decoration and furniture, the Bible helped establish a particular atmosphere in the room it occupied. Displaying the family bible created a space in which the distinction between church and home began to blur.

One of the most vivid examples of this blurring can be seen in a house design offered by Catharine Beecher and her sister Harriet Beecher Stowe, where by removing certain partitions the parlor could be transformed into a nave.[31] A bible placed on its own table or pedestal helped create this mixed sense of space by establishing, in effect, a kind of pulpit or altar within the parlor, so that domestic space became sacred.[32] The very presence of the Bible signaled the family's commitment to religious—or at least genteel—principles and marked the room as an environment that nurtured spiritual and "moral growth."[33] The home became an extension of the church with its own ability to foster spiritual growth.

Although such genuflections in American Romantic and Victorian culture may seem largely superficial, in fact this use of the Bible as an item of display in the parlor ultimately was noted in the fundamental philosophic assumptions about epistemology and virtuous behavior of the period. Scottish Common Sense philosophy, which provided America with its most prevalent epistemological system in the opening decades of the nineteenth century, had claims far beyond the narrow confines of epistemology per se.

Numerous scholars have commented on the almost immeasurable importance of Scottish Common Sense philosophy in early nineteenth-century America, noting that it was both "the official academic belief of the period" and a way of thinking best described with the noun "ubiquity."[34] It was a philosophy deeply concerned with moral action and how knowing could be channeled into proper ways of doing.

Recent scholarly discussions of virtuous or moral behavior in this period have largely focused on one of Scottish Common Sense's most popular manifestations—sentimentalism—without recognizing sentimentalism's critical connection to Scottish Common Sense philosophy.[35] Whether one attributes moral behavior to Scottish Common Sense philosophy or its better known offspring, sentimentalism, the fact remains that American culture in the opening decades of the nineteenth century was deeply marked by ideologies concerned with pursuing virtuous action. An example of this concern with virtuous action is found in the rise of the concept of virtuous citizenry. Such a citizenry was considered essential for the survival of the United States' democratic government.[36]

The connection between bibles and Scottish Common Sense philosophy returns us to Elias Boudinot, whose life and work stand as one of Scottish Common Sense's most vivid manifestations. As we have seen, when Boudinot pressed forward with his wish to establish a national bible society, he dreamed of stemming the tide of his beloved country's infidelity by placing a bible in the hands of every one of its citizens.

Serving as the ideological cornerstone to Boudinot's plan for national redemption was the notion that simply exposing Americans to biblical truth would lead to their spiritual, and thus moral, regeneration. The presumably clear and truthful teachings of the Bible would prevail. At the root of this notion stood the belief that truth was both self-evident and virtually self-enforcing.[37] Boudinot clearly adhered to certain strains of the Scottish Common Sense school of philosophy that deeply influenced both the theological and educational thinking of his day.[38]

Although Scottish Common Sense philosophy was not a monolithic entity, certain key elements appear throughout the teachings of its early proponents in the late seventeenth century to its last prominent defenders near the end of the nineteenth century.[39] Among these central elements, two stand out as particularly important for a broader understanding of how the Bible was read before the Civil War. First, Scottish Common Sense had its foundation in the view that reality could be experienced directly and accurately through one's senses. This view had one of its most important consequences in the belief that right and wrong were immediately discernible from the reality of the external world. When exposed to truth, a person would readily know the "right" from the "wrong."[40] A second basic principle of Scottish Common Sense philosophy was that people were endowed with a "moral sense" that facilitated their ability to know, and act upon, truth, in addition to the five senses of sight, hearing, touch, taste, and smell.[41]

Thus, for Boudinot and much of the Protestant leadership of the early nineteenth century, the effective inculcation of truth and the resultant promotion of virtuous behavior required first that the Bible be aggressively distributed, as people could not act on the truth unless they were exposed to it; and second, that the moral sense that would guide their actions be properly nurtured.

It is in this presumption of a moral sense that one begins to see where Scottish Common Sense philosophy and sentimentalism share common ground. Recent scholars of American sentimentalism have largely focused on various cultural practices intended to evoke primarily emotional responses.[42] The term "sentiment" as it came to be used in early nineteenth-century America cannot be separated from its Scottish Common Sense roots.[43] Scottish Common Sense's notion of sentiment was wholly wrapped up in the idea of "moral sentiment" and the "moral sense."

Consequently, sentimentalism was a set of cultural practices designed to activate the moral sense and ultimately encourage moral action. While evoking moral responses often meant evoking emotional responses as well, the goal of the sentimental was never intended to make one simply cry, sympathize, or feel remorse, but to move one to take some kind of moral action. This action most often took the form of benevolence—the extension of one's will and resources for the betterment of another.

Even though printing presses could produce millions of bibles and tracts to expose people to the truth, these same presses could not serve as the sole cultivators of the moral sense. Printing presses by themselves could not create a virtuous citizenry. The cultivation of such virtue needed to happen outside the covers of a book. Environments were required that nurtured the moral sense into transforming the appreciation of truth into virtuous action. The immensely popular minister, Henry Ward Beecher, perhaps captured this line of thinking best when he stated that the moral training of children depended most importantly on surrounding "them by such conditions . . . as will have a powerful, though indirect, influence upon their moral amelioration and upbuilding."[44]

In antebellum ideology and rhetoric, and increasingly in practice, the burden of moral education came to rest on women and the domestic environment they created and ruled.[45] As a result, the idea of a morally nurturing environment stood as the meeting place between Scottish Common Sense philosophy and the type of sentimentalism that has come to be most frequently associated with domesticity. Believing that if the proper environment could be provided, virtuous behavior would be insured and a harmonious society could be built, Americans began to look to the home as a crucial place for the moral development of their young republic.

As the importance of the home as a crucial training environment for future citizens continued to rise in the years leading up to the Civil War, the role of women also rose in importance.[46] The moral development that took place in the home gave women an almost clerical status in the realm of their domestic church.[47]

At the symbolic center of these new "domestic churches" stood the Bible, prominently displayed in the house as a symbol of truth's presence and importance within the home. The Bible could therefore be read as a sentimental artifact, an object whose mere presence infused its surroundings with a sense of the moral and the sacred, helping to make the home into an environment of moral nurture. The physical presence of the Bible underlined central components of Scottish Common Sense philosophy. It helped create a proper environment, while its presence stood as a visible, tangible representation of the "good." The physical display of the Bible complemented Common Sense's emphasis on the visible and readily apparent nature of truth. The existence and saving action of a merciful God could not be easily forgotten when the Bible was displayed as a prominent reminder of God's relationship with humanity both inside and outside the church.

4 While the size, color, and exterior decoration of bibles could communicate certain genteel and religious meanings, no less communicative were other aspects of a bible's packaging. Perhaps most noticeable among these were illustrations. One can clearly see the importance of illustrations to the Bible's content and interpretation in the products and publishing activities of the young republic's first two premier printers: Isaiah Thomas and Mathew Carey. Although their goals may have differed, Thomas and Carey both appreciated the message—and profit potential—of visual texts. They also saw how visual texts might influence the use of a particular bible edition.

Isaiah Thomas, printer, publisher extraodinaire, and philanthropist, gave the United States its first indigenous illustrated English bible when he released his magnificent folio edition in 1791. Thomas, an archetype of the self-made man, championed a strain of Enlightenment thinking that espoused social, moral, and intellectual improvement was not only the right, but within the grasp, of all people. He believed that enlightened rationality not only enabled one to better his or her position in the world, but benefited society in general by making it a more courteous, refined, and charitable place.[48]

The most visible manifestation of Thomas's belief in human potential and the benefits of refinement appears in his folio bible of 1791, an edition Thomas touted as unrivaled in either craftsmanship or content. Setting out to prove correct the post-Revolution sentiment that American products were every bit as good as their British counterparts, Thomas embarked upon his bible project with single-minded devotion. He constructed his own paper mill and bookbindery to aid the volume's production.[49] Driving his workers to the point of exhaustion, Thomas readied his luxurious folio edition (which he simultaneously produced with a more affordable quarto edition) in just over twelve months. Even the aged former printer Benjamin Franklin added his voice to the throngs that hailed Thomas's folio as the most beautiful book ever printed in America.[50]

Printed on high-quality paper, set in well-formed type, and often bound with beautifully ornamented covers, perhaps no element of Thomas's folio more clearly communicated its aspirations toward an Enlightenment aesthetic of virtuous gentility and high art than its fifty copperplate illustrations. Maintaining his emphasis on the "American" nature of his folio bible, Thomas had engaged four New England artists to produce fifty original copperplate engravings for his edition.[51] The method of copperplate engraving had long been employed in bible illustration because it produced the highest quality reproductions; pictures characterized by fine, precise lines that transferred well to paper. It was also the most expensive of the available illustration techniques. Copperplates were soft, and their lines often had to be reworked after just fifty engravings because pressure from the press tended to flatten the copperplate's grooves, thus distorting the illustration.[52]

Adding to the plates' fragility was the fact that unlike more common and inexpensive woodblock prints, copperplate illustrations had to be printed apart from the printed text because type and copperplates required differently designed printing presses. This need for different presses made copperplate illustrations more time-intensive and costly; it also produced books with pictures that necessarily had to be on different pages from the text—usually on higher quality, more expensive paper.[53] Thomas clearly chose copperplate illustrations not for their economy, but for their beauty.

Thomas's commitment to high art carried beyond the method of production into the content of the illustrations themselves. His folio's illustrations adopted the European artistic conventions of the rococo style most often associated with "the very limit of upper-class refinement."[54] Most commonly characterized by the frequent use of S and C curves, cherubs and children, clamshells and nature motifs, and a pronounced emphasis on the feminine, rococo was adopted by the eighteenth-century European aristocracy and middle class as an art form that evoked and invoked human sensibility and refinement.

Rococo's ceaseless appeal to the emotional through pleasurable sensation bears testimony once again to the importance of the senses in Enlightenment thought. The rococo style was bent on portraying beauty, often in a sensuous way, as seen in how it frequently depicted eroticized representations of classical figures in the pleasure parks and villas of European aristocracy. Thomas attempted to recodify the rococo for his bible readers by fusing beauty with certain key virtues such as honesty, courage, and wisdom in the context of biblical scenes. By linking beauty with these virtues, Thomas strove to refine his viewer's sensibilities and encourage them to think of virtuous action as a beautiful thing.[55]

The folio's illustrations are replete with rococo conventions. Thomas repeatedly employs the central rococo notion of women as moral instructors and spiritual guardians. This notion is prominent from the volume's outset, where the first plate to follow the frontispiece represents Eve as the alert overseer of creation while Adam naps (see Figure 4). Figures 5 and 6 are further examples of how the folio's illustrations foreground morally superior feminine figures. In Figure 5, Susanna virtuously resists the lascivious advances of two elders, while Figure 6 shows Esther fainting as she seeks to save her people from destruction.

In addition to using rococo motifs within the illustrations, the folio bible also surrounds the pictures with rococo framing. Elaborate scrolls relaying the dominant rococo S and C lines (see Figure 7) and cherubic figures mimicking the illustration's central action are repeatedly employed throughout the bible (see Figure 8). Rococo period artists favored the use of cherubs and cherubic figures—child-angels that neatly splice the spiritual and maternal—and nearly one-third of the folio's fifty plates contains at least one of these infant angels. Cherubs did more, however, than conjure rococo genteel overtones; they also reminded bible readers of the spiritual dimension of all human events.

Thomas's portrayal of women in the high artistic style of rococo brought with it certain problems. Dominant among these was the fact that the rococo style favored women with bare breasts, a politicized convention in Europe that emphasized the importance of the maternal, nurturing influence for the health of the body politic.[56] This convention is seen throughout Thomas's plates in everything from the obviously exposed breasts of Eve to the barely exposed nipples in pictures such as *Mary Magdalene* (see Figure 9) and *Queen Esther fainting before King Artaxerxes* (see Figure 6).

Such depictions may have evoked the high art and political conventions of European refinement, but they upset the more religiously conservative sensibilities of many of Thomas's bible readers. Upon being allowed

49

Engraved for Thomas's 8º Edition of the Bible.

GENESIS Chap. 2.

J.H.Seymour.del.sculp.

The CREATION.

FIGURE 4. *The Creation* from Isaiah Thomas's 1791 folio bible. Note the vigilant female and the male in repose. (Courtesy of the Lilly Library, Indiana University, Bloomington, Indiana)

FIGURE 6. *Queen Esther fainting before King Artaxerxes* from Isaiah Thomas's 1791 folio bible edition. (Courtesy of the Lilly Library, Indiana University, Bloomington, Indiana)

FIGURE 7. *Noah and his Family going to enter the Ark* framed by rococo artistic conventions from Isaiah Thomas's 1791 folio bible edition. (Courtesy of the Lilly Library, Indiana University, Bloomington, Indiana)

Engraved for Thomas's Edition of the Bible.

F. Le Meme delin.   Jos.ª Seymour Sculp.

GEN. III. 24.

The EXPULSION *of* ADAM *and* EVE *from* PARADISE.

FIGURE 8. *The Expulsion of Adam and Eve from Paradise* with cherubs mimicking the scene's central action, from Isaiah Thomas's 1791 folio bible edition. (Courtesy of the Lilly Library, Indiana University, Bloomington, Indiana)

FIGURE 9. *Mary Magdalene* with slightly exposed breast, from Isaiah Thomas's 1791 folio bible edition. (Courtesy of the Lilly Library, Indiana University, Bloomington, Indiana)

an early glimpse of the folio's copperplates, Jeremy Belknap thought "the position of the figures in the first plate very bad, especially Eve, whose is in a very indecent posture."[57] While Thomas was attempting to cultivate a refined sensibility through his illustrations, Belknap saw them stimulating less virtuous, totally inappropriate appetites.

Thomas's aspirations and Belknap's response reveal the brutal truth that pictures do not contain a single, readily apparent message. Although illustrations had long been used to accent or further explicate the Bible's written text, the visual commentary they provided was not always easily interpreted.[58] Pictures are frequently not straightforward interpretive devices. While illustrations may emphasize some aspect of a written narrative, they can also distract from, or subvert, the narrative they illustrate.[59] Words may say one thing, pictures another. As seen in Belknap's response to Thomas's high art aspirations, the Bible's sacred message was subverted by the "indecent" illustrations that accompanied it. What was seen as spiritual and refined by one reader could appear quasi-pornographic to another.

The complicated nature of juxtaposed visual and verbal texts becomes all the more complex when one considers economic concerns in relation to bible illustration. Forever faced with the material realities of producing books that would sell, publishers sometimes chose to illustrate their bibles as much for financial reasons as to aid a reader's interpretation of the sacred volume.

One of the clearest examples of such financial canniness and moral elasticity is found in Mathew Carey's publishing enterprise. As already noted, Carey produced more editions of the English Bible in the United States than any other publisher prior to the formation of the American Bible Society. He also illustrated dozens of his bible editions with a wide array of maps and pictures. Unlike Thomas, however, his illustrations were most often printed from woodblocks, a cheaper and cruder method of illustration, which did not have the tendency to evoke the high art aspirations of the copperplate method.[60]

If Belknap was uncomfortable with the pictures Thomas had included in his folio volume, he would have been absolutely distraught if he ever happened across Carey's bible illustrations. Carey's illustrations echo the Thomas folio's interest in the female body, but Carey puts his barebreasted women in settings that clearly fall outside the elegant and refined realm of the rococo.

Rather than placing women in the midst of peaceful garden scenes, Carey emphasized carnage and carnality by including pictures of nearnaked women being trampled, murdered, and molested. In an illustration of the Gospel story of Herod's mass slaughter of innocent children (see

Plate 16. Page 728.

Herod was exceeding wroth, & sent forth & slew all the children that were in Bethlehem, & in all the coasts thereof, from two years old and under.
Matthew. Ch. 2. V. 16.

FIGURE 10. *The Slaughter of the Innocents* from Mathew Carey's 1803 quarto bible edition. (Beinecke Rare Book and Manuscript Library, Yale University)

Figure 10), disrobed mothers are assaulted, and cherubic children fall to sword.

Neither does Carey mitigate the licentiousness of his pictures with Thomas's rococo framing devices or a strict adherence to the Bible's story line. Not only do his pictures appear without the softening influence of framing scrolls, flowers, and tapestries, but also Carey feels a freedom to fill his illustrations with nonbiblical, titillating additions. For example, Figure 11 shows a rendition of the Prodigal Son story from Carey's volume. Giving his own twist to a scene that had been a perennial favorite among bible illustrators for two centuries, Carey seems to have once again opted to follow Weems's advice to fill his bible editions with as many curiosities as possible.

In the upper right-hand corner of the picture, one finds the molestation of a screaming, bare-breasted woman; no trace of any such woman

FIGURE 11. *The Prodigal Son* from Mathew Carey's 1813 quarto bible edition. (Beinecke Rare Book and Manuscript Library, Yale University)

appears in the biblical text. Careful inspection of Carey's illustrations repeatedly reveal surprising, often sexually provocative extra-biblical details. Such additions make one wonder whether Carey knew such details would somehow give his bibles an edge over his competition's volumes. Readers could read the edifying biblical text while also enjoying the ambiguous accompanying illustrations.

In addition to using the content of his bible's illustrations to make his volumes stand out, Carey also frequently employed a formatting strategy that emphasized the pictures he included in his editions. Although the heavily individualized nature of book production in this period makes generalizations on the uniformity of various editions tricky, nearly half of the fourteen Carey bibles I have examined show that illustrations were clustered rather than spread out evenly throughout the text. Often there are five illustrations within a fifteen-page range. The effect of this clustering was further accented by the fact that Carey's illustrations frequently were printed on a heavier weight, single-sided stock used specifically for illustrations. When bound next to standard text page, these single-sided sheets stand out. In the midst of flipping through a Carey bible, one is able to find the illustrations quickly. When the illustrations are clustered together, it is easy to skip the pages between the illustrations as one moves from illustration to illustration. By placing illustrations so closely together, Carey accentuated their presence and made it possible for a "reader" to move quickly from one picture to the next, ignoring the text these pictures were supposedly illustrating.

Thus, Carey's more heavily illustrated editions could serve as picture books that drew the reader to a visual rather than verbal narrative. In this manner, the Bible's complex verbal narrative is undercut by the simpler and more physically accessible pictures that accompany the text. Biblical moments foregrounded in illustrations can take on importance far out of proportion to their textual presence; a minor biblical scene such as Obadiah fleeing Jezebel can take on the same narrative weight as Jesus rising from the dead.

Carey's binding strategy and choice of illustrative content boldly underscore how the Bible's core message never reached its readers without some form of material mediation. This mediation could exercise a profound influence on one's reading experience and interpretation of a bible. The multivalent, multilayered nature of illustrations could lead readers to find in their bibles unexpected, even unholy, messages. The levels of discourse and narrative possibilities created by juxtaposed verbal and visual texts, binding strategies, different weights of paper, and artistic conventions make it clear that more than simple religious ideologies drove bible production, distribution, and reception.

5 Even with the rise of the American Bible Society, a number of firms followed in the wake of Thomas and Carey in an attempt to turn a profit by producing bibles. Among the bibles that found particular favor with the public in the first half of the nineteenth century were a series of editions published in the small city of Brattleboro, Vermont.[61]

The instigator of this out-of-the-way bible publishing empire was John Holbrook, who defied a host of naysayers in 1816 by publishing a large family bible. His skeptics had good reasons for their cynicism. Holbrook was a complete novice in the printing trade when he took over his son-in-law's publishing business in 1815. Additionally, Brattleboro had neither the location nor the history to place it as a publishing center that could compete with Philadelphia, Boston, or New York.[62] Yet Holbrook's bibles caught on. Between 1816 and 1852, forty-two editions of the bibles were published by eight different firms connected to John Holbrook.[63]

From the beginning of his publishing career, Holbrook realized the marketing importance of good illustrations. Every one of his bible editions is filled with carefully executed engravings. The fact that Brattleboro bibles remained competitive for nearly four decades testifies to the market sensitivity exercised by the Brattleboro firms. These firms watched closely which types of bibles sold and which did not. Moreover, they were not afraid to experiment with new ideas in the content of their bible illustrations. Thus, Brattleboro bible editions offer an instructive sampling of a motif in American biblical illustration that lasted throughout the nineteenth century.

The first glimpses of this motif appeared in one of John Holbrook's earliest bible editions. From the outset, Holbrook had included a picture of the Tower of Babel in his bibles (see Figure 12). In 1818, a noticeable change appears in his Tower of Babel illustration: For the first time, it is flanked by two cuneiform tablets recently discovered in the Middle East (see Figure 13). The caption under these two tablets reads: "antiquities from Asia brought to New York in Jan. 1817 by Capt. Henry Austin and now at D. Mitchell's." The left side of the picture further reveals that one of the tablets is a "Copy of the scriptures in a fragmentary brick . . . at the Tomb of Daniel the Prophet." In adding these two tablets to the Tower of Babel picture, Holbrook helped inaugurate a trend in American biblical illustration of linking the Bible's text with contemporary travels and archaeological excavations in Egypt and Palestine. Holbrook had chosen to capitalize on the tremendous American interest in the Middle East generated by Napoléon's conquests in that region and the artifacts that began to flow to both Europe and the United States in the aftermath of European intrusions into the region.[64]

Although many Americans showed an interest in the Middle East in

TOWER OF BABEL.

102 years after the flood — 3 years preparing and 22 years in building.
Contained 8 Towers one above another, and each 75 feet high. (Hist.)
Genesis Ch.11.

FIGURE 12. *Tower of Babel* from 1816 Brattleboro bible edition. (Beinecke Rare Book and Manuscript Library, Yale University)

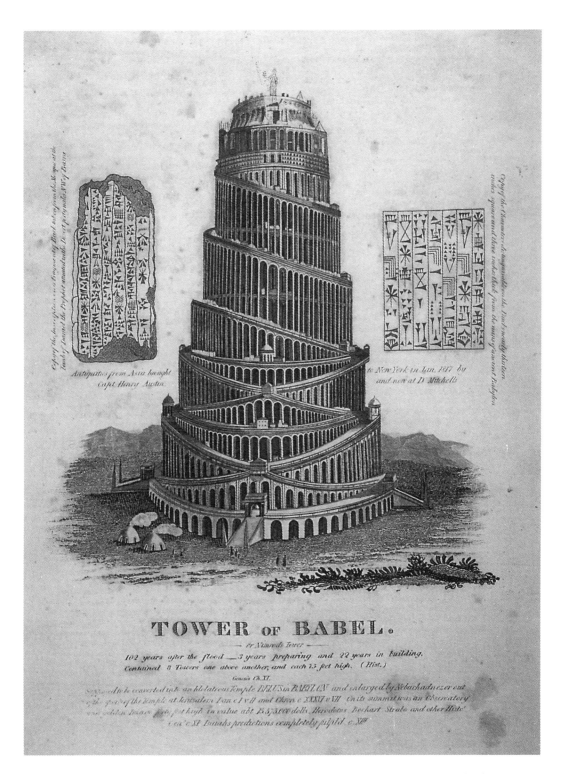

FIGURE 13. *Tower of Babel* with cuneiform tablets, from 1818 Brattleboro bible edition. (Beinecke Rare Book and Manuscript Library, Yale University)

the opening decades of the nineteenth century, it held a special allure for American Protestants.[65] Much of this appeal can be linked to Scottish Common Sense philosophy and its epistemological influences on biblical criticism.[66]

In the opening decades of the nineteenth century, American theological scholarship began to feel the first shockwaves of new trends in European biblical criticism. This criticism involved historical, chronological, and philological attacks on the accuracy of various portions of the Scriptures, placing a heavy emphasis on the need to understand the context of the Scripture writers in order to understand their messages.

Through this contextual lens, the historicity of the Bible became all-important. American biblical scholarship began to reflect a concern with the trustworthiness of the biblical text through a growing body of work concentrating on the accuracy of biblical manuscripts and traditions of interpretation.[67] Divinity programs such as the one at Harvard began to adopt the newer European views, leading more conservative Protestants to found Andover Seminary as a training ground to produce clergy untainted by the dangerous influences of the historical criticism and European rationalism.[68] As textual critics increasingly fought over the accuracy of the actual biblical text, certain biblical scholars turned from strict textual analysis to another biblical "text"—the Holy Land.

This turn toward shoring up the Bible with its land of origin found two powerful advocates in William Thomson and Edward Robinson. Thomson, a missionary in the Middle East, wrote an immensely popular, multivolume work entitled *The Land and the Book*.[69] In it, he set forth a belief in the necessary juxtaposition of the Bible with its geographical origins that gained vast popularity among antebellum Protestants. He called the Holy Land one "vast tablet whereupon God's messages to men have been drawn, and graven deep in living characters by the Great Publisher of glad tidings, to be seen and read [by] all to the end of time. The Land and the Book—with reverence be it said—constitute the entire and all-perfect text, and should be studied together."[70]

While Thomson wrote for the masses, the Congregational theologian Edward Robinson made an international reputation by journeying to Judea and writing on the Holy Land's geographical affirmation of biblical truths.[71] Robinson wrote extensively, mapping Judea physically, socially, and historically. Through these extensive scholarly writings, he founded a school of Protestant biblical apologetics that attempted to strip bare all false impressions of both the Bible's meaning and Judea by linking the study of the Bible to the Holy Land.[72]

As scholars argued over issues of biblical chronology, philology, and historicity, Robinson chose to emphasize the actual existence of the Holy

Land.[73] In true Scottish Common Sense fashion, the very existence of such sites as the town of Bethlehem, the river Jordan, and Calvary stood as tangible proofs that the Bible was true, and that the events reported in it actually took place. How could one doubt the trustworthiness of the biblical narrative when the places where Jesus was born, was baptized, and died still existed for all to see?

While travelers had ventured into the Middle East from America since the opening decade of the nineteenth century, Thomson and Robinson motivated countless Protestants to explore the Holy Land personally.[74] Protestants returned from such pilgrimages with their faith reaffirmed. One traveler wrote, "A perfect knowledge of the *Land* is needful to a perfect knowledge of the Holy *Scriptures.*" The biblical scholar Horatio B. Hackett summed up the thoughts of many pilgrims to Palestine when he wrote, "Agreement between the scriptures and the geography of the holy land . . . furnishes a direct proof of the truthful character of the sacred word."[75] The actual biblical sites located in Judea provided much-needed proof and assurance that the events in the Bible did, in fact, take place. Problems with biblical chronology and philology melted away in the face of the tangible archaeological evidence accessible in traveling to the Holy Land.[76]

Not every American Protestant enjoyed the resources to make a visit to the Holy Land. Many could, however, find bibles that brought the Holy Land to them through lavish illustrations and detailed maps. In the midst of the growing apologetic importance of the Holy Land in American Protestant thinking, biblical illustrations of the Holy Land became visual texts that allowed the bible reader to enjoy biblical sites vicariously.

These illustrations also underlined the trustworthiness of the biblical message and promised interpretive insights into the biblical narrative. By the 1830s, Brattleboro bibles unabashedly proclaimed the theological usefulness of biblical illustrations. In an advertisement frequently used by the Brattleboro Typographic Company, the publisher argued that a person is able to understand the biblical text properly only when it is coupled with the appropriate illustrations:

> it is indispensable that the reader, as far as possible, separate himself from his ordinary associations, and put himself, by a kind of mental transmigration, into the very circumstance of the writers. He must set himself down in the midst of oriental scenery. . . . In a word, he must surround himself with, and transfuse himself into, all the forms, habitudes, and usages of oriental life. In this way only can he catch the sources of their imagery, or enter into full communion with the genius of the sacred penmen.

The advertisement goes on to assert that the remarkable "tide of travel" to the East in the past few years has only served to give Bible expositors new

inhabitants committed themselves to the special protection of that deity, to whom, under this symbol, they consecrated their temples and their country.

It is very credible, therefore, that the prophet's "land shadowing with wings" should be the very country, where, as was well known, in the time of the prophet, this symbol prevailed, and was popular, and we rest perfectly assured that long before the period when Isaiah wrote, this was the *customary* symbol of southern Egypt.

Sepulchre.

ISAIAH, xxii. 16.

Tombs may be divided into—1st, those *dug below* the surface of the ground: 2dly, those built above the ground, and 3dly, those *cut* into rocks, often at considerable heights above the level of the ground.

The plate exhibits a number of sepulchres, cut at considerable heights into the rock, at Naxi Rustan, near Persepolis, in Persia, from Le Bruyn.

It is evident that these must have been works of great labor and expense; beyond the powers of ordinary persons: they must have employed many laborers, and for a long time, &c. Vain desire of something permanent! vain solicitude for a kind of terrestrial immortality, after death! This gives a spirit to the expostulation of the prophet Isaiah, with Shibna the treasurer. "What hast thou here," what lasting settlement dost thou expect? that thou hast hewed thee out a sepulchre, here, like as one heweth out, at a great height, his sepulchre: that cutteth out at a great expense a habitation, (for himself after death,) a dwelling, a residence, in a solid rock: it shall be fruitless; for the Lord shall toss thee, as a ball, into a large country, where thou shalt die, &c.

Mirage.

ISAIAH, xxxv. 7.

Generally speaking, in a desert, there are few springs of water, some of them at the distance of four, six, and eight days' journey from one another, and not all of sweet water: on the contrary, it is generally salt or bitter; so that if the thirsty traveller drinks of it, it increases his thirst, and he suffers more than before. But when the calamity happens, that the next well, which is so anxiously sought for, is found dry, the misery of such a situation cannot well be described. The camels which afford the only means of escape, are so thirsty, that they cannot proceed to another well; and if the travellers kill them, to extract the little liquid which remains in their stomachs, they themselves cannot advance any farther. The situation must be dreadful, and admits of no resource. Many perish, *victims of the most horrible thirst.* It is then that the value of a cup of water is really felt. In short, to be thirsty in a desert, without water, exposed to the burning sun without shelter, and NO HOPES

Pl. XVII.

FIGURE 14. "Illustrations of Scripture" from 1834 Brattleboro bible edition. (Library of the author)

and more accurate insight into the biblical text. In visiting the East, travelers come into contact with biblical lands that *"are still the same"* as they were in the time of Christ. They offer "at every step, some object, some idiom, some dress, or some custom of common life" that "reminds the traveller of ancient times, *and confirms, above all, the beauty, the accuracy, and the propriety of the language and the history of the Bible.*"[77]

Thus, the illustrations found in bibles served several functions. First, they allowed readers to enjoy mentally transversing the sacred environment of the Holy Land, capitalizing not only on religious interests but on the voracious appetite nineteenth-century Americans exhibited in all sorts of travel books.[78] By picking up a bible, a reader could "go forth with nomad tribes of the desert—follow their flocks,—travel with their caravans—rest in their tents—lodge in their khans—load and unload their camels—drink at their watering places . . . and listen to the strain of song or story, with which they beguile the vacant hours." Second, through "mental transmigration," bible readers were better able to "enter into full communion with the genius of the sacred penmen" and attain additional insights into the meaning of the biblical narrative. Finally, these illustrations served to confirm the accuracy "of the language and the history of the Bible."[79]

As the Holy Land became a topological apologetic for the Bible, American publishers increasingly made Holy Land pictures a central component of their illustrated bible editions. By 1836, many Brattleboro bibles not only contained numerous landscape pictures of the Holy Land, but also included introductory sections featuring dozens of pictures of historical artifacts and scenes (see Figure 14).[80] Brattleboro bibles also began to sport an extended appendix entitled "A New Geographical and Historical Index," which offered forty-six pages of connections between the biblical text and the nineteenth-century Middle East. For example, this index gave the contemporary locations of such places as the elusive Garden of Eden and Mount Sinai.[81] Brattleboro bibles became encyclopedias of biblical knowledge and scenery. One need only turn to the introductory pictures to see what a sepulchre (Isaiah 22:16) or a mirage (Isaiah 35:7) looked like.

Publishers repeatedly stressed the importance of companion pictures to serve as interpretive guides to the text, stating such additions "cannot be too highly appreciated, especially those of the character here proposed. They serve materially to illustrate the texts, and, in some cases, are almost indispensable to a right understanding of the subject."[82] This "right

FIGURE 15. *(Opposite) The Journeyings of the Children of Israel* from Mathew Carey's 1803 quarto bible edition. (Courtesy of the American Antiquarian Society)

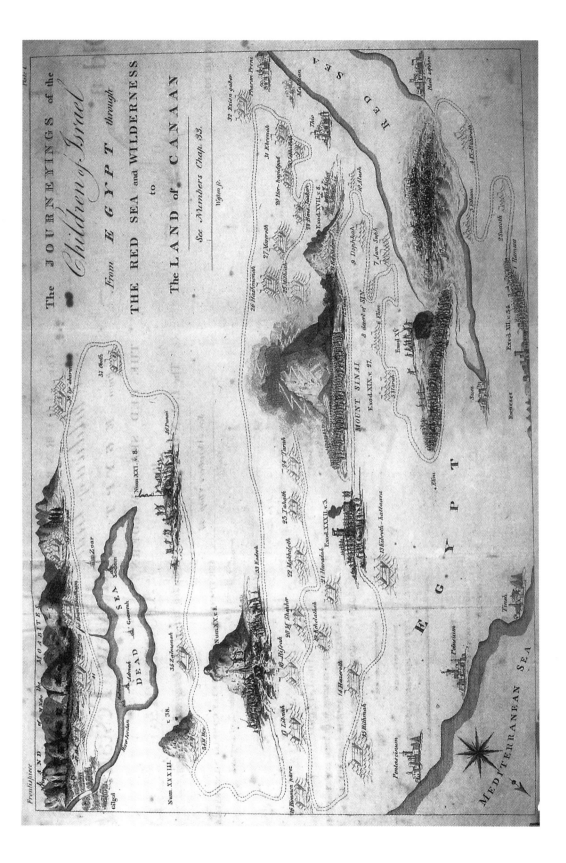

Plate 1

The JOURNEYINGS of the
Children of Israel
from EGYPT through
THE RED SEA and WILDERNESS
to
The LAND of CANAAN

See Numbers Chap. 33.

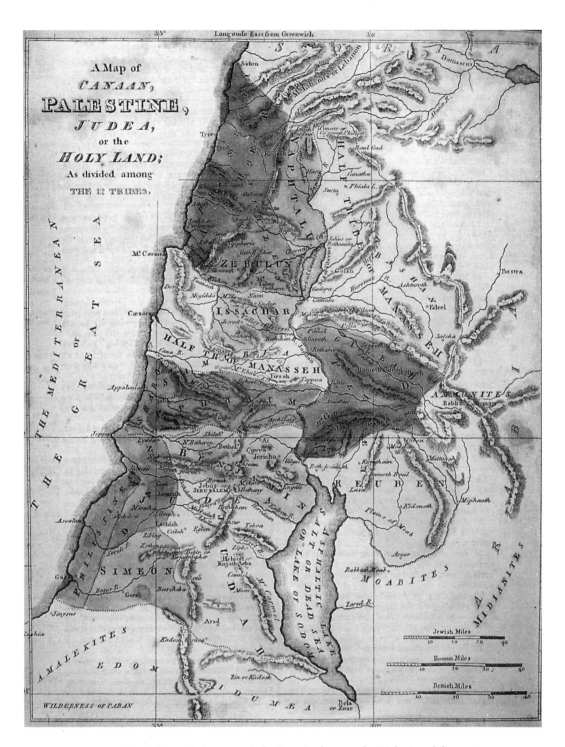

FIGURE 16. *A Map of Canaan, Palestine, Judea, or the Holy Land* from 1824 Brattleboro bible edition. (Beinecke Rare Book and Manuscript Library, Yale University)

understanding" had much to do with the Scottish Common Sense approach to reality and truth.

These illustrated entries made the truth of the Holy Land "materially" accessible to the visual sense of the reader. Since the senses could be trusted, what was seen could be accepted as truth. Pictures gave the contents of bibles a material, tangible aspect that could be more readily sensed and affirmed as true.

Along with more illustrations, commentary, and charts, Brattleboro bibles increasingly included an ever-greater array of maps of the Middle East. Maps of the Holy Land had been included in bibles for centuries. Mathew Carey had followed in this tradition, often binding as many as ten maps into his bible editions (see Figure 15). As the nineteenth century progressed, maps came to be characterized by a growing preoccupation with scientific, topographical accuracy. Maps no longer included little tents and biblical figures such as those found in Carey bibles, but focused more on complex measurement scales and accurate topographical markings (see Figure 16).[83] Scientific accuracy, not biblical narrative, became the principal concern of the maps found in nineteenth-century American bibles.

The emphasis on bringing the Holy Land to the American bible reader is vividly revealed in the difference between Isaiah Thomas's 1791 illustrated bible editions and an 1837 edition of a Brattleboro bible. While Thomas had included 50 copperplate engravings in his editions, not one of them was a map or a landscape representation of the Holy Land. An 1837 Brattleboro bible, on the other hand, boasted seven detailed maps of biblical locations and seven landscape pictures, including representations of Antioch, Thyatira, Egypt, and the Cedars of Lebanon.[84]

It would be inaccurate to say that Brattleboro bibles were only illustrated with an eye to the Holy Land because they still contained famous bible portraits such as Leonardo da Vinci's *Last Supper* and renditions of other biblical episodes. However, it is clear that historical pictures of the Holy Land—its inhabitants, flora, fauna, and material culture—came to dominate numerically the choice of illustrations in these volumes. Through the numerous additions to the Bible's core text, Brattleboro editions offered readers interpretive insights while reassuring them that God's word was true.

6 The Brattleboro and similar editions of the Bible, which attempted to seize a portion of the higher-end market, eventually developed into the huge family bibles most often associated with the nineteenth century.[85] Often weighing as much as fifteen pounds, these mega-bibles offered a wide array of expensive accoutrements, including sculpted leather bind-

ings, metal clasps, gilded pages, complex tables of information, portrait galleries, countless family record pages, extended commentaries, and hundreds of illustrations. A result of improved printing and transportation technologies, these mammoth texts and their multilayered, multivalent messages would have profound interpretive implications for bible readers.

The bible edition that served as a sort of urtext for the large family bibles of the nineteenth century was Harper and Brothers' *Illuminated Bible* of the 1840s. Weighing over thirteen pounds, printed on the highest quality paper, and illustrated with more than sixteen hundred pictures, Harper and Brothers advertised its *Illuminated Bible* as "the most splendidly elegant edition of the Sacred Record ever issued."[86] Others readily agreed, and the volume quickly became known as the most spectacular book ever printed in the United States.[87]

The idea to produce such a bible did not originally come from one of the four Harper brothers. Even though their firm was fast becoming the largest publisher in the United States, the Harpers had not printed a bible for almost twenty years when Joseph Alexander Adams, a local printer and engraver, came to them with a proposal to produce the grandest bible the United States had ever seen.[88] What promised to make Adams's edition so special was more than sixteen hundred illustrations. No previous American-made bible had ever contained more than one hundred pictures. Aside from the spectacular number of engravings, Adams wanted to distinguish his volume by the fact that the pictures would predominantly be on the same pages as the text, rather than on separate sheets bound within the text, as was the more common publishing practice.

Adams promised to accomplish this wonder through a new printing process called electrotyping: a procedure that involved coating stereotyped, woodblock, or intaglio plates with a thin layer of copper, thereby strengthening them for use in high-speed, high-pressure presses. Electrotyping allowed for large print runs of extremely fine quality text and pictures. The Harpers' *Illuminated Bible* was the first volume printed with this technology.[89]

Whether it was the Harper brothers' staunch Methodism, their keen sense of business acumen, or the allure of technological innovation that moved them to undertake such an expensive and potentially risky enterprise is impossible to say.[90] One thing, however, is clear: They believed in the project with an unrelenting fervor. They gave Adams a rare contract that allowed him both a large percentage of the edition's profits and complete charge of the edition's production.[91] They also aggressively advertised the volume by flooding "newspaper, literary periodicals, and booksellers with publicity."[92]

Rather than releasing the book all at once, Harper and Brothers decided to print the edition in fifty-four parts ranging from twenty-five to sixty-pages, at twenty-five cents each. They decided on an initial press run of 50,000 copies per installment. Subscribers could purchase the installments as they appeared and then have them bound upon the edition's completion in 1846. To make these installments more enticing, Harper and Brothers decided to print some pages in an expensive two-color format. Finally, in 1844 Harper and Brothers ordered a new set of presses specially designed to facilitate the electrotyping printing process.

The *Illuminated Bible* was an immediate success. The initial press run quickly sold out, and Harper and Brothers decided to run 25,000 copies of the entire volume in 1846. Over the next two decades, sales would remain strong enough for the firm to issue two more printings in 1859 and 1866.[93]

The volume's popularity had much to do with the rising religious importance of a home's domestic space and the growing concern with the authenticity and trustworthiness of the biblical text. The bible's appropriateness and appeal for use in the home comes across clearly in its bindings. Even with the inevitable diversity of binders who would be involved in a book that was first distributed in sheets rather than a set series of edition bindings, certain trends in how the volumes were bound can be detected.

First, the volumes tended to be elegantly and carefully bound, signaling a belief that such a beautifully illustrated book demanded an equally beautiful covering. Also, these volumes had richly ornamented gold borders. Additionally, one of the most popular styles of binding the *Illuminated Bible* in New York City involved embossing a picture of one's church on the cover (see Figure 17).[94] The placement of such a picture not only beautified the book, but displaying the *Illuminated Bible* in one's house fostered an interpretation of the family dwelling space as holy. As the volume was displayed in one's parlor, the picture emphasized the connection between the sacred space found in churches and the increasingly sacralized domestic space of the American home. The Bible was seen as a representation of the indwelling presence of the word of God in the home; it also signaled the presence of the larger community of God through the prominent display of one's church affiliation via the picture on the binding.

The interior pictures in these bibles were no less important to the book's warm reception. Clear narrative trends are present in the volume's more than 1,600 pictures. The two most noticeable motifs concern female characters and the Holy Land. The *Illuminated Bible* clearly favors representations of women and does so more in the vein of Thomas than Carey.

71

FIGURE 17. Front cover of Harper's *Illuminated Bible*. (Courtesy of the American Antiquarian Society)

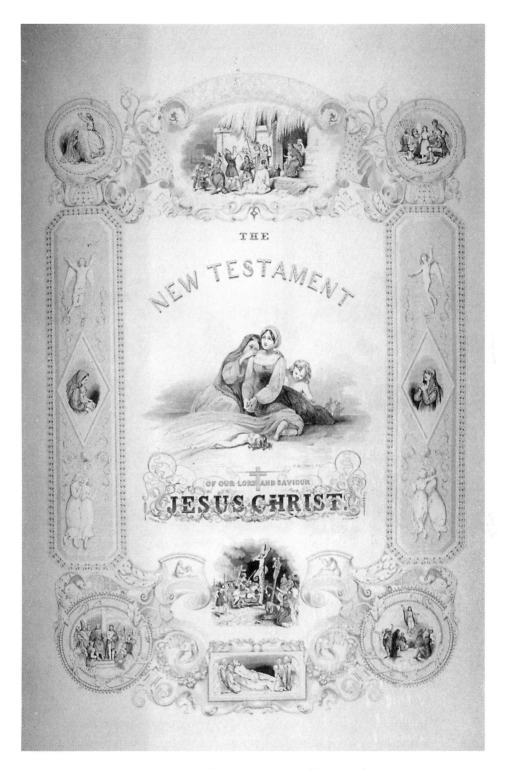

FIGURE 18. New Testament title page foregrounding "Rachel Weeping" from Harper's *Illuminated Bible*. (Courtesy of the Special Collections Department, University of Iowa Libraries, Iowa City, Iowa)

Throughout the *Illuminated Bible*, women are standard-bearers of spiritual instruction and wisdom, not victims of continual violence.

The *Illuminated Bible*'s focus on women is most apparent in the volume's New Testament title page (see Figure 18). Here, rather than highlighting the character of Jesus—the protagonist of the New Testament—the *Illuminated Bible* depicts the Old Testament story of Rachel weeping for her children. The central frame of Rachel weeping is surrounded by eight other vignettes, half of which have women as principal characters. In so prominently illustrating female biblical characters, the *Illuminated Bible* underlined the growing importance of women in American religious life.[95] In addition to foregrounding the feminine, the choice of Rachel weeping would have several profound cultural resonances with antebellum Protestant women who were all too familiar with infant mortality, fear of infant damnation, and an anxiety over failing to raise up their children as virtuous citizens.[96] As women came to be viewed as the chief guardians and educators of religious values in the nineteenth century, the *Illuminated Bible* reinforced this belief, showing woman after woman as vitally important religious figures.[97]

Amid the *Illuminated Bible*'s constant emphasis on the feminine, it is interesting to note that it was the pictures of the Holy Land that the Harpers chose to feature in marketing their bible. In stressing the Holy Land, the brothers showed their keen awareness of American Protestantism's growing tendency to attempt to settle questions about the Bible's trustworthiness by looking to the Holy Land.

On the paper covers that held the first sheets of the *Illuminated Bible*, the Harpers described their bible as a "New Pictorial Bible embellished with Sixteen Hundred Historical Engravings."[98] The word "historical" is important here. This choice of wording is but one strategy the Harpers employed to present their bible as a worthy volume for those concerned with the authenticity of the biblical text. The Harpers wanted their readers to know that their illustrations were based on historical fact, not artistic imagination.

The Harpers' use of electrotyping also served to emphasize the connection between the historical illustrations and the words of the text by directly juxtaposing the volume's visual and verbal texts (see Figure 19). Such constant juxtaposition conflated for readers historically based illustrations with the Bible's written text. The association between historical reality and biblical narrative was driven home on page after page of the *Illuminated Bible*. The illustrations also served to underline the truth and authenticity of the Holy Word by continually placing before the reader visual, almost tangible, examples of people, places, and artifacts that all supposedly had their roots in historically verifiable fact.

The manner in which the Harpers chose to advertise their Bible fur-

4 Behold, he that keepeth Israel shall neither slumber nor sleep.

5 The Lord *is* thy keeper: the Lord *is* thy shade *upon thy right hand.

6 The sun shall not smite thee by day, nor the moon by night.

7 The Lord shall preserve thee from all evil: he shall preserve thy soul.

8 The Lord shall preserve thy going out and thy coming in from this time forth, and even for evermore.

PSALM CXXII.

David professeth his joy for the church, 6 and prayeth for the peace thereof.

¶ A Song of degrees of David.

WAS glad when they said unto me, "Let us go into the house of the Lord.

2 Our feet shall stand within thy gates, O Jerusalem.

3 Jerusalem is builded as a city that is compact together:

4 Whither the tribes go up, the tribes of the Lord, unto the testimony of Israel, to give thanks unto the name of the Lord.

5 For there are set thrones of judgment, the thrones of the house of David.

6 Pray for the peace of Jerusalem: they shall prosper that love thee.

7 Peace be within thy walls, *and* prosperity within thy palaces.

8 For my brethren and companions' sakes, I will now say, Peace be within thee.

9 Because of the house of the Lord our God I will seek thy good.

PSALM CXXIII.

1 The godly profess their confidence in God, 3 and pray to be delivered from contempt.

¶ A Song of degrees.

1 UNTO thee lift I up mine eyes, O thou that dwellest in the heavens.

2 Behold, as the eyes of servants *look* unto the hand of their masters, *and* as the eyes of a maiden unto the hand of her mistress; so our eyes *wait* upon the Lord our God, until that he have mercy upon us.

3 Have mercy upon us, O Lord, have mercy upon us: for we are exceedingly filled with contempt.

4 Our soul is exceedingly filled with the scorning of those that are at ease, *and* with the contempt of the proud.

PSALM CXXIV.

The church blesseth God for a miraculous deliverance.

¶ A Song of degrees of David.

IF *it had not been* the Lord who was on our side, now may Israel say;

2 If *it had not been* the Lord who was on our side, when men rose up against us:

3 Then they had swallowed us up quick, when their wrath was kindled against us:

4 Then the waters had overwhelmed us, the stream had gone over our soul:

5 Then the proud waters had gone over our soul.

6 Blessed *be* the Lord, who hath not given us *as* a prey to their teeth.

7 Our soul is escaped as a bird out of the snare of the fowlers: the snare is broken, and we are escaped.

8 Our help *is* in the name of the Lord, who made heaven and earth.

PSALM CXXV.

1 The safety of such as trust in God. 4 A prayer for the godly, and against the wicked.

¶ A Song of degrees.

1 THEY that trust in the Lord *shall be* as Mount Zion, *which* cannot be removed, *but* abideth for ever.

2 *As* the mountains *are* round about Jerusalem, so the Lord *is* round about his people from henceforth even for ever.

3 For the rod of the wicked shall not rest upon the lot of the righteous; lest the righteous put forth their hands unto iniquity.

4 Do good, O Lord, unto *those that be* good, and to *them that are* upright in their hearts.

5 As for such as turn aside unto their crooked ways, the Lord shall lead them forth with the workers of iniquity: *but* peace *shall be* upon Israel.

PSALM CXXVI.

1 The church, celebrating her incredible return out of captivity, 4 prayeth for, and prophesieth the good success thereof.

¶ A Song of degrees.

1 WHEN the Lord turned again the captivity of Zion, we were like them that dream.

591

FIGURE 19.　Page from Harper's *Illuminated Bible*. (Courtesy of the Special Collections Department, University of Iowa Libraries, Iowa City, Iowa)

ther highlighted the connection between the Holy Land and the Scriptures. On the back covers of their installment sheet covers, one reads:

> Among other features peculiar to this edition of the Sacred Scriptures, one will be found to consist in the greater accuracy of its pictorial designs, as to architecture, costumes, localities, and characters. . . . The plates, therefore, accompanying the present work being in strict accordance with the recent important discoveries of ancient relics in the East may be regarded as *true commentary* on the text, forming a medium through which much instruction may be communicated to the mind of the reader, at the same time opening up a source of pleasureable entertainment to the eye.[99]

More than simply an endorsement of their Holy Land illustrations serving as a "*true commentary*," the Harpers wanted to stress that their illustrations also provided a source of "pleasureable entertainment" for their readers. In so closely associating the entertaining with the edifying, the Harpers were unknowingly contributing to a growing emphasis in American Protestantism on religious emotionalism.[100]

The impressions offered by pictures threatened the importance of the biblical text by leading the bible reader to concentrate more on the accompanying visual images than on the volume's printed words. Following a line of reasoning put forward by the literary critic J. Hillis Miller, once pictures and written text are juxtaposed, a competition is created between them for the reader's attention and interpretive energy.[101] This competition is most often decided in favor of the picture. Thus, any insights a picture offers into the interpretation of a text is foregrounded, often to the exclusion of what the written text might say.

In so heavily illustrating their bible, it is possible that the Harpers created a text that made readers concentrate more on the bible's illustrations than on the bible's words. This pictorial focus could encourage a radical simplification in the reader's interpretive process by highlighting one or two elements of an often extremely complex narrative at the cost of the narrative as a whole. Consequently, the heavy use of pictures in the *Illuminated Bible* in particular, and illustrated American bible volumes in general, can be seen as an important contributing factor in a shift from complicated theological reasoning to a more simple, and often emotional, discourse in nineteenth-century Protestantism.[102] The *Illuminated Bible* stands as an unrivaled example of how visual texts came to compete in more frequent and noticeable ways with the written text of the Bible.

7 While the technology of electrotyping was a key element in the development of the mega-bibles of the nineteenth century, no less important was the country's emerging railroad network. Railroads were important for two reasons: first, they allowed for an easier transport of bibles, no

small consideration when a single volume could weigh as much as twenty pounds. Second, the railroads allowed for a substantially broadened market. Using railway stops as their starting points, armies of advertising and sales agents could canvass wider areas, distributing books to an ever-larger proportion of the population. This confluence of large bibles and improved transportation networks produced the most significant results in the canvassing activities of subscription-only publishing firms in the latter half of the nineteenth century.

Differing from trade publishers like Harper and Brothers who produced their books and then distributed them for sale through both retail stores and bookselling agents, subscription-only publishers did not sell through retail stores. Instead, they sent out sales agents to canvass for buyers. A host of subscription publishing houses arose in the years following the Civil War, inundating the country with more than 50,000 agents in the course of a single year.[103] Subscription publishers would wait to obtain a predetermined number of subscriptions, often as many as 100,000, before they printed a single copy of the complete edition.[104] Publishers would send out their sales agents with canvassing samples for one or two books (see Figure 20). These samples usually included a range of specimen pages from the book itself, a table of contents, pages highlighting illustrations, fifty or so random leaves of the volume, and an assortment of potential binding materials and styles (see Figure 21).

There were definite advantages to this sales method for both purchaser and publisher. Purchasers were empowered by their choice of bindings and the convenience of having a sales agent come to them. Subscription-only selling allowed publishers to know exactly how many volumes to produce. Also, because subscription agents would also collect a small down payment with the subscription, publishers had some capital with which to work as they began their printing. Finally, subscription agents tended to have a wider reach than trade house booksellers. They penetrated deeper into less densely populated areas offering books to those who had fewer chances to purchase such luxury items.[105]

Several firms sold bibles "by subscription only" in the years following the Civil War, but perhaps the largest of these was the National Publishing Company, also known as the National Bible Press, founded by J. R. Jones.[106] Beginning in 1863, Jones produced at least a dozen English Bible editions under a variety of imprints including the National Publishing Company by perfecting the method of subscription sales.[107] Year after year, his agents would canvass the country and come back with subscription numbers large enough to justify the printing of yet another large family bible.[108]

Jones had clearly learned that while most families might already have

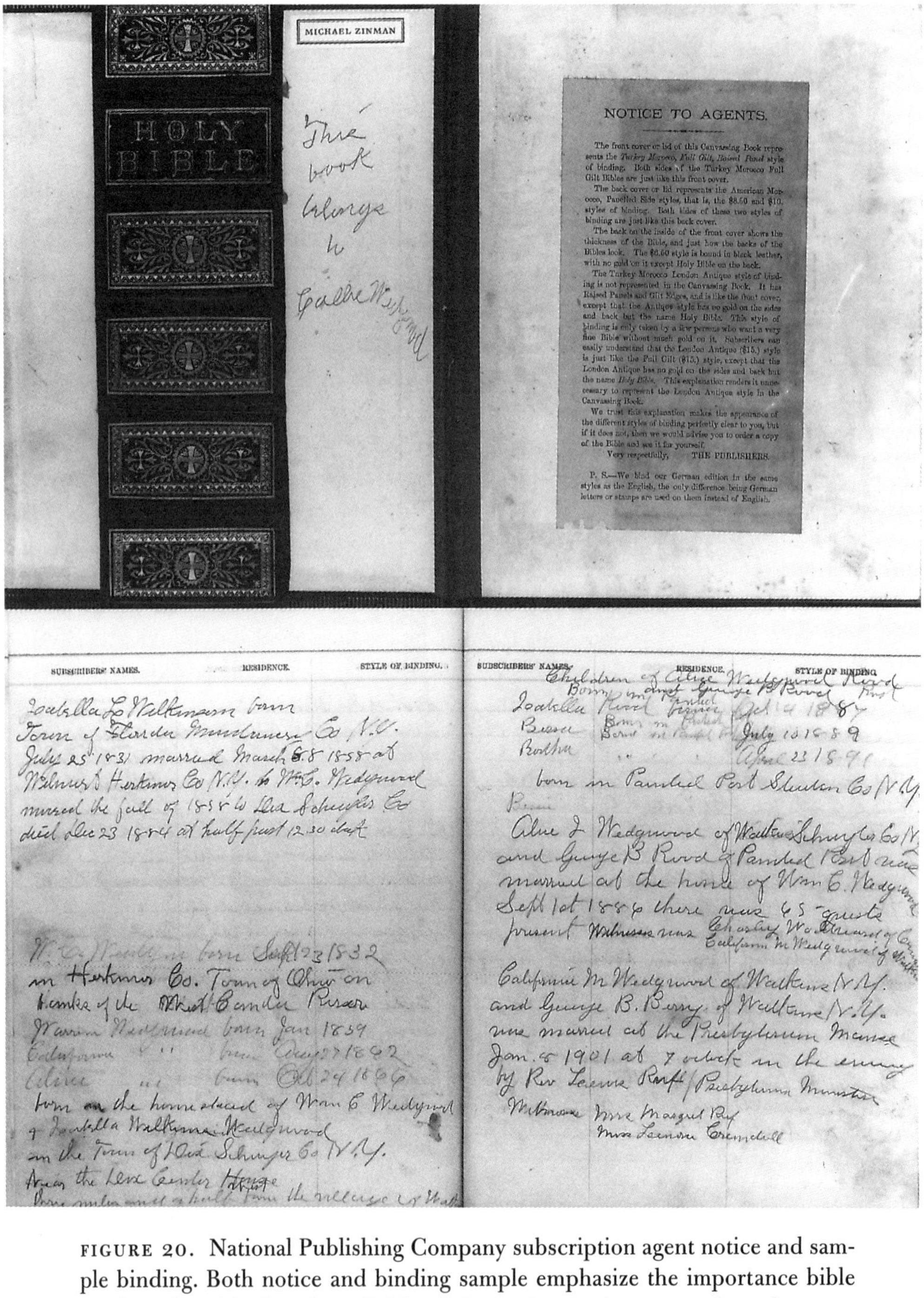

FIGURE 20. National Publishing Company subscription agent notice and sample binding. Both notice and binding sample emphasize the importance bible binding played in the sales of bibles. It is also interesting to note how the pages intended for subscription sales information have been converted into family record pages. Subscription books could take the place of a family's bible. (Collection of Michael Zinman)

a bible, they did not have a bible like the one he could offer them. An 1880 edition by M. R. Gately & Co., a publishing house aligned with R. J. Jones, shows many of the selling points for the Jones subscription megabible. For an unparalleled low price ranging between $6.50 and $15.00, customers were offered family bibles that included so much paraphernalia that they more closely resembled biblical encyclopedias than simple bibles.[109] The Gately edition—a representative National Publishing Company bible from the 1870s and 1880s—boasted "100,000 Marginal References and Readings" and "Nearly Two Thousand Illustrative Engravings"

FIGURE 21. National Publishing Company subscription books from the 1870s. Although still heavy, these thinner subscription books gave purchasers a glimpse of the finished product both inside and out, without making the subscription sales agent carry an entire bible volume. (Collection of Michael Zinman)

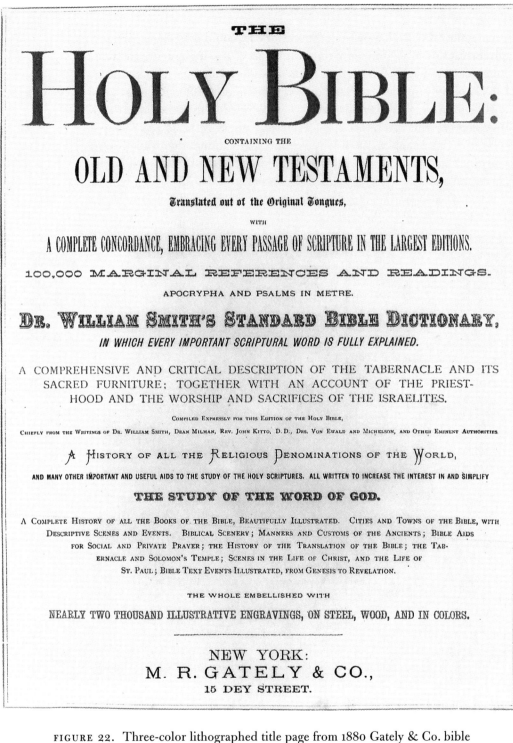

THE
HOLY BIBLE:

CONTAINING THE

OLD AND NEW TESTAMENTS,

Translated out of the Original Tongues,

WITH

A COMPLETE CONCORDANCE, EMBRACING EVERY PASSAGE OF SCRIPTURE IN THE LARGEST EDITIONS.

100,000 MARGINAL REFERENCES AND READINGS.

APOCRYPHA AND PSALMS IN METRE.

DR. WILLIAM SMITH'S STANDARD BIBLE DICTIONARY,

IN WHICH EVERY IMPORTANT SCRIPTURAL WORD IS FULLY EXPLAINED.

A COMPREHENSIVE AND CRITICAL DESCRIPTION OF THE TABERNACLE AND ITS SACRED FURNITURE; TOGETHER WITH AN ACCOUNT OF THE PRIEST-HOOD AND THE WORSHIP AND SACRIFICES OF THE ISRAELITES.

COMPILED EXPRESSLY FOR THIS EDITION OF THE HOLY BIBLE,

CHIEFLY FROM THE WRITINGS OF DR. WILLIAM SMITH, DEAN MILMAN, REV. JOHN KITTO, D. D., DRS. VON EWALD AND MICHELSON, AND OTHER EMINENT AUTHORITIES

A HISTORY OF ALL THE RELIGIOUS DENOMINATIONS OF THE WORLD,

AND MANY OTHER IMPORTANT AND USEFUL AIDS TO THE STUDY OF THE HOLY SCRIPTURES. ALL WRITTEN TO INCREASE THE INTEREST IN AND SIMPLIFY

THE STUDY OF THE WORD OF GOD.

A COMPLETE HISTORY OF ALL THE BOOKS OF THE BIBLE, BEAUTIFULLY ILLUSTRATED. CITIES AND TOWNS OF THE BIBLE, WITH DESCRIPTIVE SCENES AND EVENTS. BIBLICAL SCENERY; MANNERS AND CUSTOMS OF THE ANCIENTS; BIBLE AIDS FOR SOCIAL AND PRIVATE PRAYER; THE HISTORY OF THE TRANSLATION OF THE BIBLE; THE TABERNACLE AND SOLOMON'S TEMPLE; SCENES IN THE LIFE OF CHRIST, AND THE LIFE OF ST. PAUL; BIBLE TEXT EVENTS ILLUSTRATED, FROM GENESIS TO REVELATION.

THE WHOLE EMBELLISHED WITH

NEARLY TWO THOUSAND ILLUSTRATIVE ENGRAVINGS, ON STEEL, WOOD, AND IN COLORS.

NEW YORK:
M. R. GATELY & CO.,
15 DEY STREET.

FIGURE 22. Three-color lithographed title page from 1880 Gately & Co. bible edition. (Courtesy of the American Bible Society Library)

(see Figure 22).[110] The Gately edition was illustrated using several different methods ranging from woodblock to steel engraving to chromolithography. Like the Harper and Brothers *Illuminated Bible*, the illustrations in the Gately edition were printed directly on the pages of the written text, and favored a heavy emphasis on representations of Palestine and its inhabitants.

The Gately bible's introductory material included everything from a "Household Dictionary of the Bible" (see Figure 23) to a "History of the Books of the Bible" (see Figure 24).

The Gately edition also offered more than simple family record pages by giving its buyer a "Portrait Album" for family pictures (see Figure 25). In determining how to bind such a grand volume, the purchaser could choose from a variety of thick, sculpted leather covers with metal clasps so that the book looked like some venerable old work of art (see Figure 26).

The mega-bible editions of Jones and the Harpers stand as striking examples of how important bible packaging became to both publisher and purchaser. Beginning in the 1840s and persisting throughout the century, a trend developed in which higher-end bibles increasingly distinguished themselves not because they held a distinctive and treasured text, but because they presented that text in a particularly striking way. For a host of Americans, God's word had become more than just the written word; it was a book that exhibited its importance by its sheer magnitude and textual cornucopia. The incredible sales posted by Jones and the Harper Brothers for their respective family bible editions offers convincing evidence that the presentation of God's word was becoming as important as the word itself.

Although the materials used to bind bibles changed slowly during the nineteenth century, the presence and content of bible illustration changed radically. In the midst of these changes, publishers persistently declared that illustrations aided the reader's ability to interpret the bible's core text accurately. The exact interpretive consequences of heavily illustrating bibles may be impossible to tell; it is clear, however, that as publishers sought out ways to make the Bible's words more attractive and accessible to their buyers, they enmeshed those words in ever more complex and numerous levels of discourse. In the final analysis, any examination of the Bible in the nineteenth century must keep in mind that the volume's core text always reached its readers through various forms of material mediation.

The attempt to clarify the Bible's message was not confined to the supplements that accompanied the biblical text. The opening decades of the nineteenth century saw a growing number of American scholars and

6, 31). But the question of guilt was to be decided by the Levitical tribunal.

Music. We meet with nothing like a systematic cultivation of music among the Hebrews, until the establishment of the schools of the prophets. Music was an essential part of their practice. Professional musicians soon became attached to the court. David gathered round him "singing men and singing women" (2 Sam. xix. 35). Solomon did the same (Eccles. ii. 8; 1 Kings iv. 32). But the Temple was the great school of music, and it was consecrated to its highest service in the worship of Jehovah. It is not improbable that the Levites had practiced music, and that some musical service was part of the

Obv.: לחרות ירושלם (Heb. *lahârôth* [or *lachârôth*] *Yerû-shâlaim = of the deliverance of Jerusalem*). Bunch of fruits. **Rev.:** שמערך (Heb. *Shim'ôn = Simon*). Tetrastyle temple; above which star. AR.

worship of the tabernacle, in the private as well as in the religious life of the Hebrews music held a prominent place. It was the legitimate expression of mirth and gladness, and the indication of peace and prosperity, and on every occasion the land of the Hebrews during their national prosperity was a land of music and melody.

Mustard (Matt. xiii. 31; xvii. 20; Mark iv. 31; Luke xiii. 19; xvii. 6). The mustard tree of Scripture, the *Salvadora persica*, is found along the banks of the Jordan, near the lake of Tiberias, and near Damascus, and generally recognized in Syria as the mustard tree of Scripture. Irby and Mangles mention, in their journey in the Jordan valley, the mustard plant, which reached as high as their horses' heads. The expression "which is indeed the least of all seeds" was used proverbially to denote anything very minute.

Muth-lab'ben (Ps. ix.) has given rise to infinite conjecture. Delitzsch supposes that Muth-Labben denotes the tune or melody, with the words of the song associated with it.

My'ra, a town in LYCIA. The place where St. Paul, on his voyage to Rome (Acts xxvii. 5), entered the Alexandrian ship in which he was wrecked on the coast of Malta.

Myrrh. A gum common in Arabia, Egypt and Abyssinia. The ancients used it as a perfume and for embalming. It is bitter, whence called *gall*, and being supposed to have a property like opium, it was anciently administered to alleviate pain (Mark xv. 23).

Mys'ia (Acts xvi. 7, 8), the region about the frontier of the provinces of Asia and Bithynia.

N.

Na'amah (*loveliness*). 1. Daughter of Lamech by his wife Zillah, and sister to Tubal-cain (Gen. iv. 22 only). 2. Mother of King Rehoboam (1 Kings xiv. 21, 31; 2 Chron. xii. 13). She was one of the foreign women whom Solomon took into his establishment (1 Kings xi. 1).

Na'aman (*pleasantness*). 1. "Naaman the Syrian" (Luke iv. 27). A Jewish tradition identifies him with the archer whose arrow struck Ahab and "gave deliverance to Syria." Naaman was commander-in-chief of the army, and was nearest to the person of the king (ver. 18). He was afflicted with a leprosy of the white kind (ver. 27), which had hitherto defied cure. The circumstances of his visit to Elisha and his remarkable cure are found 2 Kings v. 1, 27. 2. One of the family of Benjamin who came down to Egypt with Jacob (Gen. xlvi. 21). He was the

son of Bela, and head of the family of the Naamites (Num. xxvi. 40; 1 Chron. viii. 3, 4).

Naamites, The, the family descended from NAAMAN (Num. xxvi. 40 only).

Na'arai, one of the valiant men of David's armies (1 Chron. xi. 37).

Na'aran, a city of Ephraim (1 Chron. vii. 28), mentioned as the eastern limit of the tribe.

Na'arath (Josh. xvi. 7, only), "a small village of the Jews, five miles from Jericho."

Na'bal (*fool*) was a sheepmaster on the confines of Judæa. His wealth consisted chiefly of sheep and goats. Once a year there was a grand banquet, on Carmel, "like the feast of a king" (xxv. 2, 4, 36). On one of these occasions Nabal refused to recognize the demand of the ten petitioners from David's encampment (xxv. 22). Abigail, Nabal's wife, appeared, threw herself on her face before him, and poured forth her petition. She returns. Nabal is at the height of his orgies, and his wife dared not communicate to him either his danger or his escape (xxv. 36). At break of day she told him both. The stupid reveler was suddenly roused. "His heart died within him, and he became as a stone." Ten days he lingered, "and the Lord smote Nabal, and he died" (xxv. 37, 38).

Na'both, victim of Ahab and Jezebel, was the owner of a small vineyard at Jezreel, close to the royal palace of Ahab (1 Kings xxi. 1, 2). The king offered an equivalent in money or another vineyard in exchange for this. Naboth refused.

REPUTED TOMB OF ESTHER AND MORDECAI AT HAMADAN.

"Jehovah forbid it to me that I should give the inheritance of my fathers unto thee." Ahab was cowed by this reply; but the proud spirit of Jezebel was roused. She had Naboth and his children (2 Kings ix. 26) dragged out of the city and despatched.

Na'chon's Threshing-floor, the place at which the ark had arrived when Uzzah lost his life in his zeal for its safety (2 Sam. vi. 6).

Na'chor. [See NAHOR.]

Nadab (*liberal*). 1. The eldest son of Aaron and Elisheba (Ex. vi. 23; Num. iii. 2). He, his father and brother and seventy old men of Israel were led out from the midst of the assembled people (Ex. xxiv. 1), and were commanded to stay and worship God "afar off," below the lofty summit of Sinai, where Moses alone was to come near to the Lord. Subsequently (Lev. x. 1) Nadab and his brother were struck dead before the sanctuary by fire from the Lord. Their offence was kindling the incense in their censers with "strange" fire, *i. e.*, not taken from that which burned perpetually (Lev. vi. 13) on the altar. 2. King Jeroboam's son, who succeeded to the throne of Israel B. C. 954, and reigned two years (1 Kings xv. 25–31).

Nag'ge, one of the ancestors of Christ (Luke iii. 25). It represents the Heb. *Nogah* (1 Chron. iii. 7).

Naha'lal, one of the cities of Zebulun, given to the Levites (Josh. xxi. 35).

Naha'liel (*torrents of God*), one of the halting-places of Israel in the latter part of their progress to Canaan (Num. xxi. 19).

Naham'ani. A chief man among those who returned from Babylon with Zerubbabel and Jeshua (Neh. vii. 7).

Nahar'ai, the armor-bearer of Joab (2 Sam. xxiii. 37), a native of Beeroth (1 Chron. xi. 39).

Nah'ari. The same as NAHARAI (2 Sam. xxiii. 37).

Na'hash (*serpent*). 1. King of the Ammonites, who dictated to the inhabitants of Jabesh-Gilead the loss of their right eyes or slavery, which roused the swift wrath of Saul, and caused the destruction of the Ammonite force (1 Sam. xi. 1, 2–11). 2. A person mentioned (2 Sam. xvii. 25) in stating the parentage of Amasa, the commander-in-chief of Absalom's army.

Nahath. 1. One of the "dukes" in the land of Edom, eldest son of Reuel the son of Esau (Gen. xxxvi. 13, 17; 1 Chron. i. 37). A Kohathite Levite, son of Zophai (1 Chron. vi. 26). 3. A Levite in the reign of Hezekiah (2 Chron. xxxi. 13).

Nah'bi, a Naphtalite, and one of the twelve spies (Num. xiii. 14).

Nahor, the name of two persons in the family of Abraham. 1. His grandfather; the son of Serug and father of Terah (Gen. xi. 22–25). 2. Grandson of the preceding, son of Terah and brother of Abraham and Haran (Gen. xi. 26, 27). He married Milcah, the daughter of his brother Haran. He was the father of twelve sons; eight of them were the children of his wife, and four of a concubine (Gen. xxii. 21–24).

Nah'shon, or Naash'on, son of Amminadab. His sister, Elisheba, was wife to Aaron, and his son, Salmon, was husband to Rahab after the taking of Jericho. He died in the wilderness (Num. xxvi. 64, 65).

Na'hum (*consolation*). Nahum "the Elkoshite," the seventh of the minor prophets. His personal history is quite unknown. It is most probable that Nahum flourished in the latter half of the reign of Hezekiah, and wrote his prophecy either in Jerusalem or its neighborhood.

Na'in, a village of Galilee, made illustrious by the raising of the widow's son (Luke vii. 12).

Na'ioth, a place in which Samuel and David took refuge together, from the jealous fury of Saul (1 Sam. xix. 18, 19, 22, 23; xx. 1).

Nane'a. The Persian goddess Nanea was invested with the attributes of Aphrodite, and represented the productive power of nature.

Na'omi, the wife of Elimelech, and mother-in-law of Ruth (Ruth i. 2, etc.; ii. 1, etc.; iii. 1; iv. 3, etc.). The name signifies sweetness or pleasantness.

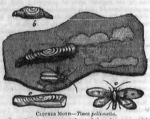

CLOTHES MOTH—*Tinea pellionella.*

a, larva in a case constructed out of the substance on which it is feeding.
b, Case cut at the ends.
c, Case cut open by the larva for enlarging it.
d, e, The perfect insect.

Na'phish, the last but one of the sons of Ishmael (Gen. xxv. 15; 1 Chron. i. 31).

Naph'tali (*wrestling*). The fifth son of Jacob; the second child born to him by Bilhah, Rachael's slave. His birth and the bestowal of his name are recorded in Gen. xxx. 8. At the migration to Egypt four sons are attributed to Naphtali (Gen.

xlvi. 24; Ex. i. 4; 1 Chron. vii. 13). When the census was taken at Mount Sinai the tribe numbered no less than 53,400 fighting men (Num. i. 43; ii. 30).

Naph'tali, Mount. The mountainous district (Josh. xx. 7), answering to "Mount Ephraim" in the centre and "Mount Judah" in the south of Palæstine.

Naph'tuhim, a Mizraite nation mentioned only among the descendants of Noah (Gen. x. 13; 1 Chron. i. 11).

Narcis'sus. a dweller at Rome (Rom. xvi. 11),

disrepute in which Nazareth stood (John i. 47) is not certainly known.

Naz'arite (one separated). The regulations for the vow of a Nazarite are given Num. vi. 1–21. Of the Nazarites for life three are mentioned in the Scriptures: Samson, Samuel and St. John the Baptist. In all the cases mentioned in the sacred history, the consecration was made by the parents before the birth. The meaning of the Nazarite vow was essentially a sacrifice of the person of the Lord (Num. vi. 2).

Neap'olis is a place in northern Greece where

being applied to in vain, Daniel declared to him both the dream and the interpretation. He was so astonished, and yet so convinced of the truth, that he fell on his face before Daniel, and acknowledged his God to be the God of gods. He made Daniel chief of the wise men and governor of the province of Babylon, and his three companions subordinate governors in the same place (Dan. ii.). Toward the close of his life, he fell into that species of monomania which leads the patient to believe that he is some animal and to act accordingly. During this period (about seven years) he thought himself an ox and dwelt in the fields. We are told that his "reason returned and he was established in his kingdom." He died after a reign of forty-three years.

Nebushas'ban, one of the officers of Nebuchadnezzar, chief of the eunuchs (Jer. xxxix. 13).

Nebuzar'adan, i. e., chief of the slaughterers, a high officer in the court of Nebuchadnezzar. On the capture of Jerusalem he was left in charge of the city (comp. Jer. xxxix. 11).

Neg'inah (Ps. lxi.). "The chief musician on Neginoth" was the conductor of that portion of the Temple-choir who played upon the stringed instruments, mentioned in Ps. lxviii. 25.

Nehel'amite, The. A false prophet, who went with the captivity to Babylon (Jer. xxix. 24, 31, 32).

Nehemi'ah. The author of the book which bears his name. He was of the tribe of Judah, and was so distinguished as to be selected for the office of cupbearer to the king of Persia. He was made governor of Judea, and his book gives an account of his appointment and administration, through a space of thirty-six years.

Nehemi'ah, Book of, is certainly not all by the same hand. The principal portion is the work of Nehemiah. The main history contained in the book of Nehemiah covers from the 20th to the 32d year of Artaxerxes Longimanus, i. e., from B. C. 445 to 433. The book throws much light upon the domestic institutions of the Jews.

Ne'hiloth. It is most likely that Nehiloth is

NAZARETH, FROM N. N. W. (From a photograph by J. Graham. Ayre.) The distant range of hills is to the S. of the plain of Esdraelon.

some members of whose household were known as Christians to St. Paul.

Nard. [See SPIKENARD.]

Na'than (a giver). 1. An eminent Hebrew prophet in the reigns of David and Solomon. He first appears in 2 Sam. vii. 2, 3, 17. He next comes forward as the reprover of David (2 Sam. xii. 1–12). In the last years of David, Nathan taking the side of Solomon, turned the scale in his favor; and at David's request assisted in his inauguration (1 Kings i. 8, 10, 11, 22, 23, 24, 32, 34, 38, 45). He left two works—a Life of David (1 Chron. xxix. 29), and a Life of Solomon (2 Chron. ix. 29). The biography of David by Nathan is, of all the losses which antiquity has sustained, the most deplorable. 2. A son of David; one of the four who were born to him by Bathsheba (1 Chron. iii. 5; comp. xiv. 4, and 2 Sam. v. 14).

Nathan'ael, a disciple of Jesus Christ, concerning whom we learn from Scripture little more than his birthplace, Cana of Galilee (John xxi. 2), and his simple truthful character (John i. 47). It is commonly believed that Nathanael and Bartholomew are the same person.

Na'um, son of Esli and father of Amos, in the genealogy of Christ (Luke iii. 25).

Nave is rendered in A. V. boss of a shield, Job xv. 26; the eyebrow, Lev. xiv. 9; an eminent place, Ezek. xvi. 31; plur. naves, 1 Kings vii. 33; in Ezek. i. 18, "rings."

Naz'arene, an inhabitant of Nazareth. Jesus the Nazarene, was one of the names of the predicted Messiah. In Acts xxiv. 5, Nazarenes is applied to the followers of Jesus by way of contempt.

Naz'areth, the ordinary residence of our Saviour, is not mentioned in the Old Testament, but occurs first in Matt. ii. 23. It is situated among the south ridges of Lebanon, just before they sink down into the Plain of Esdraelon. Of the identification of the ancient site there can be no doubt. The name of the present village is en-Nazirah, the same as of old. The origin of the

Paul and his associates first landed in Europe (Acts xvi. 11). Philippi being an inland town, Neapolis was evidently the port, and is represented by the present Kavalla.

Neba'i, a family of the heads of the people who signed the covenant with Nehemiah (Neh. x. 19).

Neba'ioth, the "first-born of Ishmael" (Gen. xxv. 13; 1 Chron. i. 29), and father of a pastoral tribe named after him, the "rams of Nebaioth" mentioned by the prophet Isaiah (lx. 7) with the flocks of Kedar.

Nebal'lat, a town the Benjamites reoccupied after the captivity (Neh. xi. 34).

Ne'bat, the father of Jeroboam (1 Kings xi. 26; xii. 2, 15, etc.).

Ne'bo, Mount, the mountain from which Moses took his first and last view of the Promised Land (Deut. xxxii. 49; xxxiv. 1). It is described as in the land of Moab, facing Jericho; the summit of a mountain called the Pisgah.

Ne'bo. 1. A town of Reuben on the eastern side of Jordan (Num. xxxii. 3, 38). 2. Nebo, Isaiah (xlvi. 1) and Jeremiah (xlviii. 1) the name of a Chaldæan god, of the Babylonians and Assyrians.

Nebuchadnez'zar. The most powerful of Babylonian kings. His father Nabopolassar having raised an immense army to quell a revolt of the Syrians, Phœnicians, etc., he was appointed to its command, and not only subdued those provinces, but overran Canaan, Moab, Ammon, Assyria, Egypt, etc., and made them tributary. He carried to Babylon, Daniel, Hananiah, Mishael and Azariah, whom he called Belteshazzar, Shadrach, Meshach and Abednego. These he caused to be trained up in all the learning of the Chaldæans, that they might serve in the court (2 Kings xxiv.; Dan. i.). He twice afterward invaded and chastised Judæa, and carried away into captivity many Jews, among whom was Ezekiel the prophet (2 Chron. xxxvi.; Ezek. xxv. 35). About A. M. 3399 his father died and he became king of Babylon. In the second year of his reign he had a surprising dream, but entirely forgot it. All the diviners

MUSTARD TREE.—Salvadora Persica.

the general term for perforated wind-instruments of all kinds.

Ne'hum. One of those who returned from Babylon with Zerubbabel (Neh. vii. 7).

Nehush'ta. The daughter of Elnathan of Jerusalem, wife of Jehoiakim, and mother of Jehoiachin, kings of Judah (2 Kings xxiv. 8).

Nehush'tan, the name by which the brazen serpent made by Moses in the wilderness (Num.

7

MICAH.—Micah was a native of Maresheth, a village near Eleutheropolis, in the west of Judah. His ministry extended over the reigns of Jotham, Ahaz, and Hezekiah, kings of Judah, a period of about fifty years, B. C. 750–698. He was contemporary with Hosea and Amos during part of their ministry in Israel, and with Isaiah in Judah. He wrote in an elevated and vehement style, with frequent transitions. His prophecy relates to the sins and judgments of Israel and Judah, the destruction of Samaria and Jerusalem, the return of the Jews from captivity, and the punishment of their enemies. He proclaims the coming of the Messiah, as the foundation of all hope for the blessed and glorious future he describes, and specifies Bethlehem in Judah as the place where he should be born of woman (Micah v. 2, 3). The prediction was thus understood by the Jews (Matt. ii. 6; John vi. 41, 42).

NAHUM.—Nahum's name signifies "Consolation." The circumstances of his life are unknown, except that he was a native of Elkosh, which probably was a village in Galilee. Opinions are divided as to the time Nahum prophesied. The best interpreters adopt Jerome's opinion that he foretold the destruction of Nineveh in the time of Hezekiah, after the war of Sennacherib in Egypt, mentioned by Berosus. Nahum speaks of the taking of No-ammon, of the haughtiness of Rabshakeh, and of the defeat of Sennacherib as things that were past. He implies that the tribe of Judah were still in their own country, and that they there celebrated their festivals. He notices, also, the captivity and dispersion of the ten tribes. The subject of his prophesy is, in accordance with the superscription, "the burden of Nineveh," the destruction of which he predicts.

THE BOOK OF HABAKKUK.

HABAKKUK, perhaps, delivered his prophecy about the twelfth or thirteenth year of the reign of Josiah (B. C. 630, 629), though the date is only conjectural, and of his personal history nothing is known. The prophet foretells the doom of the Chaldæans, and the announcement is followed by a series of denunciations

FIGURE 24. *(Both pages)* Pages from the "History of the Books of the Holy Bible" from 1880 Gately & Co. bible edition. (Courtesy of the American Bible Society Library)

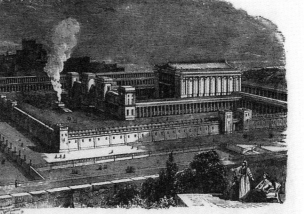

pronounced upon them by the nations who had suffered from their oppression. The strophical arrangement of these "woes" is a remarkable feature of the prophecy. The whole concludes with the magnificent Psalm in chap. iii.

ZEPHANIAH.—Zephaniah lived also in the reign of Josiah, as we learn from the superscription to the book, where the prophet traces his pedigree to his fourth ancestor, Hezekiah, supposed to be the celebrated king of that name. His date is about 630 B. C. The destruction of Nineveh, foretold in Zeph. ii. 13, occurred in 625 B. C. His prophecy contains two oracles, in three chapters, directed against idolaters in Judah, against surrounding idolatrous nations, and against wicked rulers, priests and prophets. It closes with cheering promises of Gospel blessings. His style and manner are like those of Jeremiah, during whose early years they were contemporary. His subsequent history is unknown.

HAGGAI.—Haggai is the first of the Minor Prophets who prophesied after the Captivity. With regard to his tribe and parentage, both history and tradition are alike silent. In the absence of any direct evidence on the point, it is more than probable that he was one of the exiles who returned with Zerubbabel and Jehusa. He began to prophesy in the second year of Darius Hystaspes (B. C. 520) ; and the object of his prophesying was to excite his countrymen to begin again the building of the Temple, which had been so long interrupted. In this he was successful, Darius having granted a decree for this purpose (Ezra vi.) The exceeding glory of the second Temple was, as he had foretold, that Christ, "the desire of all nations, came to it," and made the place of his feet glorious (Hag. ii. 7, 9).

ZECHARIAH.—Zechariah was the son of Berechiah, and grandson of Iddo, the priest. Ezra calls him the son of Iddo. He was a priest as well as a prophet, and succeeded his grandfather in the sacred office. He returned from Babylon with Zerubbabel and began to prophesy while yet young (Zech. ii. 4) in the second year of Darius (B. C. 520), in the eighth month of the holy year, and two months after Haggai. The two prophets, with united zeal, encouraged the people to resume the work of the Temple, which had been discontinued for some years (Ezra v. 1).

Zechariah's prophecies concerning the Messiah are more particular and express than those of most other prophets, and many of them, like those of Daniel, are couched in symbols. The book opens with a brief introduction, after which six chapters contain a series of visions, setting forth the fitness of that time for the promised restoration of Israel, the destruction of the enemies of God's people, the conversion of the heathen, the advent of Messiah, the branch, the outpouring and blessed influences of the Holy Spirit, and the importance and safety of faithfully adhering to the service of their covenant God. Chapter vii. relates to commemorative observances. Chapters ix.–xi. predict the prosperity of Judah during the

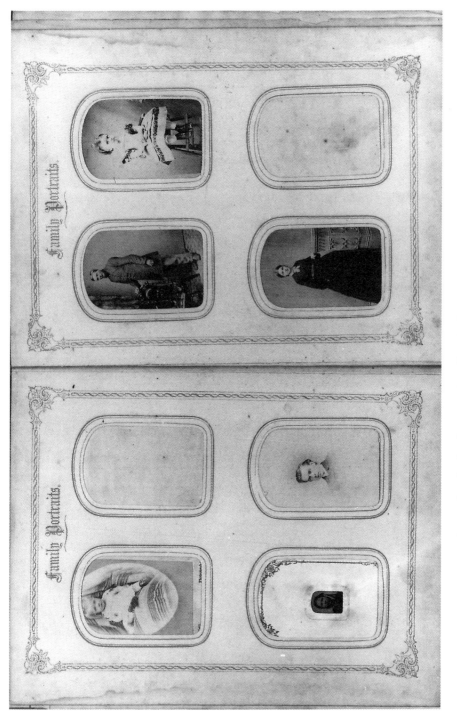

FIGURE 25. A sample of a family portrait gallery included in post–Civil War bible editions. These pictures are in a National Publishing Company bible subscription book for the *New Illustrated Devotional and Practical Polyglot Family Bible*, 187?. (Collection of Michael Zinman)

FIGURE 26. Sculpted leather bible cover from 1880 Gately & Co. bible edition.
(Courtesy of the American Bible Society Library)

lay-people attempt to refashion the Bible's core text to approximate more closely the words, and thus the truth, contained in the most ancient biblical manuscripts. These translators believed that the Bible could become a more influential text if its truth—which was self-evident and self-enforcing—could be more clearly presented to Americans. So, while publishers were attempting to clarify and distinguish the Bible by its packaging, others set out upon a quest to recover the original meaning of the Bible via more accurate and accessible translation work. Such a quest became yet one more strategy in the battle to maintain the Bible's preeminence in America's rapidly diversifying print culture.

Chapter Three

PURITY

1 In the winter of 1858, the American Bible Society was in crisis. Much of its leadership resigned, stating that the Society was no longer a safe "witness and keeper of the Holy Writ" making itself *"a manufacturer of alloy, and debasing the very standard it is pledged to circulate in its integrity."*[1] Those who left had been part of a committee appointed by the Society's Board of Managers to correct and standardize the King James Version of the biblical text.

The importance of a standard, error-free text had long been an issue in American bible production. Often printers, under the economic pressure to set type quickly, did not give a bible edition the kind of proofreading that a project of its size and complexity demanded. Although the basic content of the Bible changed little, differences in spelling, grammar, punctuation, and chapter headings were the cause of constant vexation. Certain mistakes were so notorious that the editions that contained them took on special names such as the "Wicked Bible," which commanded "Thou Shalt Commit Adultery," and the "Murderers' Bible" for a passage in the Gospel of Mark that read "Let the children first be killed," rather than "filled."[2] The Society's "Committee on Revision" was to put an end to diversity and error with a definitive "Standard Bible."[3] Such a version was to be produced by an intensive comparison of the myriad editions held in the Society's library and stock shelves. The committee worked four years to produce a purer, more accurate King James text, but it turned out to be a version that precious few American Protestants seemed to want.

When the Society's newly revised text was released in 1851, it ignited an unexpected firestorm of resentment. Critic after critic denounced the textual revisions as dangerous and unnecessary tampering. So great was the public's opposition that by 1858 the American Bible Society had the new text withdrawn in favor of King James versions they had previously published.

The Society's backpeddling infuriated those who had worked on the

Standard Bible, and as they abandoned the Society they made no secret of their displeasure.

The Society had begun the Standard Bible project as a means to clean up the typographical errors and inconsistencies of its versions; the project was never intended to revise the King James Version's core text. Typographical accuracy for American bible publishers can be traced back to Isaiah Thomas's 1791 quarto edition in which he boasted, "No cost, care or labour hath he [the editor] spared to render these Editions correct. . . . The Editor furnished himself with nearly thirty copies, printed at different times and places—from these he selected the most correct, by which to revise the whole of this work."[4] Thomas also had his edition proofread by "the Clergymen of Worcester, and by other capable persons" to insure the accuracy of his text.[5]

Other early American publishers joined Thomas in the quest for biblical accuracy. Isaac Collins, a contemporary of Thomas, published a bible edition in the same year that for decades was considered the most typographically accurate bible edition printed in America. Collins had commissioned a series of committees under the direction of Dr. John Witherspoon to correct his edition's proof sheets, and then had his own children check for errors by reading each of the proof sheets eleven more times.[6] Mathew Carey was no less concerned with textual accuracy, printing lists of the mistakes in British editions that he had found and corrected in his own editions.[7]

By the late 1820s, the editions of the bible produced by the American Bible Society had come to be recognized among American publishers as the unofficial standard biblical text. As the Society's bibles spread throughout the country, their sheer number made them easy models for other publishers to use as touchstones of biblical accuracy. Publishers increasingly advertised their editions as "Correct According to the Standard of the American Bible Society."[8] Although no wholly accepted standard text of the King James Version would ever emerge in the United States, the Society's decision to pursue the Standard Bible project makes sense in light of the rising tendency to view the Society's editions as the industry standard.

The Society was keenly aware that the public's desire for accurate bibles was based on no mere whim, but on the heartfelt belief that the bible was no common book; it contained the story of God's creative and redemptive work. Textual accuracy was more than simply an issue of good craftsmanship; it could mean the difference between orthodoxy and heresy, a life that led to heaven or a life that led to hell.[9] Accurate bibles were a matter of spiritual life and death.

In reality, the Standard Bible crisis of 1858 serves as but a small reflection of much larger translation debates that began in the late 1840s and would last until the release of the Revised Version in the 1880s. As much as traditionalists wished to keep the King James Version untouched, there was also a growing groundswell of support for newer versions of the Holy Scriptures.

The 1850s saw a number of different religious bodies engage in the debate over the need to update the King James text according to newly discovered manuscript sources and change the language of the King James Version to make it more accessible to a nineteenth-century audience. Such advocates of revision met staunch resistance from traditionalists who marshaled a host of arguments for leaving the text of the King James Version untouched, including (1) losing a centrally accepted version of the Bible would deteriorate Christian unity, (2) revision once begun would find no natural stopping point, and (3) no one had the authority to make such a revision.

Central to all the arguments against revision stood the plea that although the King James Version of the Bible was incorrect in places, it remained an accurate and adequate text.[10] The lesson that the American Bible Society had learned during the crisis of 1858 captured the overwhelming Protestant sentiment of the period, namely, that American attachment to the King James Version was "too strong to be broken abruptly."[11] The King James Version would remain firmly entrenched as the monarch of American Protestant bible versions throughout the century.

One cannot ignore, however, that even considering the King James Version's tenacious hold on the affections of nineteenth-century American Protestants, by 1880 American publishers had printed thirty-five new translations of the English bible, thirty-one of which were either created or edited by Americans.[12] The appearance of these volumes testifies to increasing doubt over the dependability and efficacy of the King James Version.[13] The emergence of such a large number of retranslations sheds new light not only on the concern in this period with biblical accuracy, but also on how biblical translation became yet another battlefield in the war to keep the Bible preeminent in the country's print culture.

2 Although some early nineteenth-century Americans would argue that the King James Version came from the hand of God, it was in reality just one in a long line of English bible translations.[14] Beginning with the extremely literal English translation of the Latin Vulgate by the Oxford theologian John Wycliffe in 1382, the English Bible started an often perilous, but sure, ascent into acceptance in English-speaking cultures.[15]

The next English translation, that of William Tyndale, appeared in 1526 and would be the first of six major English versions to appear in the sixteenth century. The others included the Coverdale Bible (1535), the

Matthews Bible (1537), the Great Bible (1539), the Geneva Bible (1560), and the Bishops' Bible (1568). These bibles marked a period of unprecedented translation work, as the tenets of the Protestant Reformation and its emphasis on the word of God began to spread throughout Europe. While these various versions differed in their source material, theological slants, and idiom, together they marked a changing attitude toward making the Word accessible to everyone.[16]

When James I ascended the English throne in 1603, there were three English versions of Scripture prominent in England: the Great Bible, the Geneva, and the Bishops'.[17] Of these, the Geneva Bible was by far the most popular, having been translated into an accessible idiom and favored by English Puritans.[18] English Puritans, however, were not entirely happy with the Geneva Bible and appealed to James I in 1604 for a "newe translation of the Bible, because those that were allowed in the raignes of Henri the eight, and Edward the sixt, were corrupt and not aunswerable to the truth of the Originall."[19] James readily agreed. For some time, he had been bothered by what he considered seditious commentary in the Geneva version, and so he gave his blessing to begin a new translation—a translation he made sure would include only philological, not political, marginal commentary.[20]

The Bishops' Bible was to serve as the root translation for the new King James Version. Its language was to be altered only when the original languages demanded it. Forty-seven scholars worked for three years on the new translation. The scholarship was advanced for its day, but the manuscripts used were often of recent date, including Latin as well as Greek and Hebrew signatures. The translators also put a premium on making the Bible accessible to the common reader.[21] In 1611, the first of three early editions of the King James Version came off the presses.

Once released, after some initial resistance, the King James Version steadily gained popularity.[22] Within fifty years of its introduction, the King James Bible had replaced the Geneva Bible as the most popular version of the Bible in English.[23] Nowhere was this more true than in New England, where Puritans were quick to adopt the King James Version over the Geneva Version.[24] Thus, beginning in the 1640s, the King James Version would become the dominant version of the Bible for Protestants in the United States.

For nearly two centuries, the King James Version would reign supreme in the United States. Only in the early years of the nineteenth century would this hegemony begin to show signs of erosion. Oddly enough, the reasons for this deterioration were similar to those that allowed for the creation of the King James Version. Once again, there was a concern that the people needed the Bible presented to them in their own common idiom along with scholarly attention paid to "original" sources. These concerns would play pivotal roles in the American bible translation battles of the nineteenth century.

3 Even though many of America's first English settlers enjoyed a high degree of education and a voracious appetite for bible reading, it is remarkable to note that Americans did not attempt translating the Scriptures into English until the early nineteenth century.[25] The first American to produce a new bible translation did not enter upon the mammoth undertaking so much to challenge the autonomy of the King James as to work through personal pain and loss. Although it might not have been strange to turn to the Bible for comfort in times of crisis, it was certainly unique that Charles Thomson would begin a thirty-year odyssey in bible translation and publication in an attempt to deal with the death of his political career.[26]

Thomson began his translation work in 1789 when, in angling for an expansion of his congressional role, he lost his position altogether.[27] For someone who had once been known as "the Sam Adams of Philadelphia" and had served as the secretary of the First Continental Congress from its inception in 1775, this loss of position was a devastating blow.[28] In his sorrow and bitterness, he returned to his estate near Philadelphia and attempted to forget that his country had forgotten him by burying himself in the gargantuan task of retranslating the Bible.

It was more than political disappointment, however, that motivated Thomson to give the last third of his life to retranslating the Bible. Unable to contribute to the development of a new nation and fulfill his desire "to die in an eminent office," Thomson sought to memorialize himself in another way.[29] He dedicated the last third of his life to attacking the religious skepticism of his day by working on a version of the Scriptures that would answer concerns about the authenticity of Jesus' claims and the Bible's credibility.

These concerns with biblical credibility and authenticity determined Thomson's choice of the Septuagint as the version he would use to translate the Old Testament portions of his new edition of the English Bible. The Septuagint version dated back to the third century B.C. when, legend has it, seventy Jewish scholars had gathered to translate the Hebrew Scriptures into Greek.

Thomson had learned that when the New Testament writers quoted from the Old Testament, they invariably used the Septuagint version of the Scriptures. Thomson was shocked to learn that no English translation of the Septuagint had ever been made. He adamantly believed that an accurate Septuagint translation could vindicate the genuineness of the Bible and its message.

Thomson thought that in order to determine whether Jesus actually fulfilled the messianic prophecies of the Old Testament, one needed to look at those prophecies as recorded in the Septuagint, since it was the version the New Testament writers employed to point to Jesus' messianic claims.[30] Such a motivation to settle decisively the concerns with textual authenticity that surrounded the issue of Jesus' divinity and credibility is underlined by the fact that the first book Thomson translated in his bible project was Isaiah, the Old Testament book most cited in the New Testament concerning the arrival of and nature of Jesus the Messiah.[31]

Thomson's achievement is remarkable for its depth of scholarship and its anticipation of two concerns that would mark American biblical translation for the next seventy years. First, Thomson was interested in the *first texts*. To strengthen further his argument concerning the Bible's reliability and authenticity, Thomson made it clear that not only had the New Testament writers used the Septuagint in their references to Old Testament law and prophecy, but also that the Septuagint offered an older version of the Old Testament than many of the Hebrew signatures used to translate various English versions of the Bible. Because of the Septuagint's age, Thomson argued that its closer proximity to biblical events made it less subject to historical errors and allowed it to claim primacy as the least corrupt text from which to make a translation.[32]

Second, Thomson was interested in *first meanings*. He was firmly convinced that he needed more than a translation of the oldest available texts to accomplish a sound revision of the Bible. He also sought the historical meanings of biblical words and phrases. He characterized his translation as an endeavor "to give a just and true representation of the sense and meaning of the Sacred Scriptures; and in doing this, I have further endeavored to convey into the translation, as far as I could, the spirit and manner of the authors, and thereby give it the quality of an original."[33] In capturing this "spirit and manner," he hoped to render more clearly the original meaning of the authors and avoid making the meaning of the Holy Scriptures "obscure" or their translation "harsh."[34]

In this concern for meaning, Thomson blazed the trail for the majority of the American translators who would follow him in attempting to put the Bible into a more understandable idiom. Thomson fashioned a bible that he hoped would make the biblical message more credible by the use of more ancient texts, more clear by the use of common idiom, and more refined by taking out ungrammatical constructions and harsh words. As a result, his changes included adjusting Genesis 1:2 from "And the earth was without form, and void" to the more Lockean "And the earth was invisible and unfurnished," and substituted the word "urine" for "piss" in Isaiah 36:12.

Thomson published his bible translation in 1808. Jane Aitken, the daughter of Robert Aitken, printed his translation as a beautifully crafted four-volume set. Although his translation garnered a great deal of respect in the scholarly community, it never enjoyed wide popular appeal.

Thomson held out some hope that his American translation would help define the young country. These hopes were ill-founded. Like the numerous other bible revisions to appear on the market before the Civil War, Thomson's Bible mounted no significant challenge to the autonomy of the King James Version. A few lone voices heralded Thomson's edition as preferable "to a version made under the authority of a foreign government," and as a "national translation" that "would stamp upon this country a character not only of independence, but of proper self respect."

But Thomson's strenuous efforts to advertise and widely distribute his bible were largely unsuccessful.[35] In respect of sales, as well as in the intent of his efforts, Thomson's translation foreshadowed the work of every other American who would attempt an English translation prior to 1880. Not one of these new versions would gain wide Protestant acceptance, and all of them would be deeply concerned with what Thomson had categorized as first texts and first meanings.

4 Thomson's clarion call to pay attention to first texts found a fervent devotee in America's second English Bible translator, Abner Kneeland. Kneeland, a Universalist minister and religious newspaper publisher in Philadelphia, advertised in 1821 for subscriptions to a new translation of the Bible.[36] Two years later, Kneeland released his *H KAINH ΔIAΘHKH* (*The New Testament, in Greek and English*). Kneeland would be the first of seven translators with Unitarian leanings who produced nearly a third of all new bible translations published in the United States before 1880.[37] More than any other single religious tradition, Unitarianism was marked by a deep interest in new English translations of the Scriptures throughout the nineteenth century.[38]

Driving this interest in new English translations was the Unitarian desire to restore the Scriptures to their "primitive integrity"—their most pure, original, and accurate form.[39] Unitarians believed that creeds had distorted the true meaning of the Bible. Centuries of Christianity had led Protestants to read the Bible in the theologically disfiguring context of creeds. Unitarians argued that these creeds (and teaching rooted in them) had greatly distorted both the message and the English translation of the Bible.

For Unitarians, the most blatant example of Christian creedal corruption came in the doctrine of the Trinity. Encapsulating the central problem with this doctrine, one Unitarian wrote "the *word* TRINITY is not to be found in the New Testament, and that it was invented by Tertullian, is a matter of little consequence; but that the doctrine itself should be nowhere stated in the New Testament, we conceive to be a matter of very great consequence."[40] Both the word and the doctrine were inventions of minds at least three centuries distant from the time of Christ. The weight of tradition and church history meant nothing to Unitarians in the face of biblical evidence that showed that the Christian belief in the Trinity was nothing more than a "modern doctrine" that had no precedent in ancient Christianity.[41]

One of the ways Unitarians chose to discredit Trinitarian doctrine involved attacking the accuracy of the biblical texts upon which the doctrine was based. Unitarians set out to prove not only that was there "no such word as Trinity in the Bible, from beginning to end," but that all verses even hinting at such a doctrine could not be found in the most ancient manuscripts of Scripture.[42]

Unitarians argued the authenticity of verses such as 1 John 5:8, which reads: "For there are three that bear record in heaven, the Father, the Word, and the Holy Ghost; and these three are one."

Unitarians claimed such verses were "spurious" texts found in "no part of the original Epistle of John."[43] They argued that all verses showing an affinity to the doctrine of the Trinity were later additions to the most ancient biblical manuscripts. Ancient texts gave no hint of the doctrine of the Trinity.

The Unitarians could forcefully mount this kind of attack because of the unusually high degree of education they could bring to bear on the argument. A number of the early Unitarian bible translators not only came from Harvard Divinity School, but also held teaching positions there.[44] Such Unitarian luminaries as Andrews Norton, John Gorham Palfrey, and George Noyes all produced English translations of at least portions of the Bible. When they questioned the accuracy of the scriptural text, they backed up their claims with arguments stemming from their specialized theological and linguistic training. This high level of education, coupled with the conviction that the Scriptures had been disfigured by the very scribes who had been responsible for the preservation and transmission of the Scriptures, provided the foundation for a massive Unitarian effort to purge the Bible's text of all its impurities.

Preceding the more scholarly translation work of Palfrey, Noyes, and Norton, Abner Kneeland stepped forward as the first American translator with Unitarian sympathies to introduce a "purer" biblical text to the United States. American editions of new Scripture translations by British Unitarians such as Thomas Belsham and Gilbert Wakefield had come to the United States as early as 1809, but these editions did nothing to deter Kneeland, who envisioned a better way to communicate the pure and accurate nature of his translation.[45]

From the outset, Kneeland offered his translation in a format that pointed to the original biblical language. Printing in parallel columns, Kneeland put the Greek text on the left side of the page and the English on the right (see Figure 27). Like Thomson, Kneeland had been preoccupied with basing his New Testament on the most ancient and accurate sources possible. His format reflected his concern with the original language and served as a constant reminder that the original was not far removed from

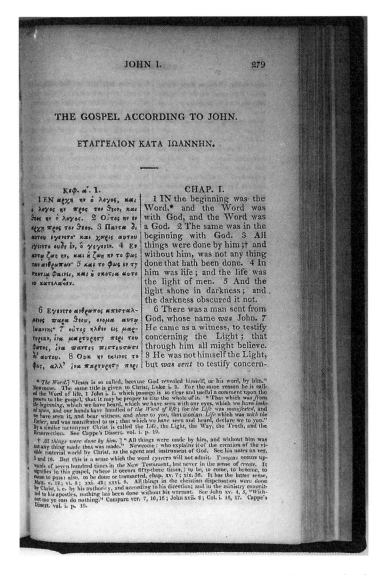

FIGURE 27. Sample page in diglot, two-column format from Kneeland's 1823 *H KAINH ΔIAΘHKH.* (Courtesy of the American Bible Society Library)

Kneeland's rendering of the Sacred Word. Moreover, Kneeland adopted the newer, more critical Greek text of the German biblical scholar Johann Griesbach for his bible's Greek version. This adoption, in itself, was a significant statement.

First published in the United States by William Wells in 1809, Griesbach's text of 1774 and 1775 was no ordinary version of the New Testament Greek.[46] It represented the most current German biblical scholarship, utilizing methods of inquiry defined by a careful attention to the intention of the biblical authors through critical and historical textual analysis.[47]

Johann Griesbach had examined the oldest manuscripts of the Scriptures he could find in the libraries of France, Germany, England, and the Netherlands.[48] His goal behind such extensive research was quite simple. He wanted to examine these manuscripts in order to provide a new compilation of the New Testament that would be more accurate than the "Received Text," the edition of the Greek text most commonly used by scholars translating the New Testament prior to the end of the eighteenth century. Griesbach's work, which was the result of his examination and compilation of over four hundred manuscript sources—some dating back six centuries earlier than the ones used for the "Received Text"—offered a groundbreaking contribution to textual scholarship.[49]

Although Griesbach's Greek New Testament had been printed in America in 1809, Kneeland's vision was to broaden the use and influence of this text beyond the narrow confines of Unitarian academia. His choice of a diglot format for his new biblical translation aided him in his goal. He would give his readers the most accurate Greek text accompanied by a new, more accurate translation of that text.

While Kneeland attacked the question of the accuracy of biblical manuscripts by completely adopting the work of Griesbach into his Bible, the questions surrounding the accuracy of an English translation of the Greek were far more difficult to address. Kneeland chose to base his own translation on the work of the English Unitarian Thomas Belsham whose "improved version" of Scripture was printed in London in 1808.[50] Although Kneeland had originally planned simply to use the London Improved Version, he decided that he wanted more changes than those offered by Belsham's version. In the end, Kneeland made few additional changes to Belsham's work, but the changes he did make are telling.

Perhaps the most striking of Kneeland's changes was his refusal to translate the Greek word *aion* as "everlasting" or "eternal."[51] Instead, Kneeland simply transliterated the adjectival form of the word from Greek to English. Thus, αιωνιον became *aionion*. As slight and innocuous as this adjustment might seem, it was based on deep theological conviction. Kneeland felt that *aionion* had been translated incorrectly for centuries. Instead of meaning "everlasting" or "eternal," it simply meant "for an age." Such a change was particularly important for a Universalist who did not believe in eternal punishment. Verses pointing to eternal punishment were thus changed to reflect a limited rather than eternal time frame.[52] Kneeland also changed verses that did not agree with his Unitarian leanings. He relegated to a footnote the portion of 1 John 5:8 that described the Father, Son, and Holy Spirit as "three are one." In his own rendering of this verse, he wrote: "For there are three that bear testimony, the spirit, and the water, and the blood, and these three agree in one."[53]

Kneeland championed his Testament as "correcting some of the monstrous errors that now exist in the Christian church."[54] This process of correction began with changing some of what he deemed the monstrous translation errors he found in the New Testament.

Kneeland's translation is intriguing for a number of reasons; not least among them is the skepticism that drove its inception. Kneeland had long struggled with doubts about the authenticity of Scripture. Although he seemed to have momentarily overcome these doubts, they eventually led him into an ill-defined pantheism that made him the center of Massachusetts's last public trial for the crime of blasphemy. (He was found guilty and spent sixty days in a Boston jail.)[55]

Scholarly treatments of Kneeland's translation are often as short as Kneeland's own belief in the bible.[56] Yet Kneeland's adoption of Griesbach's Greek text and his sectarian English translation mark this version as a critical text in English Bible translation work in America. Kneeland's quest for purity had made him face the problems of a corrupted Greek text and its effect on any attempt to arrive at the meaning of the Bible's original writers. Although his translation went largely unnoticed by American Protestantism, the textual concerns and sectarian character of his work would continually resurface in the bible translation work of the next seven decades.

5 Thomson's and then Kneeland's commitment to first texts gave momentum to the belief that better original manuscripts would lead to a better understanding of first meanings. Griesbach's New Testament would be joined by several other scholarly works and new manuscripts by the 1880s, including the Codex Sinaiticus, the Codex Vaticanus, and new Greek Testaments by Karl Lachmann (1831), Constantin von Tischendorf (eight editions between 1841 and 1872), Samuel Tregelles (six-part edition between 1857 and 1872), and Brooke F. Westcott and Fenton J. A. Hort (1881). These improved sources promised an ability to ascertain more accurately the original meaning of the Bible's writers.[57] One translator aptly captured the sentiment surrounding the much-improved biblical sources

of the nineteenth century by writing: "We are now in possession of much better means of making an exact translation than they were at the time when the [King James] version appeared. The original is now much better understood than it was then."[58]

A Greek text that sought to emulate that written by the Bible's original authors was one thing. A translation of that text which sought to emulate those authors' original meaning was another. Johann Griesbach himself had pointed to the difficulties involved in reaching beyond simply achieving a pure Greek text to translating such a text's pure meaning. Griesbach believed an accurate translation of the Greek text must always be placed within a firm understanding of its writer's historical circumstances. Accurate Greek words would be of use only if they could be translated into accurate modern equivalents. Determining what such equivalents might be required more than a knowledge of grammar and philology; it required a thorough grasp of both the passage's setting and its relationship to the "whole peculiar character of the content and the form" of the New Testament.[59]

A concern with seeking a Greek word's meaning through its textual and historical context proved to be a central issue in early American bible translation work. Having an accurate Greek text was all well and good, but if Greek sentences could not be translated into accurate English equivalents, the meaning of the Bible would remain obscure. Abner Kneeland had confronted this problem with his struggle to translate more accurately the word *aion*. To solve this problem, Kneeland left the word open to the interpretation of its reader by either translating it "for an age" or leaving it in its Greek transliterated form. Kneeland's timidity in transliterating rather than translating various forms of *aion* would not be a precedent followed by other early American bible translators. In fact, the trend in translation went markedly in the other direction. Where words were unclear, American translators increasingly substituted English equivalents that clarified the passage's meaning rather than obscured it or left its meaning to the reader's discretion. Nowhere was this more true than in the translation of the Greek word βαπτιζω.

Βαπτιζω had long been translated in English bibles by simply using variations of *baptism*, a transliterated form of the Greek.[60] The problem was that this choice of translation did not answer the long-standing debate about how the sacrament of baptism should be administered. The question was an important one. Believers in infant baptism argued from lexicons that βαπτιζω meant "to wash" and believed this washing to be a sign of God's saving action extended through Grace alone. God initiated the action; believers were simply dependent children waiting for God's offer of redemption. Baptizing children symbolized God's initiative and humanity's dependence. Others argued from lexicons that βαπτιζω meant "to dip" or "to immerse" and believed that baptism was a sign of God's saving grace linked to a person's own willingness to repent and choose to be saved. For them, immersion was a ritual associated with persons who had come of spiritual age, taking their own initiative to make a commitment to convert to Christianity.[61]

The translators of the King James Version had made no radical changes in the translation of the word *baptism*. Room for debate existed as βαπτιζω continued to stand as *baptize*. By the early nineteenth century, the quest for the original meaning of the Scriptures demanded that the ambiguity of the term finally be cleared up. The first American to seek such clarity in a bible translation was Alexander Campbell in his New Testament of 1826.[62]

Neither a history in book publishing, nor a background steeped in linguistic training led Alexander Campbell to offer a new version of the New Testament to Americans in the mid-1820s. Born in Ireland, Campbell arrived in the United States in 1809. Almost immediately, he joined the first of two churches he would pastor in Pennsylvania. Tired of petty denominational squabbles, he did not affiliate with a denomination until 1813 when he became a Baptist, having been convinced that immersion was the only proper way to baptize.[63]

In the years that followed, Campbell traveled throughout Ohio, Indiana, Virginia, Kentucky, and Tennessee preaching a gospel based on the tenets of the church found in the New Testament. Campbell's great dream was to see the Christian Church reunited. He believed such unity had been enjoyed by the primitive Christian church before the intrusion of clerical hierarchy and denominationalism. Creeds, untrustworthy clergy, and petty factionalism had fractured the cause of Christ. Campbell spent his ministry years tirelessly pounding away at the theme that a bible-centered understanding of the primitive New Testament church was the sole model of Christian living and only sure foundation for Christian unity.[64]

To unloose the power of Christianity and unify its adherents, Campbell believed that the Bible must first be unfettered. Campbell preached that "each religious party had sought to secure the Bible within its own sectarian cell," thus trammeling the sacred volume with all manner of creeds, confessions, and church structures founded on human, not biblical, precedents.[65] Campbell condemned all practices that could not be validated by apostolic example. To determine what was, in fact, validated by apostolic example, one must go to the Bible.[66]

Adopting the words of his father, Thomas Campbell, Alexander would guide his ministry by the overarching rule "where the Scriptures speak, we speak; where the Scriptures are silent, we are silent."[67] As early as 1816, Campbell began to have problems with his fellow Baptists, some of whom did not share all his radical views of primitive church restoration. Friction grew between Campbell and the Baptist association with which he was connected until he eventually broke entirely with the Baptists in 1832 to form his own denomination in partnership with Barton Stone, a fellow restorationist. Calling their new denomination the "Christian Church"—later known as the "Disciples of Christ"—Campbell and Stone began a movement that would become the fastest growing Protestant denomination in antebellum America, numbering 22,000 in 1832 and growing to around 200,000 by 1860.[68]

Campbell's belief in the absolute primacy of the New Testament's portrayal of primitive Christianity over any and all extra-biblical creeds or traditions makes his publication of his own New Testament in 1826 more understandable. In the opening volume of his first religious newspaper, Campbell wrote of his goal: "We only aim at substituting the New Testament in lieu of every creed in existence; whether Mahometan, Pagan, Jewish, or Presbyterian. . . . We neither advocate Calvinism, Arminianism, Arianism, Socinianism, Trinitarianism, Unitarianism, Deism, or Sectarianism, but *New Testamentism.*"[69]

The central place of the New Testament in Campbell's thinking moved him to give his followers a purer version of the New Testament Scriptures. So much stress was put on the all-important role of the Bible for determining what the original church looked like that Campbell felt it necessary to provide his followers with a translation of the New Testament that best captured the original meaning of the New Testament writers. Campbell felt that the King James Version suffered inaccuracies because of its translators' theological biases, the fact that it was the product of a committee of translators which invited interpretive compromise, and the reality that older, more reliable manuscripts were now available from which a translation of the New Testament could be made.[70]

Like Kneeland, Campbell turned to Griesbach for his text, believing Griesbach's Greek New Testament to be "the most nearly correct text in Christendom."[71] Then consulting the work of a number of other translators like George Campbell, James Macknight, Philip Doddridge, and Charles Thomson, Campbell sought to provide a translation that most accurately reflected the original meaning of the New Testament writers.[72] For Campbell, this meant clarifying any ambiguous terms in English, or in Greek, which existed in the King James Version.

One of the chief ambiguous terms that led to doctrinal error was the word *baptism.* For Campbell, the meaning of the word was clear. He felt that if βαπτιζω had meant "immersion" in the first century, it should mean "immersion" now. With this clarity and confidence, he substituted the word *immersion* for nearly every Greek appearance of βαπτιζω.[73] In so doing, he fired the first shot in what would become the largest bible translation battle in early nineteenth-century America.

As important as Campbell's translation was in terms of its commitment to a particular view of baptism, it would be terribly misleading to characterize the book simply as an immersion translation. For Campbell, like Kneeland, the quest for first meanings involved his translation's presentation. Campbell moved in the opposite direction of Kneeland, who sought to stress the interplay between Greek and English by attempting to create a seamless English version that drew attention to the understandable and straightforward nature of the biblical text.

Following the lead of John Locke, Campbell chose to publish his New Testament with a minimum of intrusive chapter and verse markings.[74] As Figure 28 shows, Campbell placed chapter and verse annotations only at the top of pages and at the beginning of paragraphs. The text was printed in a single column, and Campbell was most excited about his bible editions, which were clearly printed and thus could be easily read.[75] He also chose to place supplemental material at the volume's end, rather than in the margins.

Campbell's format changes sprang from his conviction that the Bible should be easy to read and understand. He strove to avoid "cutting up the sacred text into morsels," a practice of bible editors who were fond of verse markings and marginalia.[76] Campbell felt such apparatuses could kill the best attempts at understanding accurately the text's meaning. He felt that the traditional verse and chapter markings destroyed the Bible's narrative and kept the reader from engaging the larger themes and arguments of the Bible, and that annotations encouraged a piecemeal approach to reading and interpretation.

Campbell did more in his revision than simply adjust the Bible's textual format to make it easier to read and understand. He also worked hard to revise the Bible's language to make it more accessible to his readers.

Changing the Bible's format was not nearly as serious as tinkering with its language. To justify his audacity, Campbell begins the preface of his New Testament with a discussion of language: "A Living language is continually changing. Like the fashions and customs in apparel, words, and phrases, at one time current and fashionable, in the lapse of time become awkward and obsolete."[77]

Campbell dealt with the demands created by changes in language by altering words in his translation that no longer meant what they had when used by the translators of the King James Version, and by adjusting the archaic forms of certain words to more modern equivalents. For instance,

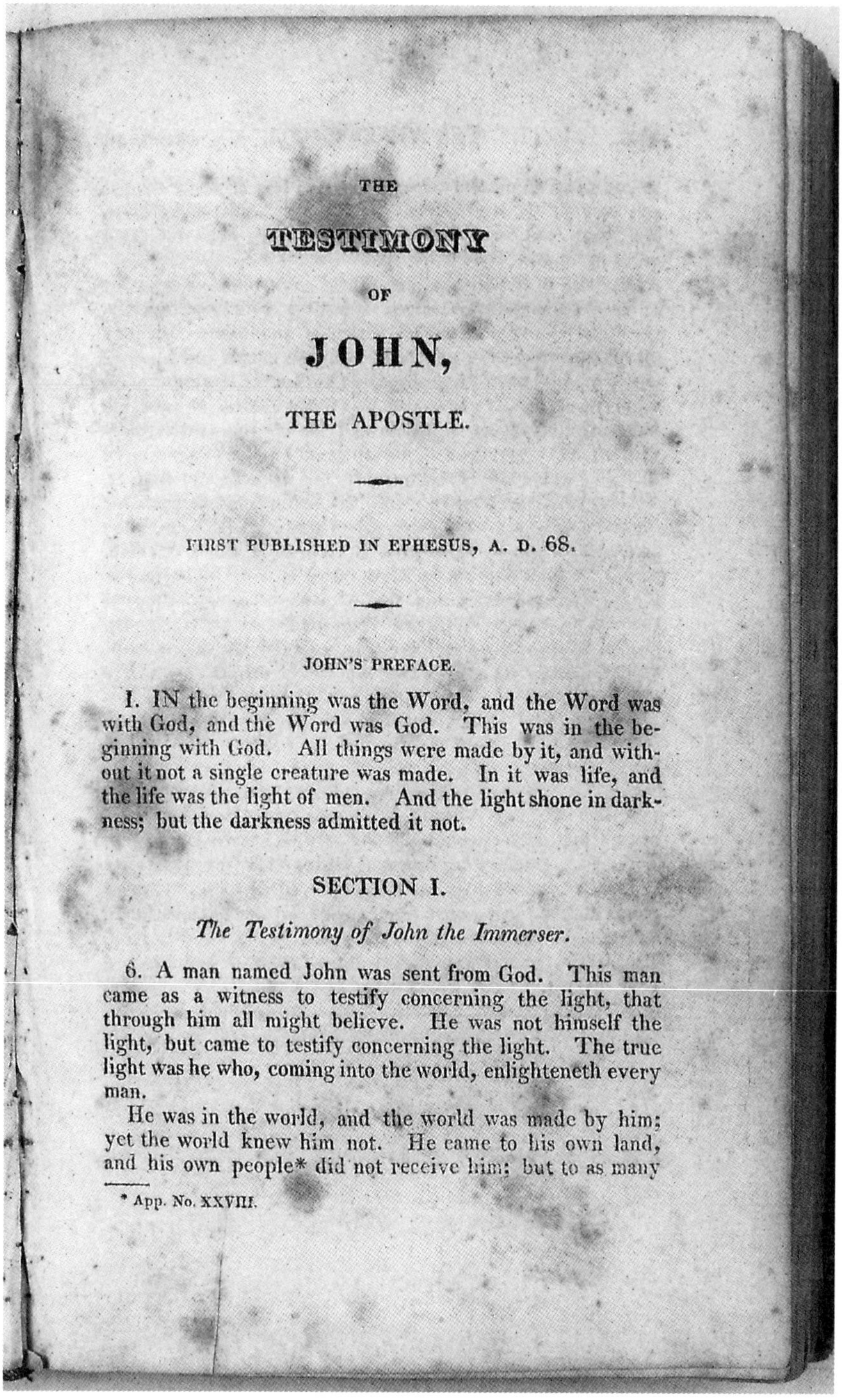

THE

TESTIMONY

OF

JOHN,

THE APOSTLE.

—

FIRST PUBLISHED IN EPHESUS, A. D. 68.

—

JOHN'S PREFACE.

I. IN the beginning was the Word, and the Word was with God, and the Word was God. This was in the beginning with God. All things were made by it, and without it not a single creature was made. In it was life, and the life was the light of men. And the light shone in darkness; but the darkness admitted it not.

SECTION I.

The Testimony of John the Immerser.

6. A man named John was sent from God. This man came as a witness to testify concerning the light, that through him all might believe. He was not himself the light, but came to testify concerning the light. The true light was he who, coming into the world, enlighteneth every man.

He was in the world, and the world was made by him; yet the world knew him not. He came to his own land, and his own people* did not receive him: but to as many

—

* App. No. XXVIII.

FIGURE 28. Single-column pages without conventional verse and chapter markings to encourage narrative flow, from Alexander Campbell's 1826 edition of *The Sacred Writings*. Notice Section I bears the title "The Testimony of John the Immerser." (Courtesy of the American Bible Society Library)

Campbell changed 1 Thessalonians 4:15 to use the word *anticipate* rather than the word *prevent*. *Prevent* had meant "anticipate" in the 1600s, but by the 1820s it only held the sense of "hindering" or "obstructing."[78] Campbell also lists the most notable changes in word forms by listing the obsolete words that he eliminates. He drops the *eth* from verb forms, changing words like *doeth* to *does* and *keepeth* to *keeps*.[79] Thus, Campbell had produced far more than an immersion version of the Bible. He had taken a step toward a modern language version—a version concerned with refashioning the text by replacing words and word forms that were no longer used or had changed meaning in the contemporary English of the period. His goal was simple: to avoid words that would "present a wrong signification or false ideas."[80]

In the next forty years, seven more bible translation projects would position themselves as versions concerned with transforming the Holy Scriptures into more understandable contemporary language. These modern language versions included the Scripture translation work of Noah Webster (1833), Rodolphus Dickinson (1833), David Bernard (1842), Hezekiah Woodruff (1852), Spencer Cone and William Wyckoff (1850), James Murdock (1851), Leicester Sawyer (1858), and H. T. Anderson (1864). Each of these translators would offer their own twists on the modernizing process. Concerns ranged from the translation of words such as βαπτιζω to standardized spelling to the accessiblity and refinement of the Bible's language. Behind all of these concerns, however, stood the overarching desire to present the meaning of the Bible in the most original, and therefore accurate, form.

Criticism of Campbell's production of a new translation was fierce. His enemies listed hubris, doctrinal error, and a spirit of divisiveness among Campbell's sins.[81] Campbell did not view his work as sectarian, but as liberating. He felt he had finally produced a pure version by which Christians could make themselves "intelligent, united, and happy."[82] In the end, his deep desire for Christian unity kept him from pushing his bible as a substitute for the King James Version. Such a substitution would be too controversial and divisive. Campbell encouraged his followers to use his bible alongside the King James Version.[83]

This kind of advice, coupled with his strong claims of biblical purity, may have rung hollow for some, but it is telling that Campbell did not advocate his version as the necessary replacement for the King James Version. Campbell's version was arguably the best-selling bible translation by an individual prior to the Revised Version, largely because Campbell enjoyed a huge denominational apparatus to spread his work. However, the King James Version still had enough sway in the first half of the century that Campbell did not dream of challenging its hegemony.[84]

6 Those who succeeded him in the baptism controversy would not show the same deference toward the King James Version. They would also not share Campbell's commitment to unity, but instead moved bible translation toward sectarianism through translations with heavy theological biases. In this tradition, one finds not only the Unitarians, but the Adventists with Nathan Whiting's New Testament of 1849 and the Mormons with Joseph Smith Jr.'s translation, which was finally published in 1867. It was midcentury Baptists, however, who created the most widely disseminated sectarian translations of the nineteenth century. The Baptist interest in retranslating the English Bible had its roots in Adoniram Judson's 1834 conflict with the American Bible Society, a controversy once again centered on issues of original meaning.

Judson, a Baptist missionary in Rangoon, Burma, had submitted his translation of the Bible into the Burmese language for publication by the American Bible Society. He had worked for nearly twenty years on his translation and fully expected the American Bible Society to eagerly publish his work. Judson's request for publication was not unique.[85] The Society had issued dozens of foreign language translations prior to Judson's and was constantly looking to publish and distribute foreign language versions whenever such translations became available.

What made Judson's translation different from the other bible versions the Society had published was his decision to render the word βαπτιζω as *immerse* in his translation. This choice, and his refusal to change it, caused the American Bible Society not only to refuse publication of his life's work, but also to pass a resolution against any such "sectarian" version of the Scriptures. It maintained that it would not publish or distribute any bibles that did not "conform in the principle of their translation, to the common English version."[86]

This emphasis on the common English version (the King James Version) as the root translation from which translators had to work raised the issue of this version's accuracy to another level. The American Bible Society was tying its translators to an English translation of the Scriptures that was increasingly coming under scholarly attack.

Not translating βαπτιζω was just one of the faults that critics found with the American Bible Society's English translation. The Baptists' larger concern in pushing for their translation of βαπτιζω as *immersion* was founded upon a concern that the original text and its original meaning be given precedence over the fallible human translations of the past.[87] The Baptists maintained that the American Bible Society was encouraging the production and distribution of error-filled texts in ignoring the primacy of the originals.

In not adopting an immersion translation, the American Bible Society alienated its Baptist constituency, which, encouraged by the model of Campbell's New Testament and a confidence that biblical accuracy demanded more than the traditional transliteration of the word βαπτιζω, split off from the American Bible Society to form their own bible society. Baptists began to resign from the American Bible Society's membership in the mid-1830s following the cry of countless Baptist associations and congregations to adhere only to translations of the Scriptures that were "undisguised and unmutilated."[88] Most notable among those to resign from the American Bible Society was the Reverend Spencer Cone, who had served as the Society's corresponding secretary since 1834. Resigning in 1836, Cone moved quickly to form and lead the Baptists' own bible society. The American and Foreign Bible Society was born.[89]

The American and Foreign Bible Society set itself up in contrast to the American Bible Society by selling itself as God's instrument "in multiplying copies of pure versions of the Scriptures, and of counteracting the effects of corrupt and mutilated translations."[90] The reference to the American Bible Society's refusal to publish immersion versions was, at best, thinly veiled. In Cone's address to the first annual meeting of the American and Foreign Bible Society, he exhorted his listeners to aid "pure and scriptural" translation work that conforms "faithfully and minutely to the originals" forever bearing in mind "the momentous truth that he who is employed in transferring the messages of heaven from their originals to another language, is bound to exercise the same accuracy and fidelity in rendering, that the inspired penmen were in recording, the communications of the Most High."[91]

For the American and Foreign Bible Society, the question of accuracy based on the original was not so much one of text as it was of meaning. Unlike the doctrine of the Trinity, the oldest Greek manuscripts included the word βαπτιζω. The issue was not whether the words were there; the issue was what the words meant.

The American and Foreign Bible Society had resolved at the first meeting of its Board of Managers that all missionaries of the board engaged in translation work "be instructed to endeavour by earnest prayer, and diligent study, to ascertain the exact meaning of the *original text*."[92] For American Baptists, this dictate meant that βαπτιζω should be translated *immerse* because there was ample evidence that this was the meaning of the original text.[93] Baptists maintained that the original language was clear about immersion; baptism by sprinkling was nothing more than a corruption of the real practice of immersion baptism to be found in the first-century Christian church. Baptists felt that since the original text was clear, the practice of immersion should be obeyed.

Cone and his compatriots supported their arguments for immersion with numerous philological sources.[94] His adversaries argued that while the word βαπτιζω did in fact carry the connotation of *immersion* in the first century A.D., the word was never used in that sense by first-century Christians. To Cone, this argument was nonsense. The word meant what it meant.[95] To say that a word carried the connotations of immersion, but that the early Christians had not used it that way was a betrayal of common sense and sound philological scholarship.

The American and Foreign Bible Society had begun with the determination to translate not only foreign versions of the Bible more accurately—true to the originals—but also the English Bible as well. To Cone's horror, this conviction evaporated in 1849 when the American and Foreign Bible Society backed away from its commitment to publish and distribute a corrected version of the Bible.

For several years now, the American and Foreign Bible Society had published an immersion version of the King James Bible, but it had decided to keep the King James Version virtually intact. Cone had long believed that this immersion version was simply the first step toward the Society's publishing a more complete revision of the King James Version. In 1850, Cone, along with another Baptist minister, William Wyckoff, offered a more complete revision of the Bible to the Society.[96] The Society balked. It feared publishing a more extensively corrected version of the King James Bible, arguing that more textual changes would "separate them further than ever from Pedo-Baptists, who [would] more than ever call them sectarian."[97]

Cone was outraged, later stating that he "would never have lifted up my finger to form the A. and F. B. Society" if he had known it would commit itself to stereotyping and perpetuating "the errors and obscurities of [the] King James Version."[98] Once again, he resigned to help form a rival bible society. This time it would be called the American Bible Union.

The American Bible Union was formed with the purpose of publishing and distributing an immersion version, as well as working on a new translation of the Scriptures that would significantly correct the *"twenty-four thousand errors"* found in the King James Version.[99] The Union attempted to gather teams of translators to accomplish its goals. Its work in the early 1850s was disastrous, since many of the translators assigned the task did not have the scholarly ability to create a high-quality translation. The controversy surrounding their incompetency almost destroyed the American Bible Union, which was reorganized and saved through appealing to more credible scholars such as Thomas Conant, Horatio Hackett, and Philip Schaff (all of whom were seminary professors specializing in ancient languages and theology) to serve on the translation team to complete an error-free version of the sacred Scriptures.[100]

The bible translations put forward by Alexander Campbell, the American and Foreign Bible Society, and the American Bible Union are best known for being immersion versions. However, it is important to place their concern with the proper translation of βαπτιζω in the context of their overarching interest in capturing as much of the original writers' meaning and spirit as possible. Immersion was only a part of the picture.

Perhaps Noah Webster, the preeminent linguist and grammarian of the early nineteenth century (and also a man who attempted his own translation of the bible), captured best the central goal of nineteenth-century bible translation when he stated that the best versions strove to never "divert the mind from the *matter* to the *language* of the Scriptures."[101]

The fallible form of the Bible often obscured the value of its contents. Modernizers, immersionists, and sectarians all positioned themselves as people who had best captured the primitive integrity of the Scriptures' oldest manuscripts, formerly lost through centuries of ecclesiastical and editorial mismanagement. They sought the "matter" of the Bible beneath the problems with its language, by purifying the translation through the use of purer original sources. Recovering the original meaning of the Scriptures meant "traveling" back in time by using the oldest available manuscripts and cultivating a knowledge of the historical setting of the Bible's authors. As more than thirty American biblical revisions showed, however, such a journey was not easy to make.

7 The numerous new versions of English Scripture that appeared prior to 1880 reveal how deeply Americans clung to the "phrases with which their spiritual life and hope have been nurtured."[102] While revisers were concerned with first texts and first meanings, Americans were predominantly interested in *their* first text, the King James Version, which to them was "the English Bible." All other bibles were "barely Bibles in English."[103] In 1863, the American Bible Union released its new version, which was perhaps the most corporate and sophisticated translation project prior to the Revised Version. It met with little enthusiasm and never approached the circulation figures enjoyed by the editions published by either the American Bible Society or the American and Foreign Bible Society.[104] No version, American or British, even appeared to threaten the ascendancy of the King James Version prior to 1880, yet the appearance of various versions did signal rising doubts and dissatisfactions with the Common Version of the bible.

What the American Bible Union had attempted in the 1850s by gathering scholars to collaborate on a new edition would be repeated with greater success in 1870 when the Convocation of Canterbury responded affirmatively to Bishop Samuel Wilberforce's resolution to form a committee for the revision of the King James Bible. The revision would take over a decade to complete.[105] The sixty-seven British scholars who were involved in the revision worked together with a thirty-four member American revision committee headed by the German Reformed scholar and devoted ecumenist Philip Schaff. These committees poured over the best and newest manuscripts to create their revision.[106] The committee members released their revised New Testament in 1881, and the entire bible appeared in 1885.

The new translation's initial reception gives some clue to the version's cultural significance. While Kneeland was begging for subscriptions for his bible project in 1823, Americans were so interested in the Revised Version that New York newsboys hawked copies of the New Testament on street corners, newspapers printed the entire New Testament in their Sunday editions, and many rural Americans traveled for miles to pick up their own copy of the revised Scriptures.[107] Advance American orders for the bible ran well over three hundred and fifty thousand, and Americans quickly gobbled up over three million copies in the opening months of the version's release.[108]

Although its initial popularity made the Revised Version the publishing event of the century, the book's popularity seemed to wane quickly. Americans seemed curious to check out the new edition, yet they just as quickly returned to their more favored King James Version.

A decade after its release, the Revised Version had attracted only five to ten percent of the nation's bible market.[109] The failure of the version to supersede the King James Version might cause one to miss the larger significance of the appearance of the Revised Version. The Revised Version offered American Protestants a serious choice for the first time about which core text would inhabit their bibles—a choice fueled by doubts about the dependability of the Scriptures and the mutability of their seemingly immutable text.[110]

The true influence of this choice would not be fully felt until a new round of biblical revision would begin in the early twentieth century. While it is true that the Revised Version crowned a steadily growing drive for a revised King James text, its primary importance was that it marked the opening of a new era in American print culture.

The Revised Version gave credence to lurking fears about the King James Version's reliability by touting itself as a version that contained thousands of changes based on new and better manuscript sources and an attention to contemporary idiom. This new version realized one of the worst fears of nineteenth-century American anti-revisionists, namely, that authorizing and introducing a new bible would deprive Americans of a primary cultural "anchor" in the form of a shared national text.[111] In one fell swoop, the introduction of the Revised Version gave credibility to doubts about the trustworthiness of the bible, while it loosened the grip of the King James Bible—a book one author called "the highest bond of unity for the English race."[112]

The release of the Revised Version opened a door to an acceptable alternative to the King James Version. This door would swing ever wider after 1880, as new translations capitalized on the fact that serious doubt had been cast upon the accuracy and efficacy of the King James text. In the forty years following the Revised Version, American publishers would release another thirty-two new biblical translations, more than doubling the translation rate of the previous century.[113] When the Revised Version appeared, Philip Schaff called it "the purest English translation and of the purest Greek Text."[114] Schaff, echoing his numerous American predecessors in translation, put his faith in the power of purity to defeat complaints that the bible was an undependable oracle of truth that was often too obscure to understand.

For others, textual purity was not enough to add ballast to the Bible in the midst of America's tumultuous print marketplace. A different kind of purity, one defined by one's nation of birth and commitment to the Protestant Bible, became increasingly important in the nineteenth century, as thousands upon thousands of immigrants flooded into the country. Just what place the Bible would have in American public institutions became an ever-growing concern as the nation grew and diversified. A purity of religious and nativist conviction played a pivotal role in determining just how central the Bible would continue to be in the education, and thus the lives, of everyday Americans.

Chapter Four

PEDAGOGY

1 Mark Twain is said to have once lampooned the all-too-common claim by Civil War veterans that a bullet-stopping pocket bible had saved their lives by recounting how a bullet had saved him from a near-fatal bible. Supposedly, Twain was walking on a sidewalk near a multistoried hotel, when for no discernable reason, a bible plummeted toward him from an open window above. Fortunately, the bible hit the "lucky bullet" he always carried in his breast pocket and was deflected harmlessly to the ground. Bullets and bibles seem to have an affinity in nineteenth-century American folklore, but their combination would become more than a narrative motif in 1844 when a group of Irish Catholics in Philadelphia shot and killed a man named George Shiffler because of bibles.

Hastily composed lithographs (see Figure 29) and songs (see Figure 30) soon immortalized him as a modern-day martyr, but Shiffler was simply unlucky enough to be among the first of dozens of Philadelphians who were killed or injured in the 1844 summer riots that wracked the city.[1] Tensions had been growing for nearly a decade between new immigrants and increasingly powerful nativist advocates who were troubled by the city's, and the nation's, growing immigrant influx. Immigrants had composed only three percent of the country's population in the 1830s; by the end of the 1840s this figure would more than double as thousands of German and Irish immigrants flooded into the United States.[2]

Opponents of such seemingly unchecked immigration did so on a number of grounds, but central to their complaints was the reality that these German and Irish immigrants were largely Catholic—a fact that posed a dire threat to democratic institutions, as well as to the Protestant heritage and moral stability of the country.[3] In fact, American Catholicism would grow throughout the nineteenth centry to become the country's largest single religious denomination by 1890.[4] The tensions between Protestants and Catholics took their most violent early forms in large eastern cities such as New York, Baltimore, Boston, and Philadelphia where the foreign-born sometimes comprised over half the city population by 1850.[5]

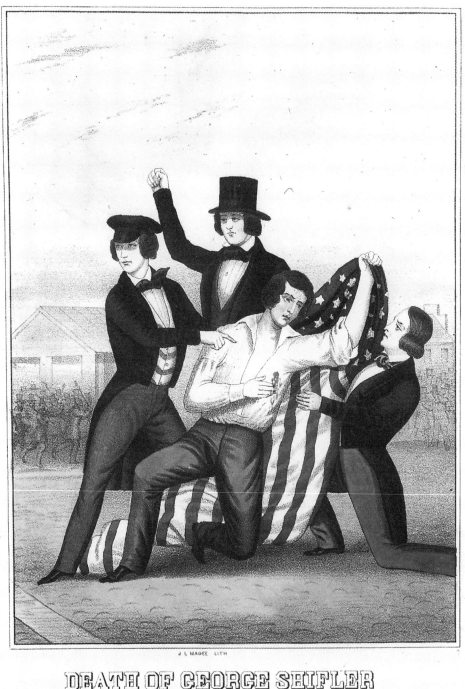

DEATH OF GEORGE SHIFLER

BORN JAN 24 1825   IN KENSINGTON   MURDERED MAY 6 1844

Pub by Wm Smith 106 SO Third St Phila

FIGURE 29. Lithograph of *Death of George Shifler in Kensington*. (Courtesy of the Library Company of Philadelphia)

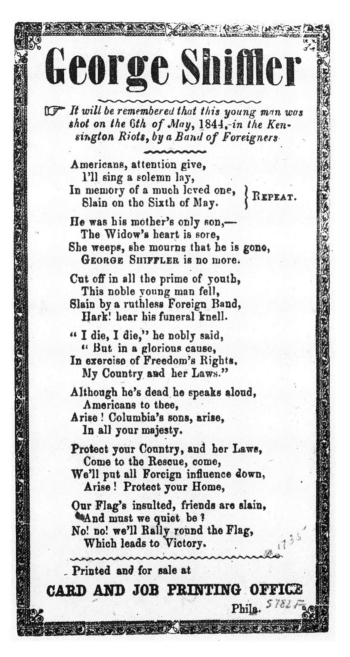

FIGURE 30. Song sheet commemorating George Shiffler's martyrdom. (Courtesy of the Library Company of Philadelphia)

Charlestown, Massachusetts, witnessed the burning of a convent in 1834, and throughout the 1830s and 1840s, party politics provided many opportunities for Catholic and anti-Catholic constituencies to flex physical, as well as electoral, muscles.[6] But these tensions in Massachusetts paled in comparison to the Philadelphia riots of 1844.[7]

The spark that would literally set the city ablaze was a letter from Bishop Francis Patrick Kenrick of the Philadelphia diocese requesting that the city's Board of Controllers for public schools permit Catholic children to use their own version of the Bible in schools and be excused from all other religious instruction.[8] Following the lead of reforms that had already been passed in New York, the Board agreed to the proposal. Over the next year, however, anti-Catholic forces misrepresented the Board's action as one entirely banning the Bible from the schools.

Fostering this misconception, native-born Americans strenuously worked to mobilize "every man who love[s] his country, his Bible, and his God . . . to resist every attempt to banish the Bible from our public institutions," and called for a public gathering in May of 1844 to protest the Board's action.[9] A rainstorm interrupted the afternoon gathering, leading the crowd to march through an Irish section of the city. Violence resulted as the mob and members of an Irish fire company exchanged shots, result-

RUINS OF ST. MICHAEL'S CHURCH, AND THE PRIEST'S HOUSE.

FIGURE 31. *Ruins of St. Michael's Church, and the Priest's House.* (Courtesy of the Library Company of Philadelphia)

ing in the deaths of several who had rallied around the Protestant call to keep "The Bible in the Public School."[10]

Just how deep anti-Catholic sentiment ran can be seen in the degree of destructive violence brought to bear upon the city's Catholic population in the weeks that followed the Board's decision. Repeatedly calling for "Blood for blood," various groups began a large-scale program of intimidation and violence against Irish Catholics.[11] Whole blocks of Irish homes were destroyed; two Catholic churches (see Figure 31), a convent (see Figure 32), and a Catholic seminary were burned to the ground, while a third church was broken into and pillaged.[12] At its height, the Philadelphia violence threatened to spread to New York, where the militaristic efforts of Bishop John Hughes averted disaster in that city.

Hughes placed thousands of armed Irish Catholics around each of New York's churches, prophesying that the city would become "a second Moscow" if Catholics or Catholic property were attacked.[13] Finally, interventions by Pennsylvania militia and the governor stopped the bloodshed in Philadelphia. The city did nothing to reimburse the Catholics for their losses, and a Grand Jury investigating the rioting attributed the trouble to

FIGURE 32. "Burning of the Nunnery or School House, On Wednesday afternoon, May 8," from *A Full and Complete Account of the Late Awful Riots in Philadelphia* (1844). (Courtesy of the Library Company of Philadelphia)

"the efforts of a portion of the community to exclude the Bible from our Public Schools."[14]

These riots reveal the violent cultural shifts Americans were experiencing in the 1840s. Among the most noted and important of these shifts was the place of the bible in the American classroom.

Although a host of simmering tensions had fostered an atmosphere in which the Philadelphia riots could take place, the role of bible reading in the schools played a critical role in propelling the violence forward. The riots highlighted the growing disquiet surrounding the use of the bible in schools across the country. American Catholics, along with numerous educational reformers, would help lay the foundation for displacing the Bible as America's most commonly read text by challenging the role of religious sectarianism in the country's public schools.

2 Too little information is available about educational practices in seventeenth- and eighteenth-century America, yet there exists substantial evidence that the Bible was long used as a primary text in schools in the years leading up to the American Revolution. The reasons for the Bible's use in schools were twofold: First, the Bible was central to the Puritan religious heritage that drove much of early American educational practices; and second, the Bible was the most common and thus most accessible printed text for Americans.[15] The conviction that all people should be able to read the Bible was a commonly held conviction among a large percentage of early Americans. It led several states to pass laws as early as 1642 requiring literacy education.[16] Consequently, the emphasis on personal Bible reading undergirded much of early American education. "The average schoolboy had only a catechism or primer, a Psalter, and a Testament, or a Bible" from which to learn reading and writing.[17]

Beginning in the mid-eighteenth century, grammars and spellers became increasingly available for the teaching of reading and writing. The best known of these was Thomas Dilworth's *A New Guide to the English Tongue*, first printed in the colonies (by the ever-entrepreneurial Benjamin Franklin) in 1747. In recounting his own early education, Noah Webster wrote that when he was young, "the books used were chiefly or whole Dilworth's Spelling Books, the Psalter, Testament and Bible."[18]

Webster would play a pivotal role in changing American schoolroom fare with the introduction of his own spellers in the 1780s.[19] Joseph T. Buckingham articulated this change when he wrote "There was not, to my knowledge, any *reading book* proper, except the Bible, till Webster's Third Book, so called, came out."[20] Webster's grammar, most commonly known as his blue-black speller because of the color of its binding, dominated the American market for the next forty years and helped pioneer a niche.[21]

Only the McGuffey Reader series would surpass its sales with figures that have been estimated to have reached forty-seven million copies between 1836 and 1870.[22]

Two things are important to keep in mind in considering the appearance and widescale distribution of grammars in the United States. First, while scholars have paid close attention to the emergence of an organized common school system in the United States in the opening decades of the nineteenth century, they have often overlooked the fact that this school system emerged at the same time as radical changes were happening in the nation's print marketplace. Between 1780 and 1860, while states initiated concerted efforts to establish uniform and accountable educational materials, changes in American print culture created an unprecedented range and accessibility of textbook material. The all-too-frequent scarcity of schoolbooks in the eighteenth century had given way to an astounding and often frustrating "multiplicity and diversity of elementary book[s]."[23]

Second, the grammars, spellers, and textbooks that began to "crowd the market" in the early nineteenth century showed a marked decrease in the amount of religious material they included.[24] The results of less religious literature flooding American schoolrooms were profound. Where the Bible, catechisms, and heavily doctrinal texts such as the *New England Primer* once ruled early literacy education, this doctrine was increasingly eschewed by school boards in the antebellum period.

By the 1820s, the Bible had almost completely receded from its role as pivotal text in teaching reading and had been relegated to a spot of daily or twice-daily devotional reading.[25] Only in the rural areas did the practice persist of pupils bringing whatever books they had to school in order to use them as textbooks. One of the major turning points in this recision of heavily religious, doctrinal material in the classroom came in 1827 when Massachusetts passed a textbook law prohibiting sectarian books in the classroom. Up until this point, Massachusetts schools had been heavily localized in their management. After 1827, a Board of Education was formed that helped centralize the pedagogical practices of the state's schools. Horace Mann served as the president of this board from 1837 to 1848.[26] Mann and his board worked hard to enforce the textbook law of 1827 (and its slightly revised form of 1835), which banned a great deal of religious reading material from school curricula in an attempt to keep sectarianism out of the classroom. Mann's work in Massachusetts served as an example for state after state, so that by the outbreak of the Civil War, there was a pronounced lack of doctrinal material in American classrooms.[27]

While Mann tirelessly attempted to keep all religious doctrine out of the schools, he remained firmly committed to keeping the Bible in the classroom. Believing that religion, just not sectarian religion, was absolutely necessary to any education that hoped to be useful in sustaining the republic, Mann argued that the Bible should be a daily part of every school's curriculum. Mann also believed that the Bible was actually a cure for sectarianism, and when read without doctrinal prejudice, its clear vision of Jesus and his moral teachings would inculcate the best virtues in students.[28] He believed that the key to proper Bible use in the classroom was simply to make sure that the Bible was read in a way that allowed it to speak "for itself without note or comment," so that its reading favored no particular religious tradition.[29]

Thus, Mann, along with other educational reformers, rallied around devotional Bible reading as a nonsectarian means of keeping a religious element in the classroom that promoted virtuous attitudes and behaviors.[30] The long-range consequences, however, of the Mannite struggle to keep classrooms nonsectarian would eventually lead to the Bible being banned from school curricula. Nonsectarian would lead to nonreligious, something Mann never intended to happen.[31]

3 Although Horace Mann and his associates ceaselessly argued that Bible reading was nonsectarian, they did not convince everyone. In reality, the Protestant bible was not the bible used by Catholics.[32]

Matters came to a head in the summer of 1840 when Bishop Hughes of New York petitioned that a portion of New York City's public education fund be used so that eight already predominantly Catholic schools might continue to operate. His petition was largely precipitated by a desire to have Catholic children read their own version of the Holy Scriptures in the classroom.

Hughes was an Irish immigrant who had arrived in the United States in 1817.[33] Having little more than his own initiative and discipline, he sought out work and educational opportunities, eventually being ordained as a Catholic priest in 1826. Serving first in Philadelphia, he moved to New York as coadjutor bishop in 1838. He immediately became a fiery spokesman for the growing Catholic community, quickly joining the fight to combat the New York City school system's clear prejudice against Catholicism.

Hughes's fight for Catholic education had its roots in the election of Governor William Seward in 1840. In the midst of growing nativist sentiment and the pressures of partisan politics, Seward was a notably openminded and openhanded individual when it came to education, which he placed at the top of his gubernatorial agenda when he entered office. Hughes made it known that he wanted to improve the quality and attendance of the state's schools and that he favored funding especially dedicated Catholic schools to help educate the vast number of Catholic children who did not currently attend schools because of education's Protestant biases.

A group of New York Catholics under the leadership of the Reverend John Powers quickly attempted to capitalize on Seward's benevolence by petitioning that a portion of New York City's public school funding be especially designated to Catholic schools. The reply was swift. Fearing the ire of Protestants and the possibility of an endless division of school funds for the special needs of various constituencies, the Public School Society of New York, a private group that had virtually monopolized the distribution of school funding in New York City since 1805, encouraged the city's Common Council against dividing school funding along sectarian lines.[34]

Drawing strength from historical precedent and Protestant solidarity, the Public School Society felt that it had little to worry about in denying the Catholic petition. After all, Bishop John Dubois had negotiated in 1834 for a similar redress of Catholic wrongs in the New York City school system and had lost at every turn.[35] Members of the Public School Society realized too late, however, that Bishop Hughes was no Bishop Dubois; they severely underestimated how forcefully Hughes would pick up the gauntlet that they had so confidently thrown down.

Hughes had been on a nine-month European trip as Powers orchestrated the petition of Catholic redress in the schools. By 1840, Hughes had joined a growing number of Catholic bishops who had lost confidence that American schooling would ever lose its Protestant biases.[36] As early as the first Provincial Council of Baltimore in 1829, when American bishops declared the necessity of establishing schools for their young whose faith was endangered by Protestant-bent schooling, American Catholics began to articulate certain means to safeguarding their children in the often anti-Catholic school systems of the nation.

Hughes quickly decided to once again petition for school funds. Rather than forsake sectarianism, Hughes proclaimed that sectarianism was vital in order to keep schools from falling into dangerous forms of deistic rationalism.[37] Proudly advocating a Catholic sectarian stance, Hughes argued that Catholics needed a portion of the school funding to insure that no school texts disparaged the Catholic faith and that all Catholic students could read their own version of the Scriptures in the classroom and not be subject to any Protestant religious instruction, including Protestant hymns and prayers.

For decades, all but mathematical school texts had depicted Catholics as murderous heretics, slovenly vagabonds, or indulgence-buying drunkards. The Protestant King James Bible was objectionable to Catholics because it did not hold the imprimatur of the Catholic Church and

121

because reading it "without note or comment" instilled in Catholic children the belief that private interpretation was acceptable.[38]

The resulting war over school funding lasted two years. Although the issues were complex, the press and majority of non-Catholics interpreted the conflict almost entirely through the lens of whether the word of God would be expelled from the common schools of the country.[39] The centrality of the Bible can be seen in the hearing granted Hughes's petition to have Catholic needs in the common schools addressed.

In October 1840, the aldermen of the city's Common Council met to consider the Catholic school question. The hearing lasted two long evenings and attracted such a crowd that hundreds remained shut out of the building where the proceedings were held. The main protagonists were Hughes, Theodore Sedgwick, and Hiram Ketchum, the last two lawyers representing the Public School Society.

In reading through the arguments presented at this hearing, one is struck by how Hughes wanted not so much preference for Catholic students, but protection and justice. He stated again and again that no Catholic religious teaching would take place in the schools during the days, but that the schools would provide a place where the Catholic religion would not be continually denigrated by classroom policies, textbooks, or personal prejudices. Hughes pronounced his case all the more important because Catholics constituted nearly one-fifth of New York City's population and Catholic students represented nearly one-third of all students currently attending the city's schools.

In response, Hiram Ketchum answered not so much with logic but by stressing the present quality of school education in the city and the danger of leaving the Bible out of the curriculum. Hughes had not asked that the Bible be removed, but rather that Catholic students not be forced to use the Protestant Bible and not be taught that private interpretation of the Scriptures is an acceptable practice.[40]

The centrality of the Bible as an issue for those arrayed against Hughes finds ample and telling expression in the second night of the hearings when a number of Protestant clergymen stood up to speak against the Catholic petition. One such clergyman was Rev. Dr. Bond of the Methodist Episcopal Church. Bond went after the bible issue with a tenacity that made even Ketchum's passionate arguments look anemic in comparison, stating that he was "sorry that the reading of the Bible in Public schools . . . is offensive to them; but we cannot allow the Holy Scriptures to be accompanied with *their* notes and commentaries . . . because among other bad things taught in these commentaries, is to be found the lawfulness of murdering heretics, and the unqualified submission, in all matters of conscience, to the Roman Catholic Church."[41] Bond then went on to read from a copy of "The Rhemish New Testament," which included an introduction to Protestants that stated the bible's notes "urged the hatred and murder of Protestants."[42] Hughes was aghast. Bond was reading from a special bible edition that had been produced in New York by Protestants to attack and mock the Catholic version of the Scriptures, yet Bond was citing it as if it was indeed an officially endorsed Catholic version of the Scriptures.

As Bond read, he made it seem that every Catholic Bible endorsed anti-Protestant hatred and that such animosity could be found in the commentary notes of any Catholic Bible. The strategy is telling because of the way Bond was able to make his case believable. He held a tangible, bound bible volume in his hand, and he quoted extensively from that edition's commentary notes. Exhibiting the material book made Bond believable.

Even though Hughes protested long and hard against the use of such a singular and nonrepresentative volume, Bond effectively furthered the arguments concerning the danger of the seemingly anti-bible stance of the Catholics by reading note after note telling how Catholics were sanctioned to see those who opposed them "chastised or executed."[43]

Bond and his fellow clergymen attacked the Catholics on the bible issue extensively in the last night of the hearings. Nevertheless, the Common Council decided to reserve judgment until further investigations into the matter could be made. Three months later, the Council announced a decision against allotting a portion of the school's funding for Catholic-sensitive schools, arguing that Catholics had no right to be treated differently than any number of other religious traditions who participated in the city's school system.

Hughes may have been disappointed by the verdict, but he was not surprised. He quickly mobilized his forces to take his petition to the next level, the state legislature in Albany.

Hughes won a resounding reversal of the Council's decision when the state legislature passed the Mclay Bill in April 1842. William Mclay, who headed the Committee on Colleges, Academies, and Common Schools, reasoned that while ninety-six percent of all children between the ages of five and sixteen attended common schools in the state, less than sixty percent attended in New York City.[44] Obviously, Mclay held, the Public School Society was failing to do its job; it had not reached out to a large enough spectrum of the city's population, and the Catholic petition served as an expression of this failure. Mclay felt that changes were necessary. He introduced legislation that took control of New York City schools away from the Public School Society and extended the state district system based on officials elected during each city election to oversee more representative and locally sensitive policies in New York City's common schools. A requirement for the disbursement of funds to individual schools was the mandate that no sectarian teaching take place during school hours.

As one might expect, the passage of the Mclay Bill did not immediately resolve the tensions between Catholics and their opponents. Rioting occurred during the November city elections of 1842, violence largely attributed to the passage of the new school law. Protestant anger during the riots manifested itself in an attack on Hughes's residence. Only last-minute intervention by the mayor and local militia kept the St. Patrick's Cathedral from being burned to the ground. One month later, news began to trickle down from Champlain, New York, that a Catholic priest had gathered up a small mountain of Protestant bibles, which local bible society members had been assiduously distributing, and had them burned publically in a street (see Figure 33). Although the story was a half-truth—only a handful of bibles had been burned by a non-ordained, renegade friar with dubious ecclesiastical connections—it was enough to spark new unrest and distrust toward the Catholics. Meetings were organized throughout the state to protest the desecration of the Holy Bible before the matter finally settled

CATHOLIC PRIESTS BURNING BIBLES AT CHAMPLAIN, N. Y., 1842.

FIGURE 33. "Catholic Priests Burning Bibles at Champlain, N.Y., 1842," from Edward Beecher's 1854 *The Papal Conspiracy Exposed*. (Courtesy of the Special Collections Department, University of Iowa Libraries, Iowa City, Iowa)

down.[45] New York was not the only state where tensions over Catholicism and bible reading ran high; in the 1840s and 1850s, Maine, Massachusetts, Pennsylvania, Connecticut, and Maryland all experienced Protestant-Catholic frictions ranging from violence to mass protests.[46]

New York City's new school law did not offer the Catholics as much as they had wanted.[47] They still did not have as much control over school funding as they had wished, and the nonsectarian stance of the law still kept them from introducing Catholic alternatives into the schools for Catholic students, while a residual Protestant-biased educational framework would continue on for years.

Also, widespread anti-Catholic sentiment also did not go away. Instead, it grew in the years to come, as seen in the popularity of the nativist Know-Nothing party of the 1850s.[48] In the midst of these difficulties, Hughes continued to pursue Catholic-sensitive schools by beginning to build a separate parochial school system.

The Mclay Bill was important, however, not only because it broke the back of the Public School Society of New York (which finally folded in 1853), but also because of its stress on nonsectarianism. New York became yet one more state in the mid-nineteenth century that passed laws against sectarian school instruction.[49] In not reasoning with the Catholics in a way that might have led to earlier and more amenable compromises, those who had fought so hard for the continuance of the Public School Society and the use of the Protestant Bible in the classroom had unwittingly helped pass a law that would lead to the secularization of classroom instruction throughout New York.[50]

This strong defense of Protestant Bible usage in the schools unintentionally opened a legal avenue—well traveled in the years to come—by which religious books would disappear from school curriculums, and even the presence of the Bible in classrooms would become a topic of heated discussion.[51]

4 Bible publishing had some interesting connections with the debates that raged over the Protestant and Catholic Bibles in American classrooms. In 1844, the strong nativist and Methodist James Harper became mayor of New York City. The other Harper brothers were critical that James—a founding brother of the Harper and Brothers publishing firm—would run for office in a time when the publishing firm had so much at stake in their risky venture of producing the *Illuminated Bible*, and the economy was still recovering from the depression of 1837. Additionally, Bishop Hughes was seemingly mobilizing Catholics to keep the Bible out of every public institution.[52]

How much James's political aspirations can be linked to his publishing business is impossible to tell. In 1844, it was commonly thought that the *Illuminated Bible* was James Harper's best campaign tool because it vividly underscored his commitment to the "good Book" when that book was seemingly under Catholic siege.[53] Harper's capitalization on a product from his publishing empire was a small example of the many ways in which publishing in general—and bible publishing in particular—had a great deal at stake in the flurry of arguments circulating in the 1840s over the Bible and textbooks in the common schools.

Catholic publishing was still coming of age when the controversies over anti-Catholic reading material became increasingly intense in the 1830s and 1840s. As early as the 1829 First Provincial Council of Baltimore, Catholic leadership called for the production of books that were free from doctrinal error and disparagement of Catholics. It would not be until 1843 that presses actually began producing Catholic textbooks in significant numbers.[54]

Bibles were a different matter, but only slightly. The Philadelphia Bible magnate, Mathew Carey, had produced the first Catholic Bible in the United States in 1790. Carey, who had actually once been a parishioner of John Hughes when Hughes served in Philadelphia, gathered subscriptions for a bible project in 1789. Upon getting 421 names, he produced one of the smallest press runs for a bible edition in the years leading up to the Civil War.[55]

The lack of demand for Catholic bibles is seen in the fact that for over a decade following Carey's first Catholic edition, no American publisher produced another Catholic version of the Scriptures. Carey alone would produce more Catholic editions of the Scriptures in the next twenty-five years: the entire Bible again in 1805 and New Testaments in 1805, 1811, and 1816. Clearly, no strong demand existed yet for Catholic bibles, and demand would remain weak until the mid-1820s when the first large waves of Catholic immigrants would begin to arrive in the United States. Beginning in 1825, a growing number of editions of the Catholic Bible would be produced in the United States, hitting a high mark of diversity in the 1850s when thirty-nine new editions of the Catholic Scriptures were produced by seven different American publishers.[56]

Catholic bibles differed from the Protestant King James Version in several key ways. Unlike Protestants who may have overwhelmingly favored the King James Version of the Bible but still had several versions available for their use, canon law emanating from the 1546 Council of Trent (which had declared the "Pre-eminence of the Latin Vulgate") forbade Catholics from reading any biblical translation that was not based on the Latin Vulgate.[57]

The Vulgate edition included several books of the Bible known as the

Apocrypha that Protestants did not consider canonical and often fought hard to keep excluded from bound copies of the Scriptures.[58] For American Catholics, the Church's commitment to *all* the books of the Vulgate meant a commitment by Church law to the Rheims/Douay Version of the Scriptures. The Rheims/Douay Version, more commonly called the Douay Version, was a vernacular translation of the Vulgate. Its New Testament had been translated in 1582, while the Old Testament followed in 1609. The version takes its name from the homes of its translation: the College of Rheims for the New Testament and Douay for the Old Testament.[59] Even though the Douay Version was the standard bible for English-speaking Catholics, it had gone through a number of revisions. Bishop Richard Challoner of London revised the Douay Version five times between 1749 and 1763, and it was one of Challoner's revised, annotated versions that Carey published in 1790.

As the bible controversy heated up in the 1830s and 1840s, it became clear that the Catholics would need to have their own editions of the Scriptures available if they were going to demand that American Catholics use only Church-sanctioned copies of the Bible in schools. There were two primary approaches to meeting the scriptural needs of American Catholics. The first was the pragmatic and immediately satisfying strategy of Bishop Hughes who worked with Catholic publishing firms such as D. J. Sadlier of New York and Boston to begin producing large and frequent press runs of editions of the Douay Bible. The Sadlier firm produced twenty-one editions of the Catholic Scriptures between 1842 and 1880. In 1845 they introduced an edition they would reprint several times in the coming years that featured the Approbation of the Right Reverend Bishop Hughes (see Figure 34).

A close examination of this 1845 edition reveals important differences between the common Protestant and common Catholic bible. Not only did the book prominently display Hughes's blessing on the volume, but the work included Bishop Challoner's annotations, which could be found at the bottom of most pages. As a consequence, the reader constantly had Catholic doctrine explained and reinforced by the bible's notes. These notes also challenged Protestant interpretation. For example, in the passage at the beginning of the Gospel of Luke where Mary states that "all generations shall call me blessed," Challoner tells his Catholic readers, "These words are a prediction of that honour which the church in all ages should pay to the blessed Virgin. Let Protestants examine whether they are any way concerned in this prophecy" (see Figure 35).[60]

The Sadlier bible editions also included an "Admonition" before both the Old and New Testaments reminding readers that the reading of the Scriptures must always be done in "due submission to the Catholic

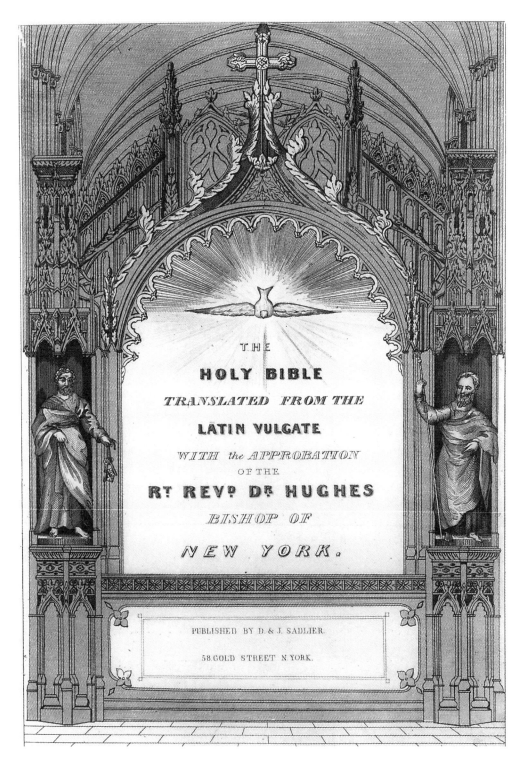

FIGURE 34. Title page noting the approbation of the Right Reverend Dr. Hughes from Sadlier's 1845 bible edition. (Courtesy of the American Bible Society Library)

Church" to guard against the errors that come from private interpretation with all its attendant dangers; scriptural interpretation must be checked by the "Pastors and spiritual Guides whom God has appointed to *govern his Church*" (see Figure 36). Catholic bibles such as the Sadlier edition also included several charts and tables not found in Protestant bibles. This material most often took the form of tables enumerating feast days (see Figure 37) or providing the biblical references for such concepts as "Extreme Unction," "Penance," "Pope," and "Transubstantiation."

Some Sadlier editions would follow the increasingly popular trend in American Catholic bible publishing of including Ward's table of errata noting the errors found in Protestant bible editions.[61] In these ways, Catholic bible editions served as a tool for their readers that both informed their faith and gave them information for combatting the constant Protestant assaults on their belief and their bible.

The second approach was far more ambitious, and far more time-consuming. Spurred on by the conflict he had helped instigate in Philadelphia, Bishop Francis Kenrick began a new vernacular translation of the Catholic Bible in the early 1840s.[62]

Trained as a theologian, Kenrick showed an openness to the higher criticism and attention to original sources that was having a serious effect on Protestant bible translation.[63] Kenrick thought that J. G. Eichhorn's theory that Moses had built upon preexisting sources to write the *Pentateuch* had merit, and Kenrick paid attention to new Greek manuscripts such as Griesbach's. In the midst of this commitment to take newer theological developments into account, Kenrick was careful to maintain the integrity of the Vulgate translation and Catholic doctrine. The notes that accompanied his text would point out where the "Greek Text or the King James differed from the Vulgate," but he would also carefully annotate how the text agreed with accepted Catholic doctrine.[64]

Kenrick's ubiquitous notes reached far beyond simple comparisons of his translation with the Vulgate. He gave his readers annotations full of extensive biblical exposition and translation clarification (see Figure 38). Such comprehensive notes were not new to American bible publishing. The immensely popular Scott's Family Bible, one of many popular "study" bible editions to appear in nineteenth-century America, contained similar internal pedagogical apparatus (see Figure 39). Since its American introduction in 1804, Scott's bible had helped shore up Calvinist orthodoxy against the Unitarian threat.[65]

Kenrick's work offered Catholics a similar bulwark of biblicism with his translation that fused an accepted Catholic biblical text with an extended commentary. Thus, while receiving criticism for some of his innovations such as using the word "repent" rather than the traditional Vulgate

17 And these signs shall follow them that believe: In my name they shall cast out devils: they shall speak with new tongues:

18 They shall take up serpents: and if they shall drink any deadly thing, it shall not hurt them: they shall lay their hands upon the sick, and they shall recover.

19 And the Lord Jesus, after he had spoken to them, was taken up into heaven, and sitteth on the right hand of God.

20 But they going forth preached every where; the Lord co-operating with them, and confirming the word with signs that followed.

THE HOLY GOSPEL OF JESUS CHRIST,

ACCORDING TO

ST. LUKE.

St. Luke was a native of Antioch, the capital of Syria. He was by profession a physician: and some ancient writers say that he was very skilful in painting. He was converted by St. Paul; and became his disciple and companion in his travels, and fellow-labourer in the ministry of the Gospel. He wrote in Greek about twenty-four years after our Lord's Ascension.

CHAP. I.

The conception of John the Baptist, and of Christ: the visitation and canticle of the Blessed Virgin: the birth of the Baptist, and the canticle of Zachary.

FORASMUCH as many have taken in hand to set forth in order a narration of the things that have been accomplished among us:

2 According as they have delivered them unto us, who from the beginning were eye-witnesses and ministers of the word:

3 It seemed good to me also, having diligently attained to all things from the beginning, to write to thee in order, most excellent Theophilus,

4 That thou mayest know the truth of those words in which thou hast been instructed.

5 There was in the days of Herod the king of Judea, a certain priest named Zachary, of the course of Abia,* and his wife was of the daughters of Aaron, and her name Elisabeth.

6 And they were both just before God, walking in all the commandments and justifications of the Lord without blame.

7 And they had no son; for that Elisabeth was barren, and they both were well advanced in years.

8 And it came to pass, that while he executed the priestly office before God, in the order of his course,

9 According to the custom of the priestly office, it was his lot to offer incense, going into the temple of the Lord.

10 And all the multitude of the people was praying without at the hour of incense.

11 And there appeared to him an angel of the Lord, standing on the right side of the altar of incense.

12 And Zachary seeing him, was troubled; and fear fell upon him:

13 But the angel said to him: Fear not, Zachary, for thy prayer is heard: and thy wife Elisabeth shall bear thee a son; and thou shalt call his name John;

14 And thou shalt have joy and gladness; and many shall rejoice at his birth:

15 For he shall be great before the Lord; and shall drink no wine nor strong drink: and he shall be filled with the Holy Ghost even from his mother's womb.

16 And he shall convert many of the children of Israel to the Lord their God:

17 And he shall go before him in the spirit and power of Elias; that he may turn the hearts of the fathers to the children, and the incredulous to the wisdom of the just, to prepare for the Lord a perfect people.

18 And Zachary said to the angel: Whereby shall I know this? for I am an old man, and my wife is advanced in years.

19 And the angel answering, said to him: I am Gabriel who stand before God; and am sent to speak to thee, and to bring thee these good tidings.

20 And, behold, thou shalt be dumb, and shalt not be able to speak until the day wherein these things shall come to pass; because thou hast not believed my words, which shall be fulfilled in their time.

21 And the people were waiting for Zachary: and they wondered that he staid so long in the temple.

22 And when he came out, he could not speak to them: and they understood that he had seen a vision in the temple. And he made signs to them, and remained dumb.

---

* Of the course of *Abia*, i. e. Of the *rank* of Abia, which word in the Greek is commonly put for the employment of *one day;* but here for the functions of a *whole week.* For, by the appointment of David, 1

Paral. 24. the descendants from Aaron were divided into twenty-four families, of which the eighth was Abia, from whom descended this Zacharias, who at this time was in the *week* of his priestly functions.

FIGURE 35. *(Both pages)* Pages, including Challoner's annotations, from Sadlier's 1845 bible edition. (Courtesy of the American Bible Society Library)

23 And it came to pass, after the days of his office were accomplished, that he departed to his own house.

24 And after those days his wife Elizabeth conceived, and hid herself five months, saying:

25 Thus hath the Lord dealt with me in the days wherein he hath had regard to take away my reproach among men.

26 And in the sixth month, the angel Gabriel was sent from God into a city of Galilee called Nazareth,

27 To a virgin espoused to a man whose name was Joseph, of the house of David: and the name of the virgin was Mary.

28 And the angel being come in, said to her: Hail, full of grace, the Lord is with thee: Blessed *art* thou among women.

29 And when she had heard, she was troubled at his saying, and thought with herself what manner of salutation this should be.

30 And the angel said to her: Fear not, Mary; for thou hast found grace with God:

31 Behold, thou shalt conceive in thy womb, and shalt bring forth a Son; and thou shalt call his name Jesus.

32 He shall be great, and shall be called the Son of the most High: and the Lord God shall give unto him the throne of David his father: and he shall reign in the house of Jacob for ever,

33 And of his kingdom there shall be no end.

34 And Mary said to the angel: How shall this be done, because I know not man?

35 And the angel answering, said to her: The Holy Ghost shall come upon thee; and the power of the most High shall over-shadow thee. And therefore also the Holy which shall be born of thee, shall be called the Son of God.

36 And behold, thy cousin Elizabeth, she hath also conceived a son in her old age: and this is the sixth month with her that is called barren:

37 Because no word shall be impossible with God.

38 And Mary said: Behold the handmaid of the Lord: be it done to me according to thy word. And the Angel departed from her.

39 And Mary rising up in those days, went into the mountainous country with haste, into a city of Juda:

40 And she entered into the house of Zachary, and saluted Elizabeth.

41 And it came to pass, that when Elizabeth heard the salutation of Mary, the infant leaped in her womb: and Elizabeth was filled with the Holy Ghost:

42 And she cried out with a loud voice, and said: Blessed art thou among women; and blessed is the fruit of thy womb.

43 And whence is this to me, that the mother of my Lord should come to me?

44 For behold, as soon as the voice of thy salutation sounded in my ears, the infant in my womb leaped for joy.

45 And blessed art thou that hast believed; because those things shall be accomplished that were spoken to thee by the Lord.

46 And Mary said: My soul doth magnify the Lord:

47 And my spirit hath rejoiced in God my Saviour:

48 Because he hath regarded the humility of his handmaid: for, behold, from henceforth all generations shall call me blessed.*

49 For he that is mighty hath done great things to me: and holy *is* his name.

50 And his mercy is from generation to generations, to them that fear him.

51 He hath showed might in his arm: he hath scattered the proud in the conceit of their heart.

52 He hath put down the mighty from their seat, and hath exalted the humble.

53 He hath filled the hungry with good things: and the rich he hath sent away empty.

54 He hath received Israel his servant, being mindful of his mercy.

55 As he spoke to our fathers, to Abraham and to his seed for ever.

56 And Mary abode with her about three months: and she returned to her own house.

57 Now Elizabeth's full time of being delivered was come, and she brought forth a son.

58 And her neighbours and kinsfolks heard that the Lord had showed his great mercy towards her: and they congratulated with her.

59 And it came to pass, that on the eighth day they came to circumcise the child: and they called him by his father's name Zachary.

60 And his mother answering, said: Not so, but he shall be called John.

61 And they said to her: There is none of thy kindred that is called by this name.

62 And they made signs to his father, how he would have him called.

63 And demanding a table-book, he wrote, saying: John is his name. And they all wondered.

64 And immediately his mouth was opened, and his tongue *loosed;* and he spoke, blessing God.

65 And fear came upon all their neighbours: and all these words were divulged over all the mountainous country of Judea.

66 And all they who had heard them laid them up in their heart, saying: What a one, think ye, shall this child be? For the hand of the Lord was with him.

67 And Zachary his father was filled with the Holy Ghost: and he prophesied, saying:

68 Blessed be the Lord God of Israel, because he hath visited and wrought the redemption of his people:

---

* *Shall call me blessed.* These words are a prediction of that honour which the church in all ages should pay to the blessed Virgin. Let Protestants examine whether they are any way concerned in this prophecy.

ADMONITION.

THE Scriptures, in which are contained the revealed Mysteries of Divine Faith, are undoubtedly the most excellent of all writings; they were written by men divinely inspired, and are not the *Words of men, but the Word of God*, which *can save our souls*, 1 Thess. ii. 13. and James i. 21; but then they ought to be read, even by the learned, with the spirit of humility, and with a fear of mistaking the true sense, as many have done. This we learn from the Scripture itself; where St. Peter says, that in the Epistles of St. Paul there *are some things hard to be understood, which the unlearned and unstable wrest*, as they do *also the other Scriptures, to their own perdition.* 2 Peter iii. 16.

To prevent and remedy this *abuse*, and to guard against *error*, it was judged necessary to forbid the reading of the Scriptures in the vulgar languages, without the advice and permission of the Pastors and spiritual Guides* whom God has appointed to *govern his Church*, Acts xx. 28. Christ himself declaring: *He that will not hear the church, let him be to thee as the heathen and the publican.* Matt. xviii. 16.

Nor is this due submission to the Catholic Church (*The pillar and ground of truth*, 1 Tim. iii. 15.) to be understood of the ignorant and unlearned only, but also of men accomplished in all kind of learning, the ignorant fall into *errors* for want of knowledge, and the learned through pride and self-sufficiency.

Therefore let every reader of the Sacred Writings, who pretends to be a competent judge of the sense, and of the truths revealed in them, reflect on the words which he finds in Isaias, chap. lv. 8, 9. *My thoughts are not as your thoughts, neither are your ways my ways, saith the Lord; for as the heavens are exalted above the earth, even so are my ways exalted above your ways, and my thoughts above your thoughts.* How then shall any one, by his private reason, pretend to *judge*, to *know*, to *demonstrate*, the *incomprehensible* and *unsearchable ways* of God!

---

* *The following Letter of His Holiness*, PIUS THE SIXTH, *to the Most Rev.* ANTHONY MARTINI, *now Archbishop of Florence, on his Translation of the Holy Bible into Italian, shews the benefit which the faithful may reap from their having the Holy Scriptures in the Vulgar Tongue*

POPE PIUS THE SIXTH.

BELOVED SON, *Health and Apostolical Benediction*

AT a time that a vast number of bad books, which most grossly attack the Catholic Religion, are circulated, even among the unlearned, to the great destruction of souls, you judge exceedingly well, that the faithful should be excited to the reading of the Holy Scriptures: For these are the most abundant sources which ought to be left open to every one, to draw from them purity of morals and of doctrine, to eradicate the errors which are so widely disseminated in those corrupt times: This you have seasonably effected, as you declare, by publishing the Sacred Writings in the language of your country, suitable to every one's capacity: especially when you shew and set forth, that you have added explanatory notes, which being extracted from the Holy Fathers, preclude every possible danger of abuse: Thus you have not swerved either from the laws of the Congregation of the Index, or from the Constitution published on this subject by BENEDICT XIV. that immortal Pope, our predecessor in the Pontificate, and formerly when We held a place near his person, our excellent Master in Ecclesiastical learning; circumstances which We mention as honorable to Us. We therefore applaud your eminent learning, joined with your extraordinary piety, and We return you our due acknowledgment for the books you have transmitted to Us, and which, when convenient, We will read over. In the mean time, as a token of our Pontifical benevolence, receive our Apostolical Benediction, which to you, beloved Son, We very affectionately impart. Given at Rome, on the Calends of April, 1778, the fourth year of our Pontificate.

PHILIP BUONAMICI, Latin Secretary.

To our Beloved Son,
Anthony Martini, at Turin.

A PRAYER BEFORE THE READING OF ANY PART OF THE HOLY SCRIPTURE.

COME, O Holy Spirit, fill the hearts and minds of thy faithful servants, and inflame them with the fire of thy divine love.

LET US PRAY:

O GOD, who by the inspiration of the Holy Ghost, didst instruct the hearts of thy faithful servants; grant us in the same Spirit, to discern what is right, and enjoy his comfort for ever: Through our Lord Jesus Christ, who liveth and reigneth one God, with thee and the same Spirit, world without end. Amen.

3

FIGURE 36. "Admonition" from Sadlier's 1845 bible edition. (Courtesy of the American Bible Society Library)

A TABLE

OF ALL

THE EPISTLES AND GOSPELS

FOR ALL

THE SUNDAYS AND HOLY-DAYS THROUGHOUT THE YEAR;

AND ALSO, OF THE

MOST NOTABLE FEASTS IN THE ROMAN CALENDAR.

It must be observed, that the Verses at which the Epistle or Gospel begin and end are set down after the Chapter.

ADVENT, 1 Sunday, Epistle Rom. xiii. 11. 14. Gospel Luke xxi. 25. 34.
2 Sunday, Epistle Rom. xv. 4. 13. Gospel Matt. xi. 2. 10.
3 Sunday, Epistle Philip. iv. 4. 7. Gospel John i. 19. 28.
4 Sunday, Epistle 1 Cor. iv. 1. 5. Gospel Luke iii. 1. 6.
Christmas, 1 Mass, Epistle Tit. ii. 11. 15. Gospel Luke ii. 1. 15.
   2 Mass, Epistle Tit. iii. 4. 8. Gospel Luke ii. 15. 21.
   3 Mass, Epistle Heb. i. 1. 12. Gospel John i. 1. 14.
St. Stephen, Epistle Acts vi. and vii. 54. 49. Gospel Matt. xxiii. 34. 39.
St. John, Epistle Eccl. xv. 1. 7. Gospel John xxi. 20. 24.
Holy Innocents, Epistle Apoc. xiv. 1. 6. Gospel Matt. ii. 13. 18.
St. Thomas Cant. Epistle Heb. v. 1. 7. Gospel John x. 11. 17.
St. Sylvester, Epistle 2 Tim. iv. 1. 9. Gospel Luke xii. 35. 41.
Circumcision, Epistle Tit. ii. 11. 15. Gospel Luke ii. 21, 22.
Epiphany, Epistle Isai. lx. 1. 7. Gospel Matt. ii. 1. 13.
1 Sunday, Epistle Rom. xii. 1. 6. Gospel Luke ii. 42. 52.
2 Sunday, Epistle Rom. xii. 6. 16. Gospel John ii. 1. 12.
Name of Jesus, Epistle Acts iv. 8. 12. Gospel Luke ii. 21.
3 Sunday, Epistle Rom. xii. 16. 21. Gospel Matt. viii. 1. 13.
4 Sunday, Epistle Rom. xiii. 8. 11. Gospel Matt. viii. 23. 28.
5 Sunday, Epistle Coloss. iii. 12. 18. Gospel Matt. xiii. 24. 31.
6 Sunday, Epistle 1 Thess. i. 2. 10. Gospel Matt. xiii. 31. 36.
Septuagesima, Epistle 1 Cor. ix. 24. x. 5. Gospel Matt. xx. 1. 17.
Sexagesima, Epistle 2 Cor. xi. 19. xii. 10. Gospel Luke viii. 4. 16.
Quinquagesima, Epistle 1 Cor. xiii. 1. 13. Gospel Luke xviii. 31. 34.
Ash-Wednesday, Epistle Joel ii. 12. 20. Gospel Matt. vi. 16. 22.
1 Lent, Epistle 2 Cor. vi. 1. 11. Gospel Matt. iv. 1. 12.
2 Lent, Epistle 1 Thess. iv. 1. 8. Gospel Matt. xvii. 1. 10.
3 Lent, Epistle Ephes. v. 1. 9. Gospel Luke xi. 14. 29.
4 Lent, Epistle Gal. iv. 22. 31. Gospel John vi. 1. 15.
Pass. Sunday, Epistle Heb. ix. 11. 15. Gospel John viii. 46. 59.
Palm-Sunday, Epistle, Phil. ii. 5. 11. Gospel Matt. xxi. 1. 10. and chap. xxvi. xxvii.
Maunday-Thursday, Epistle 1 Cor. xi. 20. 33. Gospel John xiii. 1. 15.
Good-Friday, Epistle Exodus xii. 1. 12. 1. Gospel John xviii. xix.
Holy Saturday, Epistle Coloss. iii. 1. 4. Gospel Matt. xxviii. 1. 7.

6 M

Easter Sunday, Epistle 1 Cor. v. 7. 8. Gospel Mark xvi. 1. 7.
Easter Monday, Epistle Acts xx. 37. 43. Gospel Luke xxiv. 13. 35.
Easter Tuesday, Epistle Acts xiii. 26. 33. Gospel Luke xxiv. 36. 47.
Low-Sunday, Epistle 1 John v. 4. 10. Gospel John xx. 19. 31.
2 Sunday after Easter, Epistle 1 Peter ii. 21. 25. Gospel John x. 11. 16
3 Sunday, Epistle 1 Peter ii. 11. 18. Gospel John xvi. 16. 22
4 Sunday, Epistle James i. 17. 21. Gospel John xvi. 5. 14.
5 Sunday, Epistle James i. 22. 27. Gospel John xvi. 22. 30.
Ascension, Epistle Acts i. 1. 11. Gospel Mark xvi. 14. 20.
6 Sunday, Epistle 1 Peter iv. 7. 12. Gospel John xiv. 26. xvi. 4.
Whit. Sunday, Epistle Acts ii. 1. 11. Gospel John xiv. 23. 31.
Whit. Monday, Epistle Acts x. 42. 48. Gospel John iii. 16. 21.
Tuesday, Epistle Acts viii. 14. 17. Gospel John x. 1. 10.
Trinity-Sunday, Epistle Rom. xi. 33. 36. Gospel Matt. xxviii. 18. 20
Corpus Christi, Epistle 1 Cor. xi. 23. 29. Gospel John vi. 56. 59.
2 Sunday, Epistle 1 John iii. 13. 18. Gospel Luke xiv. 16. 24.
3 Sunday, Epistle 1 Peter v. 6. 11. Gospel Luke xv. 1. 10.
4 Sunday, Epistle Romans viii. 18. 23. Gospel Luke v. 1. 11.
5 Sunday, Epistle 1 Peter iii. 8. 15. Gospel Matt. v. 20. 24.
6 Sunday, Epistle Rom. vi. 3. 11. Gospel Mark viii. 1. 10.
7 Sunday, Epistle Rom. vi. 19. 23. Gospel Matt. vii. 15. 21.
8 Sunday, Epistle Rom. viii. 12. 17. Gospel Luke xvi. 1. 9.
9 Sunday, Epistle 1 Cor. x. 6. 14. Gospel Luke xix. 41. 47.
10 Sunday, Epistle 1 Cor. xii. 2. 11. Gospel Luke xviii. 9. 14.
11 Sunday, Epistle 1 Cor. xv. 1. 10. Gospel Mark vii. 31. 37.
12 Sunday, Epistle 2 Cor. iii. 4. 9. Gospel Luke x. 23. 37.
13 Sunday, Epistle Gal. iii. 16. 22. Gospel Luke xvii. 11. 19.
14 Sunday, Epistle Gal. v. 16. 24. Gospel Matt. vi. 24. 33.
15 Sunday, Epistle Gal. v. 25. vi. 11. Gospel Luke vii. 11. 16.
16 Sunday, Epistle Eph. iii. 13. 21. Gospel Luke xiv. 1. 11.
17 Sunday, Epistle Eph. iv. 1. 6. Gospel Matt. xxii. 35. 46.
18 Sunday, Epistle 1 Cor. i. 4. 9. Gospel Matt. ix. 1. 8.
19 Sunday, Epistle Eph. iv. 23. 28. Gospel Matt. xxii. 1. 14.
20 Sunday, Epistle Eph. v. 15. 21. Gospel John iv. 46. 53.
21 Sunday, Epistle Eph. vi. 10. 17. Gospel Matt. xviii. 23. 25.
22 Sunday, Epistle Philip. i. 6. 11. Gospel Matt. xxii. 15. 21.

223

FIGURE 37. Table noting Sundays, holy days, and notable feasts in the Roman Catholic calendar from Sadlier's 1845 bible edition. (Courtesy of the American Bible Society Library)

THE HOLY GOSPEL OF JESUS CHRIST

JOHN.

CHAPTER I.

THE DIVINITY AND INCARNATION OF CHRIST. JOHN BEARS TESTIMONY TO HIM.
HE BEGINS TO CALL HIS DISCIPLES.

1. IN the beginning[1][a] was the Word,[2] and the Word[b] was with God,[3] and the Word was God.[4]

2. This was in the beginning with God.[5]

3. All things were made through[c] Him:[6] and without Him was made nothing that was made.[7]

4. In Him was life,[8] and the life was the light of men:[9]

---

[1] Before all things, from eternity. With Moses the beginning is connected with the creation, and consequently limited. John says nothing to restrict its meaning. It is clear that he had in view the exordium of Genesis.

[2] Some moderns have fancied that the evangelist borrowed his ideas about "the Word" from Philo the Jew, or from Plato: but it is easy to show the wide difference between his teaching and theirs. He was utterly unacquainted with the writings of the Pagan philosopher; and left nothing which could confirm or favor them. The doctrine as well as the style of John savors not of Grecian discipline. More probably he had in view what is written in the sacred books concerning Wisdom.

[3] In intimate union. "Since the evangelist declares that the Word was with God, he manifestly shows that there is one Son, who subsists in Himself, and one God the Father, with whom the Word is." St. Cyril Alex.

[4] The identity of the Word with God is here affirmed: yet a personal distinction has been already declared. The Word was with God the Father, and was God, equally as the Father, although personally distinct.

[5] Repetitions, enforcing what was already said, are familiar to this evangelist.

[6] The Father may be said to create through the Word, who, being the same God, does whatever the Father does, by an inseparable operation of the Divine Nature.

[7] Not even a single created thing exists without the concurrent action of the Son : "Since then the evangelist declares that creatures were made by Him, He plainly teaches that He is different from created nature, and that by His ineffable power all things were produced from nothing." St. Cyril. Alex. "All things, from the angel to the worm." St. Augustin.

[8] The Word was the source of life.

[9] The principle of life which emanates from the Son, spreads light over mankind, gives animation to inert matter. Supernatural truth—the light and life of the soul—comes likewise from the Divine Word.

[a] *Infra* 17 : 5; Eph. 1 : 4; Col. 1 : 17.

[b] 'Ο λογος, "The Word," is the reason and wisdom of the Deity—it specially denotes the second Divine Person, to whom it is here appropriated.

[c] διά is used also to express the original source. 1 Cor. 1 : 9.

FIGURE 38. Sample page from Francis Kenrick's 1862 New Testament. Notice the large amount of commentary accompanying the text. (Courtesy of the American Bible Society Library)

declares him to be "an Israelite indeed:" and he confesses Jesus as "the Son of God and the King of Israel," 46—49. Jesus promises that he shall see still greater things, 50, 51.

IN ªthe beginning was ᵇthe Word, and the Word was ᶜwith God, and ᵈthe Word was God.

Gen. 1:1. Prov. 8:22,23; Eph. 3:9. Col. 1:17. Heb. 1:10. 7:3. 13:8. Rev. 1:8,11. 21:6. 22:13. b 14. 1 John 1:1,2. 5:7. Rev. 19:13. c 18. 16:28. 17:5. Prov. 8:22— | 30. 1 John 1:2. d 10:30—33. 20:28. Ps. 45:6. Is. 7:14. 9:6. 40:9—11. Matt. 1:23. Rom. 9:5. Phil. 2:6. 1 Tim. 3:16. Tit. 2:13. Heb. 1:8. 2 Pet. 1:1. Gr. 1 John 5:7,20.

2 The same was in the beginning with God.

3 All ᵉthings were made by him; and without him was not any thing made that was made.

e 10. 5:17—19. Gen. 1:1,26. Ps. 33:6. 102:25. Is. 45:12,18. Eph. | 3:9. Col. 1:16,17. Heb. 1:2,3. 10—12. 3:3,4. Rev. 4:11.

NOTES.

CHAP. I. V. 1—3. The other Evangelists leave us to collect the Deity of Christ, from his miracles and doctrine, and from the various declarations and displays of his glory and perfections, which they record: but John opens his gospel, with an express avowal and statement of this fundamental truth. He declares, that "In the beginning was the Word." (Marg. Ref.) Nothing could precede this, that man can know, but an immeasurable incomprehensible eternity. (Note, Gen. 1:1.) Time began, when the creation was called forth into existence by the Word himself: and "in the beginning, the Word was," that is, from eternity. Critics have shewn, that there is an important difference between "in the beginning;" and "from the beginning:" the context, however, generally fixes the meaning. "The devil was a murderer," or manslayer, "from the beginning;" but this he could not be, ere man existed. (8:44.) —Some imagine that the evangelist referred to the speculations of Plato and his disciples, in the term "the WORD," or the LOGOS, which that philosopher used: but it is not likely that he would at all countenance such speculations, as those of that philosopher, which seem originally to have been borrowed from Revelation, though they were at length so distorted and darkened, as to be little better than atheism.—The Jews 'were constantly taught in their synagogues, that 'the Word of God" was the same as God; and 'that by "the Word all things were made:" which 'undoubtedly was the cause, why St. John deliv- 'ered so great a mystery in so few words, as speak- 'ing unto them, who at the first apprehension un- 'derstood him. Only that which they knew not 'was, that this "Word was made flesh," and that 'this Word made flesh was Jesus Christ.' Bp. Pearson. The same learned divine, shews, that this way of speaking was in use, before Platonism was at all introduced among the Jews: and Jerom, in his note on Ez. 1:24, says, that the Septuagint translate the words, rendered in our version "the voice of the Almighty," the voice of the Logos, or second person in the sacred Trinity. The clause, however, is at present wanting in some copies of the Septuagint; and in others, the words τοῦ λογου, do not appear to be a translation of the original word Shaddai, but of that rendered speech.—"As the voice of a mighty one: when they went, there was the voice of speech, like the voice of an host."—The word may probably be taken, in its 'ordinary signification: though we may certainly 'conclude, that this was the appearance of the 'second person in the sacred Trinity; both be- 'cause he appears under the resemblance of a 'man (26), and from what hath been said on this 'subject, upon Is. 6:1.' Lowth. (Notes, Is. 6:1—4. Ez. 1:15—28.)—It is indeed probable, that the apostle referred to expressions, often made use of by the ancient Jewish writers, who spoke of "the Word," in language not very dissimilar from that of the ancient fathers of the church, and other Christian divines; who, endeavoring to explain a mysterious subject, and to add further information, to that which the scripture has afforded us,

VOL. V.　　　　57

have only darkened it, and laid it open to the objections of infidels. I apprehend, however, that St. John especially regarded the doctrine of the Old Testament, in what he declared. We have in many places observed the clearest intimations of distinct persons called JEHOVAH, in the writings of the ancient prophets; (Notes, Is. 48:16. Zech. 2:6—13. 4:8—10. 6:14,15.) and Solomon especially speaks of Wisdom, in language very similar to that which John here uses concerning "the Word." (Notes, Prov. 8:22—34.) But the apostle "spake as he was moved by the Holy Spirit," and could refer to no higher authority than his own: he expressly states the doctrine, as a divine testimony; and we should endeavor to ascertain his meaning, according to the most simple and obvious interpretation of his words; and explain occasional intimations on the same mysterious subject by his words, and not his words by other intimations.—The title of "the Word" is peculiar to this Evangelist, at least with but few exceptions; it may signify Reason, and is nearly equivalent to Wisdom, as speaking by Solomon. Probably, the title is given to Christ; because by him the perfections, will, and secret counsels of God are made known to man; especially his hidden and deep thoughts of wisdom and love in our redemption; even as a man communicates his secret purposes and counsels to others, by his word: and by him exclusively; for all prophets shine by his light, and report his testimony. 'The plainest 'reason, why this essential "Son of God" is styled '"the Word," seems to be this; that as our words 'are the interpretation of our minds to others, so 'was this "Son of God" sent to reveal his Father's 'mind to the world.' Whitby.—It follows, "The WORD was with God." The apostle had not here mentioned Christ as "the Son of God;" and therefore he did not say "the Father," but God. The Word existed, and was with God, when no creature had been produced. (Notes, 1 John 1: 1—4.)—"And the WORD was GOD." Christianity was doubtless intended to deliver the world from idolatry, that principal work of the devil: it would therefore have been the most palpable absurdity, to suppose that one of its divinely inspired teachers should use those expressions, at the opening of his gospel, which were exactly suited to draw the whole Christian church into a new species of idolatry, and which could scarcely fail to have that effect. Yet this must be the consequence of supposing the person, of whom he here spake, to have been a mere creature, however highly exalted. The article is not indeed prefixed to the word rendered "God," but the rules of grammar require that it should be omitted, to distinguish the predicate from the nominative before the verb: and the word is frequently thus used even of God the Father; so that scarcely the shadow of an objection can be drawn from that circumstance. And what can we understand by this testimony, "The Word was God," but that he was possessed of the same divine nature and perfections with the Father; participated the same glory and felicity; and was in every respect as fully entitled to the adoration of all rational crea-

[449

FIGURE 39. Representative page from Scott's Family Bible, Samuel T. Armstrong 1832 edition. Note that only three verses are actually cited on the page. The rest of the page's content consists of various levels of commentary, including chapter introduction, time-line date, cross references, and theological commentary. (Library of the author)

"to do penance," Kenrick offered American Catholics a new vernacular bible coupled with a rich commentary that assured their theological view, aided their personal reading, and testified to the sufficiency of all versions based on the Vulgate.[66]

Kenrick's version would appear in six volumes between 1849 and 1862, but Kenrick never completed a revision of the entire Bible. He had intended his translation and its notes to be the best answer against the constant Protestant claims that the Catholic Bible was a hopelessly outdated mistranslation of the Scriptures contaminated further by the inclusion of spurious books. Kenrick's work would also never receive the official sanction of the American Catholic Church, whose leadership decided not to elevate the new bible to the country's primary version of the Scriptures in 1884's Third Council of Baltimore. The Church hierarchy endorsed Kenrick's work as a version worthy of attention and acceptable for study, but they did not elevate it above the Challoner versions already in use. This moderate reception of Kenrick's new bible indicated the Church hierarchy's relative comfort with the quality and quantity of Catholic bibles currently available, as Church leaders did not feel it necessary to endorse Kenrick's version in order to meet the needs of American Catholics.[67]

5 While the American Catholic Church hierarchy worked to strengthen Catholic publishing in order to disseminate more widely its own version of the Scriptures, it also continued its efforts in establishing a more effective parochial school system. As early as the First Provincial Council in 1829, the Church had stated the need for religiously oriented instruction for their young. This stance was reiterated in the First and Second Plenary Councils of Baltimore in 1852 and 1866 and finally became official policy in the Third Plenary Council of 1884 when all churches were instructed to establish schools for Catholic youth.[68]

In the midst of this push for parochial education, Catholics continued to seek aid from the state governments, reasoning that currently Catholics were paying tax dollars for an educational system they could not fully endorse or participate in.[69] Such repeated calls for funding once again became the topic of wide debate in the 1870s. Partly as a result, Catholics once again suffered from the waves of anti-Catholic sentiment that pulsated through American Protestantism.

Much of the Catholic-Protestant tension of the 1870s found its roots in two widely publicized pronouncements of the Catholic Church. The first of these was Pope Pius IX's 1864 *Syllabus of Errors*. The *Syllabus* was a list of errors meant to combat a growing religious liberalism within the Catholic Church, but it included a number of strong statements on how Catholic children should be educated with a strong religious orientation.

The second pronouncement was the Vatican decree of 1870 that proclaimed, "The Roman Pontiff cannot err in defining matters of faith and morals" and that all Catholics were subject to his guidance in these issues.[70] American Protestants feared this decree as yet another manifestation of the Pope's desire for total control in all realms of life. As one writer put it, the decree would make "civil legislation on all points of contract, marriage, education, clerical immunities, mortmain, even on many questions of taxation and Common Law subject to the legislation of the Church, which would be simply the arbitrary will of the Pope."[71]

Protestant anti-Catholic feelings were not calmed by rampant rumors in the wake of Garibaldi's 1870 capture of Rome that said the pope was looking to transfer the papal see to the United States.[72] These rumors, coupled with papal pronouncements and continued Catholic intransigence on bible reading in the common schools, once again fanned the flames of anti-Catholic sentiment. Even Thomas Nast of *Harpers Weekly* entered into the Catholic controversy. When William M. (Boss) Tweed maneuvered to win Catholic votes by passing a law in 1869 sympathetic to parochial school funding, Nast joined a host of furious New Yorkers who saw such a move as aiding the Catholic menace in its desire to corrupt the nation's youth (see Figures 40 and 41).[73]

The debates about the use of the Bible in public schools differed, however, from their antebellum predecessors in that the postwar years saw an escalating number of court cases and legislative movements to define the role of the Bible in the common schools. No longer were these debates confined to school boards and city governments. State legislatures increasingly became involved, as did the federal government.

The federal Congress in this period continually declined to take a stand on funding parochial schools and classroom bible reading, but between 1870 and 1888 eleven attempts were made to secure an amendment to the United States Constitution that would specifically forbid government financial aid to any parochial or denominational school.[74] The issue of funding parochial schools was intense enough that in 1875 President Ulysses S. Grant made a number of speeches clearly stating his position that no denominational schools should be funded by the government. Grant held that religious matters should be left "to the family, altar, the church, and the private school supported entirely by private contributions."[75] As Catholics continued to push for funding, their desire for funding fueled Protestant acrimony toward the Catholic Church and its implicit criticism of the country's supposedly godless school system.[76]

Alongside the issue of school funding, state courts and legislatures found themselves more frequently debating the place of the Bible in the classroom.[77] Although a number of states would affirm the nonsectarian nature of bible reading, a pivotal case took place in the early 1870s when the Supreme Court of Ohio ruled to forbid the common practice of reading a portion of the Bible at the opening of each school day. The case, *Minor v. Board of Education of Cincinnati*, not surprisingly had its roots in the relationship between Catholicism and Protestantism.

What developed into the "Cincinnati Bible War" had begun with the idea of combining the city's common schools with the Catholic schools.[78] To make this consolidation more palatable to the Catholics, the school board proposed resolutions against religious teaching of any kind in the schools and the discontinuance of daily bible reading. The consolidation never took place, but the resolutions were voted on and passed in 1869,

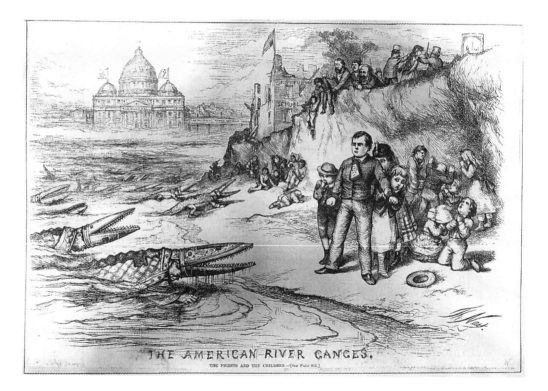

FIGURE 40. Thomas Nast's "The American River Ganges" from *Harpers Weekly*, September 30, 1871. One of Nast's many anti-Catholic cartoons, this one captures the deep sense of danger Protestants felt from Catholic interventions in the nation's public school system. A Vatican-like Tammany Hall stands in the background as does a destroyed public school flying an inverted American flag, a sign of distress. Boss Tweed, who favored subsidizing Catholic schools with public funds, is seen lowering children to their death, while a schoolboy armed only with a Holy Bible "breastplate" takes his stand against the oncoming Catholic menace. (Courtesy of the American Antiquarian Society)

ROMISH POLITICS—ANY THING TO BEAT GRANT.

IRISH ROMAN CATHOLIC INVADER. "The Y. M. C. A. want the Bible in the public school, assuming that this is a Christian country. *We want the Priest, the Brother, and the Sister in our public schools, not assuming, but endeavoring to effect, that this is a Catholic country."—St. Louis Western Watchman, July 13, 1872.*

FIGURE 41. Thomas Nast's "Romish Politics—Any Thing to Beat Grant" from *Harpers Weekly*, August 17, 1872. The battleground is the public school, with the issue being the presence of the Bible. The combatants are an "Irish Roman Catholic Invader" and the Protestant newspaper magnate Horace Greeley. Grant's stance against government funding for parochial schools was an unpopular stance with Catholics as seen in the cartoon's caption. (Courtesy of the Indiana University Library, Bloomington, Indiana)

despite the absence of their original goal. Almost immediately, the protests began, and the issue quickly took on the hue of the old Catholic versus Protestant debate on the place of bible reading in the common school. A temporary restraining order was granted in November 1869 against having these resolutions enforced, and the battle would now take place in the city's and state's courtrooms.

The arguments by those who wanted the resolutions repealed in *Minor v. Board of Education of Cincinnati* were fairly standard when it came to bible reading in the schools.[79] Religion was necessary to morality, and thus to the national welfare. Those arguing for the resolutions did not differ with these views, but stressed a line of argument that would reverberate with growing resonance in the decades to come, namely, that religious instruction should be taught in private settings, such as the church and the home, and that repealing the resolutions created, in effect, a state-established Protestant Christianity.

Two of the three superior court judges ruled in 1870 that the resolutions be repealed. Their ruling seemed more propelled by their own personal views and religious convictions, and in 1872 Ohio's Supreme Court reversed the decision. One result of this reversal was that Ohio school boards were allowed to decide on the level of religious education and bible reading they would allow. A larger consequence of the decision, however, was that a precedent had been set that forbade school boards the prerogative of forcing bible reading and other religious instruction on pupils. Significant winds of change had begun to blow.

Minor v. Board of Education of Cincinnati is not important because it represented the norm in the United States in the period; one could argue just the opposite, as several states had passed laws specifically endorsing or commanding bible reading in the classroom. A climate of religious leniency toward bible reading in American public schools would persist until the 1960s.[80]

The real importance of the Cincinnati case is twofold. First, it was a clear decision against the nation's Protestant conception of itself. Many legislatures utilized a line of argument that the United States was founded on Christian principles, and thus bible reading was permissible in the nation's classrooms.[81] The Cincinnati case argued for religious freedom over a Protestant-centered conception of religion in the United States. Second, the case stood as an early harbinger for a starker view of the separation of church and state that would gain growing support throughout the twentieth century. This conception held that bible reading was obviously sectarian and violated both the rights of individuals and the Constitutional call for a separation of church and state.

This clear call for a separation of church and state would find striking affirmation in the Wisconsin Supreme Court ruling of 1890. Here, in *Weiss v. The District School Board of Edgerton*, the court ruled that since reading of the Bible is an act of worship, taxpayers could not be compelled to contribute to the support of common schools because the state's constitution clearly states that "No man shall be compelled to support any place of worship."[82] Instead the church, not the state, should work to offer the "priceless truths of the Bible . . . in the church, the Sabbath and parochial schools," religious meetings, and in the home.[83] The court argued that mingling "church and state corrupts religion and makes the state despotic."[84] Thus, *Minor v. Board of Education of Cincinnati* and *Weiss v. The District School Board of Edgerton* stood as a precedents for displacing the Bible in the American classroom.

These two cases clearly showed that arguments about the Bible's place in American education had moved from the realm of denominational squabbling before school boards to higher levels of the country's court system. *Minor v. Board of Education of Cincinnati* marked a legal moment when thenceforth laws and their interpretation would play a larger and larger role in determining the place of the Bible in America's public institutions, and consequently, the country's cultural life.[85]

A stronger conception of the separation of church and state, coupled with a receding notion of the United States as a Protestant country, would lay the foundation for the ultimate recision of bible reading in the American classroom and other public institutions. Such a recision would have profound consequences reaching beyond debates over whether such a move signaled a slide toward a godless culture.

A widespread familiarity with the King James text, partly propagated by the nation's schools, gave the United States a shared text from which to speak and anchor a common memory. Lincoln could call the nation away from being "a house divided," and Frederick Douglass could characterize his life as weeping "near the rivers of Babylon" because such terminology had deep resonances with vast segments of the American population.[86] As the Bible receded from the nation's schools and other public institutions, so did its power as a binding force for American linguistic practice, narrative convention, and national self-perception. A text that had provided the nation with a source of shared cultural memory and language for nearly two centuries would find itself increasingly "ghetto-ized" among specific more Protestant segments of the nation's population.

Grammars replaced the Bible as literacy textbooks in the opening decades of the nineteenth century, and the 1840s inaugurated an era in which the institutional roles of the Bible in the public sphere became hotly contested topics. Meanwhile, a growing number of evangelical Christians turned not to institutional, but narrative, means in an attempt to draw readers to the Sacred Scriptures. Early in the nineteenth century, Protestants deplored fiction as an insidious form of writing that drove women to ruin and parents to an early grave. But by the 1850s, writers such as Harriet Beecher Stowe, Susan Warner, Maria Cummins, and Joseph Holt

Ingraham had successfully adapted the biblical message into the incredibly popular form of the novel.[87] The biblical message once again found itself in a new wineskin. But for those concerned with the centrality of the Bible in American culture, there were once again unforeseen consequences of storing wine in this kind of skin.

Chapter Five

POPULARITY

1 Nineteenth-century Americans did not simply purchase and preserve the new bibles of their era—they altered, amended, and expanded their texts. For example, one bride meticulously sewed portions of her bridal dress into her bible to commemorate her wedding day. Other bible owners stored important personal correspondence in their copies of the Scriptures. Anticipating the portrait gallery inserts that would proliferate in bibles after the Civil War, Sewall S. Cutting and his family joined themselves to the biblical text by pasting family photographs along with extended written accounts of their relations into their copy of Harper's *Illuminated Bible*. In this manner, the Cuttings joined their own pictorial narrative to the heavily illustrated biblical account already included in the Harper Bible.[1]

Americans also placed themselves textually inside the Bible with inscriptions, as when James Blakely wrote in his 1817 bible: "When I am absent from this place / and numbered with the dead / remember that you saw my face."[2] James Wilson Griffith echoed this sentiment with more flair when he recorded in his bible:

> This book my name shall
> ever have when I am
> dead and in my grave
> and hungry worms my
> body eat then you may
> read my name
> complete 1831.[3]

Women, as well as men, wished to memorialize themselves by inscribing their names in a timeless book. Abigail Torr wrote:

> Abigail Torr is my name
> New England is my nation
> Durham is my dwelling place
> and Christ is my salvation

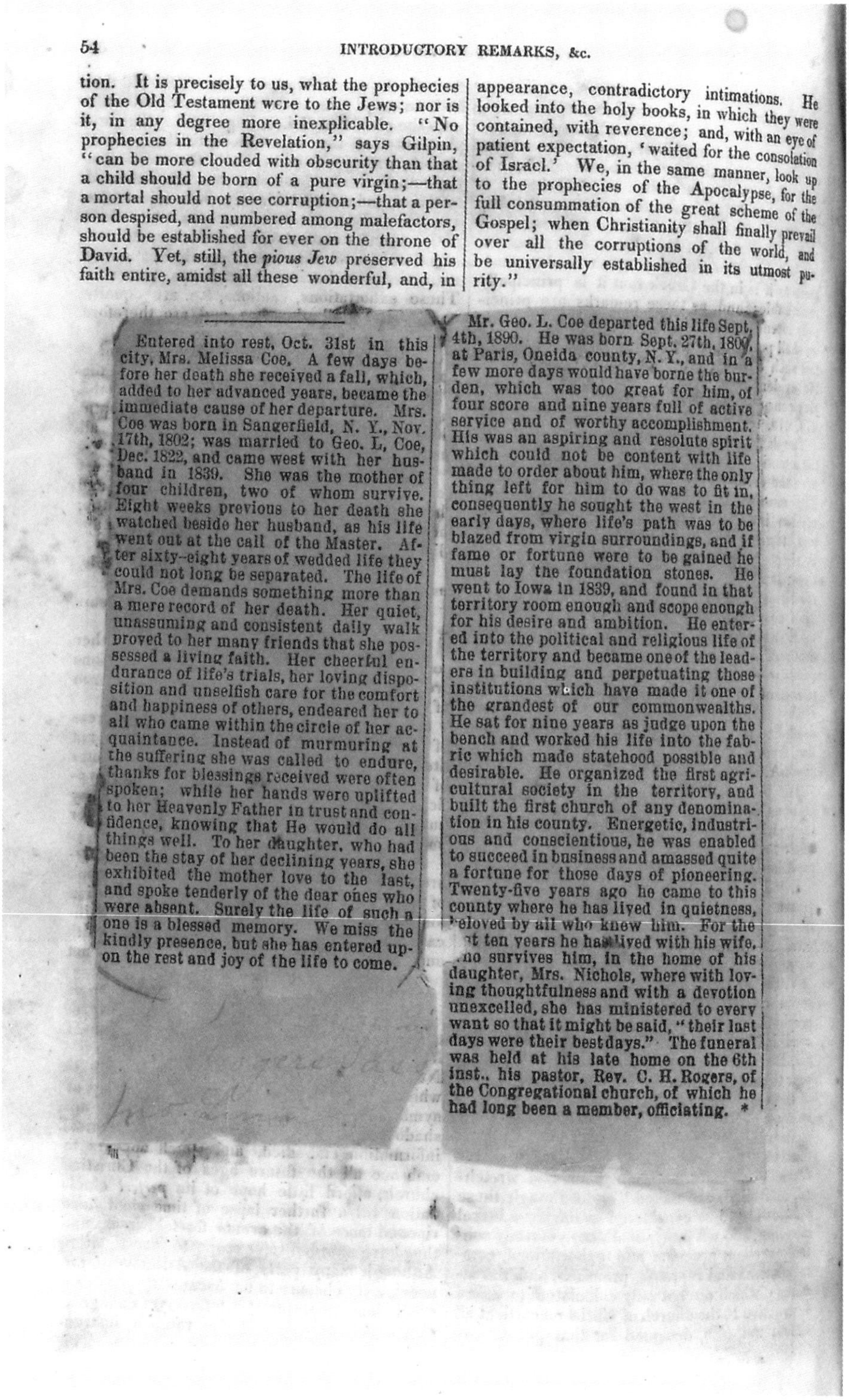

tion. It is precisely to us, what the prophecies of the Old Testament were to the Jews; nor is it, in any degree more inexplicable. "No prophecies in the Revelation," says Gilpin, "can be more clouded with obscurity than that a child should be born of a pure virgin;—that a mortal should not see corruption;—that a person despised, and numbered among malefactors, should be established for ever on the throne of David. Yet, still, the *pious Jew* preserved his faith entire, amidst all these wonderful, and, in appearance, contradictory intimations. He looked into the holy books, in which they were contained, with reverence; and, with an eye of patient expectation, 'waited for the consolation of Israel.' We, in the same manner, look up to the prophecies of the Apocalypse, for the full consummation of the great scheme of the Gospel; when Christianity shall finally prevail over all the corruptions of the world, and be universally established in its utmost purity."

Entered into rest, Oct. 31st in this city, Mrs. Melissa Coe. A few days before her death she received a fall, which, added to her advanced years, became the immediate cause of her departure. Mrs. Coe was born in Sangerfield, N. Y., Nov. 17th, 1802; was married to Geo. L. Coe, Dec. 1822, and came west with her husband in 1839. She was the mother of four children, two of whom survive. Eight weeks previous to her death she watched beside her husband, as his life went out at the call of the Master. After sixty-eight years of wedded life they could not long be separated. The life of Mrs. Coe demands something more than a mere record of her death. Her quiet, unassuming and consistent daily walk proved to her many friends that she possessed a living faith. Her cheerful endurance of life's trials, her loving disposition and unselfish care for the comfort and happiness of others, endeared her to all who came within the circle of her acquaintance. Instead of murmuring at the suffering she was called to endure, thanks for blessings received were often spoken; while her hands were uplifted to her Heavenly Father in trust and confidence, knowing that He would do all things well. To her daughter, who had been the stay of her declining years, she exhibited the mother love to the last, and spoke tenderly of the dear ones who were absent. Surely the life of such a one is a blessed memory. We miss the kindly presence, but she has entered upon the rest and joy of the life to come.

Mr. Geo. L. Coe departed this life Sept. 4th, 1890. He was born Sept. 27th, 1800, at Paris, Oneida county, N. Y., and in a few more days would have borne the burden, which was too great for him, of four score and nine years full of active service and of worthy accomplishment. His was an aspiring and resolute spirit which could not be content with life made to order about him, where the only thing left for him to do was to fit in, consequently he sought the west in the early days, where life's path was to be blazed from virgin surroundings, and if fame or fortune were to be gained he must lay the foundation stones. He went to Iowa in 1839, and found in that territory room enough and scope enough for his desire and ambition. He entered into the political and religious life of the territory and became one of the leaders in building and perpetuating those institutions which have made it one of the grandest of our commonwealths. He sat for nine years as judge upon the bench and worked his life into the fabric which made statehood possible and desirable. He organized the first agricultural society in the territory, and built the first church of any denomination in his county. Energetic, industrious and conscientious, he was enabled to succeed in business and amassed quite a fortune for those days of pioneering. Twenty-five years ago he came to this county where he has lived in quietness, beloved by all who knew him. For the last ten years he has lived with his wife, no survives him, in the home of his daughter, Mrs. Nichols, where with loving thoughtfulness and with a devotion unexcelled, she has ministered to every want so that it might be said, "their last days were their best days." The funeral was held at his late home on the 6th inst., his pastor, Rev. C. H. Rogers, of the Congregational church, of which he had long been a member, officiating. *

FIGURE 42. *(Both pages)* Family record page with pasted-in newspaper clipping from 1834 Brattleboro bible edition. (Library of the author)

NAMES.	BIRTHS.			DEATHS.		
	Month.	Day.	Year.	Month.	Day.	Year.
Mr Edward Trask Born May 10						
Miss Roxey Trask Born March 18						
and was Married February 10						
These their Children						
Melissa Trask Born November 17 1800 Sayer						
Israel Trask						N Y
Israel H Trask Born						
Proctor P Trask Born						

> When I am dead and buried
> and all my bones are rotten
> When this you see remember me
> that I may not be forgotten.[4]

As these verses show, immortality was on the minds of many nine-teenth-century bible inscribers. In fact, the immortal nature of the book was probably the reason behind many an inscription. Whatever families might part with by accident or necessity, they usually held on to the family's bible tenaciously.[5]

In addition to poetic musings, one of the most popular means of verbally inserting oneself into the immortal biblical narrative was through the "family record" pages. To send a strong message about the bible's longevity, some publishers bound their bible editions with nearly one hundred pages of family record leaves.[6]

Perhaps literally interpreting John's exhortation that Christians should lead lives worthy of being recorded in God's Book of Life, American Protestants meticulously used family pages to record not only names and dates, but places of birth, occupations, causes of death, and important personal characteristics—often supplemented with newspaper clippings or handwritten narrative accounts (see Figure 42).[7] Through such insertions, people quite literally fused their personal narratives to the biblical narrative. Consequently, the Bible served American Protestants not only as the Book of Life, but also as the book of their lives.

In addition to materially interleaving themselves into their bibles, Americans also sought to place themselves figuratively in their bibles. The growing emphasis on the Holy Land as a tangible biblical apologetic, German biblical criticism's stress on historical context, and a marked interest in the church of the New Testament all combined to foster a view among many American Protestants that any understanding of the Bible was directly dependent upon one's ability to imagine oneself as a character in the "grand drama" of which God was both "author" and "chief personage."[8]

For example, Alexander Campbell stressed throughout his ministry that to understand the Bible one must imagine oneself "in Judea, in Rome, or in Corinth, and not in these places in the present day; but . . . nearly two thousand years before we lived at all." Bible readers "must mingle with the Jews in their temples and synagogues . . . must visit the temples and altars of the Pagan Gentiles . . . must converse with Epicurean and Stoic philosophers—with Pharisees and Sadducees—with priests and people, that died centuries before" they were born.[9] The palpable nature of the Holy Land, coupled with a rising concern with the historical settings of biblical stories, propagated a view that to understand the biblical drama, one needed to project oneself onto the historical stage of that drama.

In pursuing their place in God's drama, American Protestants began to turn to fictional adaptations of biblical stories. Whereas most Protestants decried fictional writing as an insidious and corrupting influence in the early 1800s, by the 1850s a wide variety of fiction was winning acceptance among Protestants as a viable means for people to become imaginative participants in the Bible's narrative.[10]

As a result, quasi-fictional narratives based on the Bible appeared with greater frequency as the nineteenth century progressed. These new religious narratives found one of their most popular forms in the evolving genre of the life of Christ.[11] From Paul Wright's *The New and Complete Life of Our Blessed Lord and Saviour Jesus Christ*, which went through fourteen printings from 1785 to 1818, to Lew Wallace's unprecedented blockbuster, *Ben-Hur: A Tale of the Christ* (1880), Americans increasingly turned to these biographies of Jesus as a way to connect with the biblical narrative without having to confront the complex text of the Bible.

The figure of Jesus, which readers all too often found obscure in the New Testament, appeared more accessible through the fictional representations of the Christ found in religious fiction. After all, the historical Jesus had lived nearly two thousand years earlier, spoken a foreign language, and been part of an exotic, Middle Eastern culture. Americans who wished to find their place in the biblical drama found in fiction a more comprehensible expression of the God who had shown Himself most tangibly in the person of Christ.

The more accessible narrative content and strategies of religious fiction worried many Protestants; they feared that such fiction would make the Bible seem a "wearisome book."[12] While religious fiction might point readers to the Bible's story, it also gave them an excuse not to read it. Although its popularity would steadily grow throughout the nineteenth century, as the evolution of the most popular versions of the life-of-Christ literary genre shows, fiction proved a capricious means of drawing American readers to the Sacred Scriptures.

2   The two most pronounced characteristics of early American retellings of Jesus' life involved describing Jesus in his historical setting and portraying him as the ultimate model of moral behavior.

The nineteenth-century life-of-Christ literary genre involved creating a sense of geographic and temporal travel for the reader. Writers, publishers, and editors of this genre operated on the assumption that readers would be able to understand the relevance of the figure of Christ for their own lives only if they could imaginatively accompany him in his original, historical settings. The success of such mental transmigration was judged by the moral consequences elicited by exposure to the figure of Jesus.

147

MARK, V. 28 &c.

A Woman miraculously HEALED *of a* BLOODY ISSUE.

FIGURE 43. *(Both pages)* Durell's use of a Thomas 1791 bible folio plate, "A Woman miraculously Healed of a Bloody Issue," in his edition of Paul Wright's *The New and Complete Life of Our Blessed Lord and Saviour Jesus Christ* (1803). Note that the usual "Engraved for Thomas's Edition of the Bible" has been effaced from this illustration. (Courtesy of the Library Company of Philadelphia)

was *not come to call the righteous, but sinners to repentance ;* and to blame him for conversing with publicans and sinners was as great a piece of absurdity as to blame a physician for visiting the sick. This answer from the great Friend and Redeemer of lost sinners, was far from satisfying the haughty self-conceited Scribes and Pharisees: and as they made great ostentation of their fasting and abstinence, they took this opportunity to give themselves consequence on that account ; and joining with John's disciples, presumed to blame our great Redeemer because his disciples were not so frequent in this practice as themselves. To this our Lord replied, that the present was not a time for fasting, for his disciples need not fast and mourn in the presence of their Master, any more than the friends of the bridegroom need

fast and afflict themselves while they enjoyed his company. *But,* said he, *the day will come, when the bridegroom will be taken away from them, and then they shall fast.* Intimating by this, that the calamities, troubles, and afflictions which they would suffer after the death of their Master, would oblige them to fast and mourn ; but the corrupt nature of man, which was the cause of his coming into the world, required different treatment ; the rent would not be patched up with mortification, fasting, or any external performances ; such treatment as this would be like sewing a piece of new cloth on an old rotten garment, which would only make the rent worse, or putting new wine into old leather bottles, which would burst as soon as the liquor fermented.

CHAPTER XIII.

CHRIST *healeth a Woman of an inveterate Issue of Blood ; Raises Jarius's daughter from the dead : Gives sight to two blind Men : Delivers a possessed Person from the evil Spirit : And, returning to Galilee, chooses his twelve Apostles out of his Disciples : Then, repairing to Capernaum, cures the Centurion's Servant.*

WHILE the blessed JESUS was disputing with the Scribes and Pharisees in the house of Matthew, whom he had lately called into the number of his disciples, an afflicted father, in all the agonies of distress, hastily pressed into his presence. This was Jarius, the ruler of the Jewish synagogue in Capernaum, and the cause of his present affliction was the dangerous illness of his daughter, who lay at the point of death.

Having earnestly implored the assistance of our great Redeemer in this distressing case, the Lord of life graciously condescended to comply with his request, and accordingly accompanied the distressed father to his house ; and great multitudes of people, who were desirous of beholding the miracles of Christ, crowded around and pressed to behold what the divine Instructor would do on this great occasion.

But as they passed through the streets of the city, the attention of the surrounding

multitudes were turned to a woman, who came behind the Son of God, and touched the hem of his garment. This woman had been afflicted twelve years with a terrible disorder, which had baffled the force of medicine. She had spent her whole substance on physicians, but could obtain no relief ; but hearing of the miracles performed by the blessed JESUS, she was so fully convinced of his divine power, that she concluded if she could but touch his clothes she should be made whole. Nor was she deceived, for she no sooner touched the border of the garment of our great Redeemer than her issue of blood dried up ; and she felt such a flow of vital spirits, and uncommon gladness warm her heart, that she was fully convinced that she had received a cure.

The blessed JESUS, who knew the hearts of all men, was not ignorant of the minutest circumstance attending this affair ; he knew the woman's thoughts, and was

It was commonly thought that the surest way to know whether you were one of the Lord's characters in His "grand drama" was the degree to which your contact with Jesus had moved you to lead a more Christ-like life, modeling your biography, so to speak, on the New Testament narrative.

The emphasis on influencing readers by exposing them to Christ's historical setting found its first widely popular treatment in Paul Wright's *The New and Complete Life of Our Blessed Lord and Saviour Jesus Christ*. An Anglican vicar in England, Wright first published his "complete, authentic, ample, accurate, instructive, universal, and full account" of the life of Jesus in London in 1785.[13] The volume quickly crossed the Atlantic, and by 1803 it was available to Americans readers in four American and three British editions.

Wright presented his readers with what he claimed were the "real facts" of Jesus' life, culled from both the Gospel accounts and extra-biblical writers.[14] Unabashedly using the writings of "prophane *authors* of undoubted *authority*, who were contemporaries with the *Evangelists* and *Apostles*," Wright sought to give his readers "a variety of useful particulars relating to our Blessed Saviour, not included in the Scripture History" in order to illustrate more fully the cultural milieu in which Jesus lived.[15]

Wright wanted his portrayal of the life of Christ to do more than simply bolster Christians' confidence in the reliability and accuracy of the Gospel accounts by filling out the historical setting in which Jesus had lived; he also wanted it to cause his readers to see Christ as the subtitle proclaimed: "That Great Example, as well as Saviour of Mankind."[16] He offered Jesus as humanity's chief role model by providing a running commentary to Jesus' life that had the goal of representing "*real religion* in its *native colours*, as taught by Christ himself." Wright's main goal was to "enable even the most ignorant *Christian* to give account of the *faith* that is in him."[17]

Following Wright's lead in blurring the boundary between sacred and secular texts, American publishers were quick to capitalize on the volume's professed close association with the Bible. William Durell of New York City employed several techniques to bolster the association between Wright's book and the Bible. Still extant copies of Durell's editions of *The New and Complete Life* show that they were set in a folio format with ornamented leather bindings that invoked associations with folio bibles of the day.[18] Durell did not stop with binding *The New and Complete Life* like a bible, he illustrated it like a bible as well. Durell purchased the copperplate engravings of Isaiah Thomas's 1791 folio edition of the Bible, effaced Thomas's name from the plates, and then used them to illustrate his 1803 edition of Wright's *The New and Complete Life* (see Figure 43).[19] Such associative formatting strategies nicely complemented Wright's desire to have his book serve as an apologetic to the authenticity of Christ's life.

In order that his portrayal of the life of Christ might guide readers into leading Christ-like lives, Wright used a narrative strategy that allowed his readers to follow Jesus' life from its beginning to its end. By adopting a chronologically linear form of a *"Harmony* of the *Gospels,"* Wright presented the life of Jesus as one smooth, continuous whole.

In this way, Wright gave his readers an accessible narrative that saved them the usual work of piecing together the entire story of Jesus' life from the four Gospel accounts. Wright wished to give his readers all the available sources on Christ's life that were "of undoubted *authority"* in order to avoid and "rectify *errors* which too many are apt to run into" by attempting to fill in the narrative gaps of their Savior's life by using their own, often misguided, imaginations.[20]

Inseparably woven into the richly detailed texture of his chronological presentation was Wright's own sustained theological commentary on Christ's life. Paradoxically, Wright's running commentary, coupled with his attention to narrative detail, simultaneously historicized and dehistoricized Jesus' life. The immense amount of particulars Wright included on every phase of Christ's life gave the reader a vivid historical sense of Jesus' life.

Wright's commentary then demystified these particulars by pointing out the relevance of Christ's actions and teachings for his readers. For example, Wright drove home the lesson that from "the pride, envy, obstinate perverseness, and implacable resentment of the Pharisees," we should not be surprised to "find the same malicious insinuations in different shapes levelled against ourselves, if we are enable to embrace the truths of the gospel."[21]

Through this style of historicized biographical commentary, Wright connected the problems that faced the earliest Christians with his eighteenth- and nineteenth-century readers. By collapsing Christ's narrative with that of his readers, Wright hoped to motivate in his readers a *"firm faith* in the *merits* of our Blessed Redeemer, and to recommend the *practice of every Christian virtue."*[22]

3 Joseph Smith Jr.'s *The Book of Mormon* was perhaps the most audacious rendering of Christ's life to appear in the nineteenth century. It followed in the tradition of Wright's book—blurring the sacred and common through rhetorical, binding, and illustrative practices.

Scholars most often point to an anonymously written 1837 novel entitled *Zerah: The Believing Jew* as the first work of fiction to include a representation of Jesus.[23] But Smith's 1830 representation of Jesus appeared earlier and was much more influential.[24] Smith's rendition of the Christ, like Wright's, historically contextualized Jesus as a moral example, but with an interesting twist. Smith's Jesus appears as a visitor to America in the first century, thus offering American readers a role model who actually visited their native land.

Smith was twenty-five years old when he finally convinced the skeptical Palmyra printer E. B. Grandin to publish *The Book of Mormon*.[25] His life had been deeply marked by hardship and poverty. Having moved seven times in fourteen years, Joseph, his parents, and eight siblings finally settled on a small farm in Palmyra, New York, around 1816.[26] By 1825, the Smith family numbered eleven, and they had been reduced to a life of poor tenant farmers through the machinations of a dishonest land agent. Smith's chronic poverty and nomadic existence led him to treasure hunting and religious revivalism in hopes of bettering his life.[27] He had little luck with either. He could neither locate hidden treasures with seer stones or divining rods, nor settle on joining a specific religious denomination.

In the midst of this continuing poverty and confusion, two angels reportedly visited a fourteen-year-old Smith in a prayer time, telling him that all religious denominations "were corrupt," and that God would show him the form of true religion if he would wait.[28] Seven years later, the Lord allowed Smith to obtain gold plates—buried in the earth like other treasures he had sought—which would reveal to him a long-lost chapter in Christianity's history.

From these plates Smith translated *The Book of Mormon*, a 600-page book that defies easy description. It is a tale of two families and their descendants; one family flees Jerusalem in 600 B.C. via boat and eventually settles in America, while the other family also crosses to America, but this time after the failure of the Tower of Babel. Various heirs of these families develop into warring factions and eventually destroy each other, leaving only scattered traces of their existence in the form of American Indians. Both families kept records prior to their destruction, and it is these records that Smith uncovers in the form of gold plates.

Smith carefully oversaw the book's production through almost daily visits to Grandin's shop, and there is little doubt that the book's binding style intentionally echoed the bible editions of the day.[29] *The Book of Mormon* emerged just as the American Bible Society's first General Supply was at its height, and the most common bibles supplied by the Society were the 1829 Minion and the 1830 Non-Pareil editions. The Society distributed 300,000 copies of the latter edition alone.[30] Smith's *The Book of Mormon* was bound in such a way that it looked strikingly similar to these Bible Society editions. All three editions were bound in brown leather with a twin gold bars impressed on the spine at regular intervals. The volumes also bore a black label imprinted with gold letters on the spine bear-ing the volume's name. It would be hard for even the most casual observer to miss how much Smith's book looked like a bible.

One of the most striking characteristics of Smith's book is its language. Smith wrote imitating King James English, playing on the long-standing association of Elizabethan English with the sacred propagated by the predominance of the King James Bible. No longer the common idiom in nineteenth-century America, the unique Elizabethan English conjured up visions of the sacred for American readers. Many of the later arguments against revising the King James Bible revealed how many Americans saw Elizabethan English as the only appropriate language in which to enfold the holy words of Scripture.[31]

Smith judiciously wrote his book in an idiom that constantly invoked the holy cadences of the King James Bible. While Alexander Campbell was taking the *eth* endings off words, Smith was putting them on. Thus, when Warren Foote came across *The Book of Mormon* in 1833 he was overwhelmed by the linguistic similarities between Smith's book and the Bible. So striking were the similarities between Smith's book and the Bible that Warren Foote, who proudly proclaimed that he had "read the Bible three times through by course, and could bring almost any passage of scripture to my mind," converted to Mormonism.[32]

It is important to note, however, that although *The Book of Mormon* invoked the Bible and many read it "side by side" with their King James Version, Smith was offering more than simply a new sacred, bible-like text.[33] He was offering a book more "authentic" in its sources, and thus more accurate in its message than the Bible.[34] Unlike the Bible, *The Book of Mormon* was not a message that had been passed down from one century to the next through mutilated and partial manuscripts. B. Pixley, a Baptist preacher and early critic of Mormonism, was angered by Smith's statements of biblical corruption and the need for a better text. He wrote in 1832: "The Gospels too, we are given by them [Mormons] to understand, are so mutilated and altered as to convey little of the instruction which they should convey. . . . Our present Bible is to be altered and restored to its primitive purity, by Smith, the present prophet of the Lord, and some books to be added of great importance, which have been lost."[35]

The Book of Mormon stood as an answer to a mutilated Gospel record. It was a record that Smith had translated directly from the original plates used by writers and editors that predated all the available biblical manuscripts—and even many of the Bible's actual writers—by hundreds of years. While revision debates would rage throughout the nineteenth century centering on the purity of textual source materials and translations, Smith offered American Protestants no mere revision, but an uncorrupted biblical text. Other claims to purity paled in comparison.

Much of the genius of Smith's work was how it placed the character of Jesus not in the traditional, historical setting of Judea, but in America. As innovative as this might sound, Smith's connection between ancient Israel and America was not new.

Elias Boudinot was one among many early nineteenth-century Americans who built upon James Adair's 1775 monumental history of the American Indians to argue the connection between Hebrews and Native Americans.[36] Boudinot dedicated his last book-length writing project, *A Star in the West*, to this connection, convinced that the surest way to deepen a "sense of the certainty of the prophetic declarations of the Holy Scriptures" and draw "attention to the truth of divine revelation" was a convincing treatise on America's links to the Holy Land.[37] No longer were the American shores simply a place where a new nation had been founded; it was the stage upon which God's ongoing redemptive drama was being enacted. Native Americans may have been the ragged remnant of the once-proud inhabitants of the Holy Land, but their mere presence pointed to the cosmically significant role of the United States in the history of the world.

Smith took the association of America with the Holy Land to unprecedented heights in his *Book of Mormon*, repeatedly calling the American continent "a land which is choice above all other lands." To accommodate the need to explain biblical passages and the reality of the Holy Land in the Middle East, Smith reasoned that the flood had carried Noah with his family away from the lands surrounding Eden.[38] As a result, the opening story in *The Book of Mormon* concerning Nephi's escape to the Americas by boat reversed Noah's own journey.

Whereas American Puritans had rhetorically identified America with the Holy Land, and Adair and Boudinot had linked the Holy Land to America through the Indians, Smith would claim that the United States was the actual geographic location of the Garden of Eden. Thus, America became not *like* the Holy Land, or some sort of spiritual or typological successor to the Holy Land, but the site of God's original work in the world. In Smith's view, rather than being a new country with little history, America was the place where human history began.

Smith could not pinpoint the exact location of the Garden of Eden, but he determined it to be somewhere in northwestern Missouri, approximately marked by a place he named "Adam-ondi-Ahman." As early as 1832, Smith began talking about "Adam-ondi-Ahman," but it was not until the late 1830s that Smith identified it as a geographic site near Eden.[39]

The 1830s had been a turbulent decade for Smith and his followers. Located primarily in Kirtland, Ohio, and Jackson and Clay Counties, Missouri, the Mormon Church in the 1830s would enjoy a steady growth. This growth brought with it an increasing distaste for Mormonism among the new religious tradition's neighbors. By 1838, persecution by neighbors coupled with internal dissent among his followers forced Smith to flee Kirtland and head to Missouri.[40] One great benefit that Missouri enjoyed over Ohio was the fact that the Missouri legislature had agreed to set aside two counties, Caldwell and Daviess, for exclusive Mormon settlement in an attempt to end the enmity between Missouri Mormons and non-Mormons.[41]

Soon after his arrival in Missouri, Smith declared that the region was "Adam-ondi-Ahman," the very place where Adam had dwelt after his expulsion from Eden, and the place that Christ would gather and reappear to his followers in the last days.[42] It must have been a source of tremendous encouragement and comfort for Smith's followers that this land, which finally promised to be a safe haven, was also both the cradle of Western Civilization and the place where human history would culminate with Christ's return.[43] In reality, the comfort would be short-lived. Through threat and practice of violence, Missouri non-Mormons soon forced the vast majority of their Mormon neighbors to move to Illinois.

The special nature of North America did not begin with Smith's revelations concerning Eden in the late 1830s. They had, in fact, begun years earlier in *The Book of Mormon*. Here, Smith recounted the history of the remnant of the lost ten tribes of Israel after they left Palestine and traveled to North America. Whereas Boudinot and others settled for associating North America with the Old Testament by linking it with a remnant of God's Chosen People, Smith associated North America with the New Testament. He claimed that after arriving in the New World, the displaced Israelites prospered for a time and built great civilizations. More important, Smith said the Israelites had been visited by Jesus Christ in the New World after his death and resurrection in the Middle East. Jesus' visit led them into a long period of peace and prosperity; it also established the Christian Church in North America.[44]

By recording Christ's visit to North America, Smith offered his own unique—and stunningly American—life of Christ. Smith taught that Christ was not some distant, exotic figure stranded in a remote Middle Eastern location. He described Christ as a messiah who had physically visited the Americas.

Smith proposed that one did not need to know arcane historical lore or the geography of Palestine to understand Jesus and his teaching; one could gain such understanding by exploring American history and the American landscape. For instance, Smith found in the numerous earthen mounds located throughout the Northeast ample testimony that God had been at work in America centuries before any Europeans set foot in North America. Smith declared that the hill Cumorah near his Palmyra home—

where he had found the golden plates—was the spot where the ultimate destruction of the ancient American civilizations had taken place in a titanic battle.[45]

In describing Jesus' supposed visit to the Americas, Smith created a closer link between the Christian Messiah and Americans who had little or no knowledge of the Holy Land. At the same time, Jesus' visit imbued the land that would eventually become the United States with an importance and history that had previously been reserved only for the tiny region of Judea.

Smith's representation of Jesus is marked by certain recurrent characteristics. The first of these is that the Jesus who appeared in America was the resurrected divine Christ. The inhabitants of America never saw the earthly, human Jesus. Smith underlined Christ's divine nature in a number of ways, including cataclysmic natural disasters that signaled his coming and Jesus' disembodied voice preaching from heaven so that it was "heard among all the inhabitants of the earth upon all the face of this land."[46] Smith represented Jesus as a powerful, supernatural being who could command both heaven and earth.

Smith built upon the supernatural qualities of Jesus by portraying him as a messiah bent on two activities during his visit to the Nephites: religious instruction and compassionate action. Through this double thrust, Smith showed Christ as the ultimate example of moral behavior. Jesus arrives in the midst of the Nephites, one branch of the lost Israelites, by descending out of heaven clothed in a white robe.[47]

According to Smith's narrative, after letting them touch the wounds in his hands and side to satisfy them as to his divine, resurrected nature, Jesus enters into a long discussion on right doctrine and proper morality. In his opening statements, Jesus cuts through doctrinal ambiguity with crystal-clear teaching concerning the Trinity and the proper mode of baptism.[48] Thus, doctrines that had been the source of rancorous debate and hundreds of pages of written theological discussion in antebellum America were decisively settled in Jesus' opening remarks to the inhabitants of America.[49] Smith underscores the force of these religious teachings by repeatedly emphasizing Jesus' divine authority to settle doctrinal problems. He is portrayed as coming from God and being invested with authority from God.[50] Not only does Smith's Jesus have religious authority, he later passes on this authority to the Nephites so that they will be able to establish a Christian Church in America complete with old and new versions of the Scriptures, the Holy Spirit, and the Protestant sacraments of baptism and the Last Supper.[51]

While a great deal of scholarly attention has been paid to the manner in which Jesus so clearly settled issues of doctrinal dispute in his teachings to the Nephites, almost no attention has been paid to how this teaching was done.[52] The Jesus of *The Book of Mormon* was not only the ultimate arbiter of antebellum Protestant controversies, but a savior principally characterized by an intensely compassionate demeanor. Though Smith's Jesus did not skirt the issue of judgment (most often directed against those who oppress the weak), his interactions with the Nephites are full of descriptions of his merciful feelings toward them.

For example, Jesus is so impressed by the faith of the Nephites that his "joy is full. And when he had said these words, he wept, and the multitude bear record of it, and he took their little children, one by one, and blessed them, and prayed unto the Father for them. And when he had done this, he wept again."[53] In the entire New Testament, Jesus only weeps twice. Here, in the space of two sentences, he is so moved by the spiritual need of the Nephites that he quickly matches that number before going on to show a wide range of sympathetic emotions. Smith portrays Jesus as a savior whose "bowels is filled with compassion" and "mercy."[54] Nowhere are these descriptions of Jesus found in contemporary English translations of the traditional Gospel accounts. The Jesus protrayed by Smith has a sensitivity of temperament that makes him aware of the need around him and moves him to attempt to meet that need.

John Peters reinforces this connection between a sensitive anatomy and moral action by arguing that in early Mormon theological writings, as in the New Testament, "bowels" connoted the source of one's ethical affections.[55] Feeling something in one's bowels was more than experiencing intense emotion; it was the beginning of moral action because the intensity of emotion compelled ethical behavior. Jesus' "bowels" are filled with compassion and mercy, leading him not only to weep, but also to heal the sick, teach the ignorant, give ecclesiastical authority to the Nephites, and stay with his listeners well beyond the time he told them he needed to depart.

In portraying Jesus as such a compassionate Savior, Smith makes Jesus a moral example by endowing him with an outstandingly developed moral sense. Jesus' attentiveness to the needs of others, his commitment to benevolence and his perpetual inclination toward virtuous action all testify to the fact that Smith's Jesus exhibited a moral sense of striking proportions. Smith underlined the presence of such a well-developed moral sense both by portraying him as an untiring agent of care and compassion and by having him adapt and incorporate the New Testament's best-known summary of moral teaching, the Matthean Sermon on the Mount, into his teaching to the Nephites.[56]

Smith described Jesus as being not only remarkable for his own large moral sense, but also committed to developing the moral sense in all with whom he came into contact. Jesus's time with the Nephites is brief, and so is his teaching to them, but the moral element of his character makes it a priority for him to give the Nephites his longest New Testament discourse on moral and virtuous behavior.

In Smith's depiction of Jesus as the ultimate moral example, it should not be forgotten that he placed his figure of Jesus not in the Holy Land, but in America. Such a change of venue laid the foundation for Smith's eventual proclamation that America, not Judea, had long been God's true Holy Land.

Smith emphasized the divinely favored nature of America not only by having Jesus visit the lost ten tribes of Israel in the New World, but by having him favorably describe these lost Israelites when he met them. In Smith's narrative, Jesus describes the American Nephites as having a far greater faith than the Jews, telling them that "there are none of them [the Jews] that have seen so great things as ye have seen; neither have they heard so great things as ye have heard."[57]

In giving the ancient inhabitants of North America greater faith than the Jews, Smith portrayed North America as a holier land than ancient Judea because it was filled with holier people. Between his depiction of Jesus as the ultimate moral example and ancient North America as a land capable of greater faith, and thus greater holiness, than ancient Judea, Smith put forward in *The Book of Mormon* a life of Christ that transposed America with the Holy Land and promised a restoration of that holiness if the reader would but heed the fact that Jesus had visited America and would visit it again at the end of time.

Although sales of Smith's book began slow, by 1880 thousands of copies had been distributed in the United States via thirty-seven British and American editions.[58] Much of the book's popularity was due to the fact that it functioned as an integral part of a new religious tradition that offered Americans the chance to once again restore and enjoy Eden-like bliss in the United States.[59] By offering Americans a version of Jesus' life in which the Savior had so clearly articulated the special nature of America and its inhabitants, Smith gave his readers a chance to be a part of the biblical drama in a way that no other Protestant denomination could claim.

Smith taught that Americans no longer needed to look to the Middle East as the primary stage of God's redemptive drama; instead that stage was all around them with its divine locus somewhere near "Adam-ondi-Ahman." In the 1830s, Americans need only listen to the living Prophet of Mormonism and his *Book of Mormon* to find their place on that stage, remembering that the drama was more linked to their own country than it was to some faraway land in the Middle East.

4 Whether the United States was the cradle of Western Civilization or not, Joseph Smith Jr.'s general concern that the figure of Jesus Christ serve as a "light" that would guide Americans to salvation was shared by a number of religiously oriented authors who followed him.[60] By the 1850s, the novels of several of these authors enjoyed a popularity that was unprecedented in American publishing. Susan Warner's *The Wide, Wide World* (1850), Harriet Beecher Stowe's *Uncle Tom's Cabin* (1852), and Maria Cummins's *The Lamplighter* (1850) all sold well over 100,000 copies in the decade before the Civil War.[61] Reluctant to denominate their work as "novels," these authors saw their books as religious parables or true stories that could expose readers to the truths and values of the Bible by placing scriptural themes and archetypes in more contemporary settings.[62]

Consequently, these novels were not biographies of Christ; instead, various characters in these books served as reflections of Christ's teachings and personality. Ellen Montgomery in *The Wide, Wide World* and Gertie Flint in *The Lamplighter* reflected Christ's suffering, patience, and perseverance, while Uncle Tom and Eva in *Uncle Tom's Cabin* embodied the Savior's compassionate lifestyle of sacrificial love. In writing these books, Warner, Stowe, and Cummins hoped to motivate their readers to live more Christ-like lives not by giving them actual portraits of Jesus to emulate, but by placing examples of Christ-like behavior before them. They offered Americans accessible and imitable pictures of Christ by assigning his core attributes to commonplace figures such as little girls, day laborers, businessmen, housewives, ministers, farmers, and even slaves. In this manner, Christ's divinity became human, and the promise was held out that humans could become more divine.

The heavily moralistic writings of Warner, Stowe, and Cummins reveal that by the mid-nineteenth century fiction had become a tremendously popular purveyor of religious lessons. Justifying the use of such religious fiction, authors pointed to its good moral effects. It was advocated as a powerful new weapon in the battle to transform the United States in its every aspect into a more God-centered, moral nation.[63]

Those who advocated the use of religious fiction for moral education, however, remained slow to associate too closely the techniques of fiction with the truth of the Bible. Portraying scriptural themes in fiction was one thing; incorporating actual biblical episodes and adding new content to them was another. Until the unprecedented successes of *The Wide, Wide World* and *Uncle Tom's Cabin* testified to the appeal—and potential usefulness—of religious novels, authors hesitated to fictionalize the biblical narrative. Religious novels that sold in the hundreds of thousands of copies, however, tempted some Protestants to rethink the role of fiction in the moral instruction of their nation.

In 1855, Joseph Holt Ingraham offered Americans a new type of morally edifying religious fiction in his life of Christ, *The Prince of the House of David*. While Smith's *The Book of Mormon* would slowly gather momentum to become one of the nineteenth century's best-selling accounts of the life of Christ, Ingraham's fictionalized biography of Jesus skyrocketed to popularity almost immediately upon its release, selling 180,000 copies before 1858 and remaining in print for more than 100 years.[64]

Looking back upon Ingraham's early career as an author, it is not surprising to find that he was among the pioneers in placing the figure of Jesus into a sensational work of fiction. Ingraham spent the early portion of his authorial career writing cheap adventure fiction.[65] He was so prolific that he has been described as single-handedly accounting "for nearly ten percent of the fiction titles published" in the 1840s.[66]

While such a claim might be optimistic, Ingraham did enjoy great success as a fiction writer, but for reasons not entirely clear he chose not to continue his writing career. Instead, in 1847 he began studying theology and four years later was ordained an Episcopalian priest. Early in this clerical period of his life Ingraham was so embarrassed by his novels that he is said to have destroyed any of them he could find.[67]

By 1850, however, Ingraham's antipathy toward his former career mellowed, and he once again picked up the pen to compose a fiction series entitled "Letters from Adina," which appeared in the Episcopalian publication *The Evergreen*.[68] This series eventually became the immensely popular *The Prince of the House of David*. Ingraham would follow up *The Prince*'s success by fictionalizing the story of Moses in *The Pillar of Fire* (1859) and the story of King David in *The Throne of David* (1860). Neither of these books, however, approached the resounding popularity of *The Prince of the House of David*.

That Ingraham was determined to produce a biography of Christ that would serve as an agent of religious edification and moral change appears not only in the book's content, but in its narrative strategy as well. Ingraham chose to write *The Prince* in the form of an epistolary novel. Evoking moral pieces as old as the epistles of St. Paul and as recent as Samuel Richardson's *Clarissa*, Ingraham chose to depict a young Jewish girl by the name of Adina who wrote letters to her father while she visited the Holy Land. Her time in Palestine exactly coincides with the three-year ministry of Christ, making her letters an exposé of his activities. Believing that American readers had grown tired of lifeless Bible stories, Ingraham filled Adina's epistles with a bold mixture of biblical truth and sensational melodrama in order to "tempt" readers to consider the divinity of Christ.[69] Adina's letters give the reader stirring subplots centered on treachery, love, friendship, and misplaced religious devotion, as well as a compelling picture of Jesus as God "veiled in the flesh."[70]

Although Ingraham hoped to attract readers through the addition of melodramatic subplots, he was careful to follow the lead of Warner, Stowe, and Cummins in not highlighting the fictional components of his book in its early editions. Truth was a central issue for Ingraham because he wanted *The Prince* to serve as a tool of religious and moral education. This goal came across clearly in his book's preface where he writes: "For the Israelite as well as the Gentile believer this volume appears; and if it may be the means of convincing one son or daughter of Abraham to accept Jesus as Messias, or convince the infidel Gentile that He is the very son of the Lord and Savior of the world, he will have received his reward."[71]

Ingraham wanted this book to convince all who read it that Jesus was "the very son of the Lord and Savior of the world." To underline the truthfulness of his tale, Ingraham gave his book the deceptive subtitle: "*Three Years in the Holy City . . . by an Eye-Witness, All the Scenes and Wonderful Incidents in the Life of Jesus of Nazareth*."[72] Accompanying this eyewitness account in the early editions of his book, Ingraham constantly referred to himself as the book's editor, not its author.[73] He carefully gave the impression that all he had done was take a historical record from the first century and make it accessible to his readers.

Ingraham was interested in giving his readers a Jesus that "was *man*, as well as God!" He stresses Christ's humanity again and again as he shows the Savior as someone who is "seen, conversed with, eaten with, as a man!" Added to incessant depictions of Jesus in "domestic intercourse and friendly companionship" are Adina's lengthy and meticulous descriptions of the Holy Land and its customs.[74] Not only did these extended descriptions provide apologetic ammunition for American Protestants; they also reinforced Christ's corporeal nature. Jesus was depicted as a physical man who walked, talked, ate, and slept in a tangible, geographic location. In portraying Jesus in his earthly setting, Ingraham made it clear that Jesus was a savior who had indeed suffered the pains and enjoyed the pleasures of human existence.

Perhaps most striking in Ingraham's portrayal of the "man Christ Jesus" is his choice to represent the Savior as a man who suffered from a chronic headache.[75] Nowhere in the traditional Gospel accounts is there even a hint of such a malady. Adina records that Jesus seemed to her "weary and pale, and . . . seemed to suffer, as from time to time he raised his hand to his temples."[76] Here, one gets an early glimpse of Jesus' propensity toward headaches, a condition that is not just an annoying discomfort to the Savior, but a pain that is often so intense that it forces him to stoop in pain.[77] Ostensibly, Jesus is given headaches as just one more way to humanize him.

Jesus tells his followers: "It is not mine to escape human infirmities by any power my Father hath bestowed upon me for the good of men. It behooves me to suffer all things."[78] By stressing his suffering, Ingraham created a savior with whom his readers could more easily relate. They may not know what divinity felt like, but everyone had experienced suffering. Jesus' headaches, and the humanity to which they pointed, made Jesus a more accessible, and thus imitable, savior.

Headaches did far more than signal Jesus' humanity; they signaled American readers that Jesus had a physical constitution of great spiritual and moral sensitivity. In antebellum America, the headache was a malady almost entirely associated with women. As one physician explained in 1827, the woman "is far more sensitive and susceptible than the male, and extremely liable to those distressing affections which for want of some better term, have been denominated nervous, and which consist chiefly in painful affections of the head."[79] In portraying Jesus as suffering from a headache, Ingraham had feminized Christ.[80] This pronounced emphasis on the feminine played into antebellum beliefs in the more biologically sensitive, thus more religiously attuned, bodies of women.[81] In giving Christ a sensitive physical constitution, Ingraham laid the foundation for the spiritually superior nature of Christ.

Ann Douglas has argued that there was a pronounced trend in the feminization of American Protestant views of morality in this period. Pointing to a wide variety of religious figures who stressed Christ's meekness and compassion over his undeniable authority and omnipotence, Douglas argues that Christ became a divine figure predominantly associated with the more feminine traits of nurture, sympathy, and mercy.[82] Douglas notes that "One clergyman, writing in 1854 on 'The Woman Question,' not content with asserting that the 'womanly element predominated' in Christ, likened woman very specifically to the Messiah: 'She must open the long disused page of beatitudes among us, for manly energy rots among its husk, having dismissed reproving meekness and poverty of spirit. Let woman offer them an asylum; let her rise and take the beautiful shape of the Redeemer.'"[83] Not only had Christ become a "womanly" redeemer, but by the mid-1850s, women were being ideologically positioned as national redeemers.[84]

The morally redemptive character of women was trumpeted by numerous writers of the period. Edward Mansfield in his treatise on the legal rights of women wrote: "To every one of the race (Adam alone excepted) she [woman] has been prior in being, and prior in moral influence."[85] Sarah Hale, the educational reformer and magazine editor, worked hard to associate women with a redemptive moral influence. In her epic tome, *The Woman's Record*, Hale traces women's superior moral nature all the way back to the Garden of Eden, where "man was ordained to become the Worker or Provider; the Protector; and the Lawgiver. Woman was to be the Preserver; the Teacher or Inspirer; and the Exemplar."[86]

These are but two examples of how a wide range of American literature cultivated a belief in the moral superiority of women in this period.[87] This moral superiority carried with it great responsibilities. Women were rhetorically positioned as the most important moral influence on the nation's citizenry. Through their responsibilities in educating the young and providing morally uplifting domestic environments for the men in their lives, women were seen as critical factors in the United States' ability to survive and thrive.

The pivotal role of women as religious agents of moral influence was given more than a passing nod by Ingraham himself who dedicated his book "To the Daughters of Israel," using this term for American women who, like Adina, might be persuaded of Christ's messianic mission.[88] Ingraham then goes on to fill his book with an emphasis on the female.

He adjusts his gospel narrative to stress that the gentle disciple, John the Beloved, was Jesus' best friend, not the more militant and manly Peter. The book's original illustrations underline feminine and maternal spirituality as well. In the frontispiece, Jesus' head is surrounded by a host of female angels (see Figure 44), and the book's first illustration shows a rather maternal Jesus calling children to him (see Figure 45). Even Ingraham's descriptions of the houses Jesus enters portray a feminine touch, as readers are told such domestic details as Mary and Martha owned a table where "a richly worked book-cover of silk and velvet" lay "with the Letters 'I.N.'," which stand for "Jesus, of Nazareth."[89] It would seem that even first-century Hebrew women had a specially dedicated space for the family bible and were concerned with morally nurturing environments.

In choosing to feminize Jesus in particular and emphasize the feminine in general, Ingraham created a novel full of encouragement and apologetic resources for women who were attempting to execute their responsibilities as the nation's chief moral agents. This concern is also evident in Ingraham's portrayal of the story's narrator, Adina. Although Adina is but a young woman, she exercises a great deal of moral influence in the book, particularly over the men in her life.

Adina's letters to her father include several extended apologetic arguments on Christ's divinity and the value of his teaching. Such arguments, laced heavily with Bible verses, show that Adina has not only an obvious intelligence and broad knowledge of the Scriptures, but also a moral sensitivity not shared by the men around her. Her well-reasoned letters could

FIGURE 44. Frontispiece of Jesus surrounded by a host of female angels from 1855 edition of Joseph Holt Ingraham's *The Prince of the House of David*. (Library of the author)

FIGURE 45. "Jesus Blessing Little Children" from 1855 edition of Joseph Holt Ingraham's *The Prince of the House of David*. (Library of the author)

easily be used as model arguments for Ingraham's women readers who could identify with Adina's struggle to "moralize" the men around her.

The success of *The Prince* was perhaps the most visible sign of a growing shift in American Protestant thinking about the moral uses of fiction. Ingraham's desire to "tempt" readers back to the Bible's central character reveals that for many Protestants the goal of attracting people to the scriptural message was worth the cost of mixing truth with fiction.[90]

Residual, yet strong, resistance among certain segments of the American Protestantism would remain, however, until another account of the life of Christ appeared. Lew Wallace's *Ben-Hur* would topple what remained of what Carl Van Doren has called the remaining "village opposition" to fiction as it became the best-selling novel in nineteenth-century America.[91]

5 At first glance, Lew Wallace might seem an unlikely character to win a large Protestant audience for his religious fiction. Unlike Ingraham, Wallace had embarked on writing *Ben-Hur* not out of desire to convince people of the truths of Christianity, but because he wanted to write a best-selling book. Wallace had simply taken note that the Bible was the best-seller of all time, and that any book associating itself closely enough with the Bible had a good chance of riding on its coattails.[92] He even subtitled the book "A Tale of the Christ" to emphasize its biblical character, although Jesus only makes cameo appearances within its pages. Jesus as moral example is almost totally absent in Wallace's work, making *Ben-Hur* a notable exception in the life-of-Christ genre.

In fact, aside from the book's subtitle, one is hard pressed to really consider *Ben-Hur* a biography of Christ. Wallace obviously knew what he was doing, however, for his all-but-invisible Christ kept various Christian doctrinal issues from hindering the book's acceptability among a broad spectrum of both religious and nonreligious readers. First published in 1880, *Ben-Hur* succeeded beyond Wallace's greatest hopes; by 1893, Harper and Brothers touted it as the best-selling novel of the century, and in 1922 the firm was still producing 1,000,000-copy press runs of the book.[93] In 1899, a play based on the book began a twenty-one-year tour of the country, selling more than 20,000,000 tickets.[94]

Although previous scholarship on *Ben-Hur* has emphasized its tremendous popularity, little attention has been given to the reasons for it. Most often the book's popularity is chalked up to its melodramatic qualities; after all, it is an engaging story of the young Jew, Judah Ben Hur, whose life is full of illicit love affairs, murder plots, bloodcurdling adventures, and friendships marked by extreme loyalty or acrimonious betrayal.[95] No reasons are ever explicitly offered for why a Protestant readership—still leery of novel reading—would not only read *Ben-Hur*, but recommend it to their friends and go as far as to adopt it as a common text in their Sunday schools.

The reasons for its success among religious readers have much to do with the way its contents melded with certain prominent Protestant currents of thought in the late nineteenth century. Early in *Ben-Hur*, Wallace describes the state of affairs in first-century Judea: "The line of prophets, long extinct in Israel, was now succeeded by a line of scholars."[96] In the climate in which Wallace was writing, it would have been easy to replace the word "Israel" in this sentence with "the United States" and thus to see a parallel between the cultural climate of Palestine in the time of *Ben-Hur* and the United States in the last two decades of the 1800s. The last two decades of the 1800s were a time when the great prophets of the American church were being replaced by the great scientific theorists and theories of the day.[97] Principal among these theorists were Charles Darwin and Auguste Comte.

American theologians, ministers, and eventually parishioners increasingly had to confront the religious implications of Comtean and Darwinian thought. By the end of the century, German Higher Criticism was mixing with these two schools of thought to offer American Protestantism a host of new theoretical challenges. For instance, Darwin's evolutionary theories of natural selection "offered a thoroughly nonteleological means of explaining natural history, a means of explaining organic evolution that needed no recourse to the idea of design or designer."[98]

Darwin's thoughts on evolution propagated a scientific theory that explained the history of the world in terms of a causal link of adaptations. The fittest of a species had survived and reproduced over time. As innocuous as this idea may sound, it had profound theological implications. Darwin proposed a system that no longer required a God to organize and orchestrate the world.

Perhaps even more important, at the root of Darwinism stood a strong call for scientific evidence. Darwin's theories were so powerful because they were presented with so much commonsense knowledge to back them up. Darwinists claimed the theory of evolution could be proved simply by looking at any animal in the natural world and tracing back its development through various stages.[99]

Auguste Comte's epistemological theories of causality reached the height of their influence in the 1880s and accented Darwin's ideas on natural selection.[100] The idea of linear causation lay at the root of Comtean thought. Comte did not believe in any supernatural causal force. He viewed causation as a horizontal, not vertical, process. For him, causation meant an invariable time sequence: "x caused y if it invariably preceded y. There was no concept of x being a power; x was merely something invariably precedent. All humanity could know, Comte wrote, were the 'connections and sequences of phenomena.'"[101]

Thus, like Darwin, Comte stressed that no higher power need be responsible for any given event. Comte argued that all which could be known about the cause of a present event was what immediately preceded it. No hand from heaven was reaching down to direct humanity and the world. Vertical causation simply did not exist. The world was simply following a course that at some point had been set in motion and could be influenced only by making adjustments on a horizontal level of causation.

Darwin's and Comte's reliance on horizontal causation challenged all forms of nonphenomenal knowledge. Evidence, not faith, became the cornerstone for determining the truth. As the religious historian Jerry Brown has noted in his history of biblical criticism in nineteenth-century America, such a cornerstone only added fuel to the fire of Higher Criticism that was already burning down the credibility of the Bible.[102]

The pressure brought to bear by Comtean and Darwinian ideas of causality was intense because causal proof to validate the Bible simply did not exist. Antecedents to the Bible and its stories were difficult, if not impossible, to find. If found, it was difficult to prove their authenticity and accuracy. This tension between biblical and scientific authority eventually erupted in a clear fissure between science and religion in the 1880s, occasioning a number of Protestant conferences that addressed the tensions between faith and science.[103] The old order of American Protestantism had been based on a relationship between faith, science, and the Bible. In an age that so highly esteemed science, it was important that the Bible be a scientifically reliable document that taught scientifically verifiable material.[104]

The spreading acceptance of Darwinism and Comtean thought changed the dynamic between faith and science, creating a Protestant line of thinking that relegated science and religion to separate spheres. As the religious historian George Marsden has argued: "Religion would no longer be seen as dependent on historical or scientific fact susceptible to objective inquiry; religion had to do with the spiritual, with the heart, with religious experience, and with moral sense and moral action—areas not open to scientific investigation. Thus science could have its autonomy, and religion would be beyond its reach."[105]

Swirling amid this intellectual milieu, one can discover reasons for *Ben-Hur*'s unprecedented popularity. Chief among these were Wallace's perfectionist historical tendencies. Before sitting down to write the novel, he traveled to the Library of Congress in Washington and combed through the library's one-quarter of a million volumes for anything he could find on the Jews and the first-century Roman Empire. He was passionate in his search for accurate details concerning politics, geography, and even botany.

Nineteenth-century Protestants had long viewed history as acceptable reading material, since history provided both insights in human nature and validation of Christian doctrine.[106] Wallace's painstaking historical research resonated with religious readers who saw in the book a means of answering the call for scientific validation for the existence and authority of Christ and his teachings.

It took Wallace weeks to locate an accurate description of a Roman trireme, but once he found one, he was quick to spend five pages of *Ben-Hur* incorporating a painstakingly detailed portrait of this Roman battleship. He noted everything about the ship, often including the Latin names for the vessel's various parts. His description of the trireme also includes footnotes that serve to document and provide corroborative evidence for the material he is presenting to his readers. He put the same effort into accurately depicting the famous chariot race of the book. Here, the reader is once again not only given the excitement of the actual race, but also fully introduced to every aspect of Roman chariot racing, from the placement of certain segments of the audience to various chariot constructions.

Because of Wallace's attention to historical detail in depicting the novel's background, readers felt that they were acquiring accurate information about first-century Palestine. Thus, the book clearly became more than a simple adventure tale. Readers could learn things about the time in which Jesus lived and point to the educative qualities of the book as a reason for reading it. Through the tremendous historical detail, they could imaginatively transport themselves to first-century Judea. They could point to the obvious historicity of the book's setting as a reason to believe in the historicity of the figure of Jesus.

In keeping with his obsession for historical accuracy, Wallace was also committed to giving his readers exact dates and extensive genealogies, which similarly served as testaments of verification. The best example of this preoccupation with exact dating comes early in the book when Wallace writes: "Following the Hebrew system, the meeting of the wise men described in the preceding chapters took place in the afternoon of the twenty-fifth day of the third month of the year; that is to say, on the twenty-fifth day of December. The year was the second of the 193d Olympiad, or the 747th of Rome; the sixty-seventh of Herod the Great, and the thirty-fifth of his reign; the fourth before the beginning of the Christian era."[107] Use of mulitple-calendar dating systems enabled Wallace to pinpoint the date and thereby encourage readers to believe that the historical event actually took place. A verifiable date is great evidence to prove that an event actually took place.

Wallace uses genealogies throughout his story in a similar way, namely, to attest to the truth of certain otherwise problematic fictional and biblical claims. Near the beginning of the novel, for example, Joseph and Mary are given housing in a hopelessly overcrowded Bethlehem because they can trace their ancestry through the line of David. Later, Judah is comforted by his mother when she tells him that he is of a noble race that can be traced through Jewish registries for centuries. Still later, Judah is required to show proof of his lineage so that Simonides, a former servant of the Hur household, will believe him to be a descendent of the house of Hur. Finally, the incredibly wealthy and powerful Arab, Ilderim, keeps a thorough genealogy of his chariot horses. He can trace their ancestry back for centuries, and this aristocratic pedigree lends credibility to the claim that they are the fastest horses in the world.

Genealogy is the technique that the Bible uses often to prove the lineage of many of its characters. In Wallace's novel it also becomes a means of invoking the scientific idea of systematic linear regression. Just as Comtean thought emphasizes that one can know phenomena only through an analysis and isolation of prior causes, a genealogy gives a written record of those prior causes.

Although Wallace is concerned with historical accuracy throughout the novel, this concern reaches its apex in his geographic depiction of the Holy Land. He spent hours of painstaking research, as he later recalled: "I examined catalogues of books and maps, and sent for everything likely to be useful. I wrote with a chart always before my eyes."[108] His demand for precision paid off. Upon actually visiting the Holy Land a few years after the book's publication, he concluded that his descriptions were so accurate that he would not change anything he had written. In a tradition dating back to the first Brattleboro bible editions, *Ben-Hur* capitalized on Protestants who eagerly accepted the Holy Land as a biblical apologetic. The story of Christ was true because the Holy Land existed. That his painstaking descriptions of the Holy Land were important can be seen in the respect these descriptions garnered from the religious community. Sunday school teachers and Protestant clergy were quick to use *Ben-Hur* as a text in their religion classes for gaining a precise picture of the Holy Land. One writer recalled the use *Ben-Hur* was put to in the years following its first release: "Superintendent, pastor, and stray visitor, called on for a few remarks, reminded everybody at least once in three months that the most vivid picture of the Holy Land in the time of Christ was in *Ben-Hur*."[109]

Equally important, however, when considering the popularity of *Ben-Hur* is how the novel profited from one of the most profound results of the growing separation of religion and science in late nineteenth-century

Protestantism, namely the increasing emphasis on the emotional in religion over the rational. Capturing this emphasis, the prominent New York minister Henry Ward Beecher made it a cardinal rule in his preaching and his homiletic teaching that Christians were to strive to inspire the heart and leave the development of the mind to other fields. Viewing the goals of preaching and evangelism as an appeal to sentiment and emotion, he argued that their purpose was to kindle the "nobility of a heart opened when God has touched it." As he saw it, "While we are taught by scientists in truths that belong to the sensual nature . . . we need the Christian ministry to teach us those things which are invisible."[110]

For all its emphasis on authentic history, *Ben-Hur* was a novel that consistently espoused a belief that faith is always more a matter of feeling than it is of cold, hard logic. Wallace makes this clear at the beginning of the story by having the three wise men agree that the Savior will teach a "new lesson—that Heaven may be won, not by the sword, not by human wisdom, but by faith, love, and good works."[111]

This message is reinforced later in a confrontation between Judah Ben-Hur and his nemesis, Messala. By contrasting the passionate hero Judah Ben-Hur with the calculating villain Messala, Wallace encourages the reader to put more emphasis on the heart than on the head. Criticizing Judah for "too much passion," Messala extols the virtues of coldhearted, Roman trained logic. Romans have come to rule the world because they have learned to rule their emotions, Massala declares. It is Judah's passion for his faith that leads him away from a partnership with Messala. Although Judah's dedication to his passion results in his being placed in the galleys as a slave, it is his passionate revenge that cripples and defeats Messala at the end of the book. In this way, Wallace demonstrates that passionate feelings make a victorious hero; logic destroys, feeling ennobles; logic misdirects action, feeling empowers and properly guides action.

By so clearly setting forth the primacy of feeling over thought in both the words of his characters and through the romantic plot, Wallace makes *Ben-Hur* a parable of the power and saving agency of faith. *Ben-Hur* thus encourages readers to be more concerned with their religious feelings than with the scientific questions that might plague their more rational faculties.

As has been noted earlier, *Ben-Hur* was a book supposedly written about Jesus, but largely without Jesus. It most clearly offered an exciting adventure tale, and less clearly a religious message. The demands of narrative plot took precedence; issues of doctrine receded into the background. This frequently enabled religious readers to emphasize various elements within the book—such as its historical accuracy or even its subtitle—as a justification for reading it. Protestant readers could pick and choose religious elements of the book to rationalize their reading of it, when, in fact,

the book may have been appealing to some primarily because of the "secular" titillation it provided.

Ben-Hur capitalizes on spectacle at the cost of actual biblical content;
the discipline and perseverance involved in grappling with complex ideas
are overshadowed by the emotional gratification. The Protestant readers of
the late nineteenth century were able to appropriate *Ben-Hur* as a Christian apologetic. At the same time, the book helped pave the way for a kind
of Christianity less interested in a reasoned argumentation and more interested in simple entertainment and emotional stimulation.

In commemorating Lew Wallace upon his death in 1905, one com-
mentator celebrated the fact that *Ben-Hur* had achieved what no other
work of religious fiction had ever done: it had gone "straight to the heart
of solid puritans, who thank Heaven! Are still the backbone of America."[112] The question that needs to be asked is whether or not, in the end,
Ben-Hur made these so-called Puritans less religiously solid and the biblical backbone of America more brittle.

6   The lack of doctrinal orientation and disciplined religious thinking
fostered by *Ben-Hur* realized the worst fears of those who stood
against Protestants reading religious fiction. Charles Wesley Andrews, perhaps the most vocal and articulate writer against the use of religious
fiction, spent a great deal of time attempting to destroy the credibility of
religious novels in general, and Ingraham's work in particular.

In his widely distributed pamphlet entitled *Religious Novels: An Argument Against Their Use*, Andrews lamented *The Prince*'s popularity,
recording that it had sold 20,000 copies in ten months when the much
more factual *The Christ of History* had sold only 2,500 copies in the same
period.[113] For Andrews, such sales statistics told a simple story: religious
novels were drawing people away from books, including the Bible, that offered them real truth. Quickly dismissing the argument that religious
fiction offered people a doorway by which to enter the faith, Andrews argued that such fiction only deceived readers into thinking they were getting some modicum of truth, when, in fact, they were developing a craving
for fiction as "uncontrollable as that for strong drink."[114]

Andrews's pamphlet is one long diatribe against the belief that religious truth could take any form and still be efficacious. His argument was
a simple one: Truth always needed to be presented in nonfictional forms
or it ceased to be truth. Religious fiction deceived its readers by portraying itself as true, and it encouraged lazy thinking that was not well suited
for the rigors that concerted bible reading demanded.

Andrews claimed that those who read "trashy" religious fiction kept
themselves from receiving truth by wasting their time in not reading the

Bible, and they ruined their ability to discern truth when they did do Bible reading. Reading the Scriptures and other useful pieces of nonfiction demanded a level of intellectual discipline and intensity that extended exposure to fiction undermined. It was Andrews's opinion that far from helping conform Americans to a more "heavenly character," religious fiction paved the road to ruin.[115]

Andrews's vitriol proved no match for the enormous popularity of religious fiction as clearly evinced in the resounding sales and Protestant adoption of Wallace's *Ben-Hur*. Yet, there was merit in the fear that religious fiction could help marginalize the Bible by offering bible stories that were easier to understand and more exciting to read. While such fiction pointed readers to the Bible's story, it also gave them an excuse not to read it. Religious fiction might base itself upon the biblical narrative, but it could also give people a distaste for the Bible's complexity and density. Although the reasons for the Bible drifting from the center of American print culture are complex, religious fiction proved an unreliable ally in the battle to keep the volume preeminent in that print culture. Fiction offered a glimpse of the Bible, but readers often felt no need to peer beyond that glimpse.

In many ways, *Ben-Hur* stands as a parable for the place of the Bible and the biblical narrative in nineteenth-century American culture. Just as Jesus had been shunted from the main plot of Wallace's novel, the Bible increasingly found itself on the periphery of American print culture. Even Sunday Schools could displace the Bible with *Ben-Hur* when it came to descriptions of the Holy Land.

People might own a bible, display it, and selectively read from it, but they also had a growing number of ways to avoid engaging it in all its dense complexity. Its core text could be invoked, but one need not necessarily grapple with that text because pictures, marginal commentary, encyclopedic introductions, and now fictionalized bible stories all created ways in which readers might access the Bible without having to confront the Bible itself. Fictional bible stories became yet one more means of diluting the biblical narrative, while at the same time splintering and weakening the Bible's voice in a print culture where thousands of simpler and more immediately rewarding printed materials were calling for the attention of readers.

POSTSCRIPT

Eulogizing George Livermore after his death in the summer of 1865, the president of the Massachusetts Historical Society at the time, Robert C. Winthrop, proclaimed that among Livermore's extensive contributions to New England society and culture was "his beautiful library—with its remarkable collection of . . . the Sacred Scriptures."[1] Livermore, a successful Boston merchant with a voracious antiquarian appetite, had spent much of his life collecting complete or partial editions of the Sacred Scriptures. Upon his death, Livermore's library contained almost 600 bibles or portions of bibles, including the personal bible of Martin Luther's disciple Philip Malanchthon, a complete Coverdale bible, and both editions of John Eliot's Indian bible.[2]

As impressive as Livermore's biblical collection was, it paled in comparison to John Pierpont Morgan's. Morgan—banker, railroad baron, steel magnate, savior of the United States Treasury—began seriously collecting books in the 1890s.[3] By the time of his death in 1913, his library included nearly 20,000 volumes, including the greatest private collection of the Scriptures in existence.[4] Among his myriad biblical editions, Morgan had managed to acquire three of the forty-eight extant variants of the Gutenberg bible.[5]

No longer simply a religious guidebook for life, bibles had become collectable commodities, and the libraries of Livermore and Morgan provide stunning examples of how by the nineteenth century the Bible was anything but a monolithic entity. Since the time of Christ, the Scriptures had undergone myriad revisions incited by complex ideological, technological, and economic concerns. Bible collections bear vivid witness that once the Word had become words, those words and their presentation were in a constant state of flux.

American-made bibles were an echo, albeit an immensely magnified one, of the diversity in scriptural reproductive trends that had been active since the time of monastic scribes.[6] What was peculiar to nineteenth-century America was the unprecedented growth of the country's publishing industry and the unprecedented diversity of bible editions that appeared in its publishing marketplace. Even with the incredible growth in American bible production, by the 1880s it was clear that the Bible no longer enjoyed its preeminent place as the most-read text in the United States. One minister captured the sentiment of the times when he wrote in 1884: "The fact that the Bible occupies a somewhat different place in the thoughts of well-instructed Christians from that which it held twenty-five or fifty years ago is a fact that cannot be denied."[7]

Reasons for the Bible's drift from the center of the nation's print culture are either too complicated or too uninteresting to garner much serious attention. Aside from Grant Wacker's thoughts on the role German Higher Criticism played in the Bible's fracturing influence, treatments of American literature, education, religion, and reading tastes never directly address why the Bible lost its preeminence.[8]

Obviously, reasons behind the Bible's changing role are complex, but this study has posited that central, and almost totally unexplored, components to explaining the Bible's changing role in American culture find their roots in the diversification of the country's print marketplace and bible editions themselves.

The explosive growth in bible edition diversity and production had a number of momentous consequences. First, the very attempts to make the Bible more accessible both physically and intellectually ultimately contributed to making this special book less special. Put another way, in mass-producing the Bible and producing it in so many different formats and translations, its producers often made the Scriptures appear more ordinary than extraordinary. At its core, the American mass production of bibles and the resultant diversity of biblical editions highlighted the mutable nature of a supposedly immutable book.

With a prescient and prophetic voice, the Episcopal Bishop Arthur Cleveland Coxe led a crusade against the diversification of bible editions before the Civil War arguing, among other things, that different editions of the Bible would erode faith in the Bible's sacred and unique nature. Coxe contended that tampering with the Bible risked destroying "the feeling, so healthful and so prevalent, that the Bible is a book above change, and too holy to be subjected to experiments."[9] Although Coxe helped win certain battles, for example, getting the American Bible Society to repeal its use of a revised version of the King James in the 1850s, he was on the side that lost the war. Fulfilling Coxe's worst fears, the image—accurate or not—that the Bible was a cohesive, unchanging text began to disintegrate in the minds of Americans as nearly 2,000 editions of the English Bible poured into the American marketplace. These different editions, with their varying translations, illustrations, commentaries, formats, and bindings contributed to a notion that the Bible—far from being an unmediated, unchanging text produced by the hand of God—was a human production, open to the failings inherent in any work wrought by human hands.

A second factor that helps explain the Bible's changing role is the increased access to different bindings and biblical illustrations. These bindings and illustrations helped create bibles that were purchased for reasons aside from the words they contained. Bindings increasingly became tools to mark levels of gentility and social status, not simply provide an appropriate protection reinforcing the Bible's precious words.

The growing number of biblical illustrations also served to de-emphasize the volume's words. Although pictures had accompanied the biblical text for centuries, early nineteenth-century changes in print technology transformed biblical illustration from a handful of illustrations to thousands of images. As more and more illustrations began to accompany the biblical text, their presence enabled readers to bypass the Bible's complex written narrative in favor of the images that sat in juxtaposition to that text. These vast numbers of pictures, increasingly mounted on the same page as the biblical text, could serve to remove the Bible's words from the main field of a reader's interpretive attention. Readers found themselves able to skim over difficult or boring passages in favor of simply enjoying the pictures that purportedly illustrated those passages. Thus, the Bible's many complex narrative strands were frequently reduced to the interpretation offered by a single image, an image often only loosely based on a single aspect of the narrative it purportedly illustrated.

A third factor that explains the Bible's changing role is the fact that the diverse bible editions exercised a profound influence in the development and functioning of important national institutions. Not only did various new biblical translations cause bible societies and other voluntary organizations to split and reorganize, but also, religious traditions such as the Unitarians, Mormons, and Disciples of Christ used their own biblical translations to distinguish and validate their beliefs. The fact that Catholics and Protestants used different versions of the Bible led to confrontations in the nation's public school and court systems, ultimately laying the foundation for the Bible's declining role in school curricula. This diminishing role would lead the less overtly Protestant segments of the nation's population to become increasingly less familiar with the text, depriving the nation of a textual anchor for shared cultural memory and communication.

Finally, the growth in United States publishing created an environment that began to drown out the Bible's "written preaching" in a deluge of other printed "noise."[10] The Bible was facing hitherto unimagined competition for readers as reading material became accessible to a degree unprecedented in American, and even world, history. Here begins a dilemma that still persists among those most invested in distributing the Scriptures: How does one attract readers to the Bible's message when new media and broader spectrums of information are continually threatening not only the relevance of the biblical message, but the material and narrative forms that message has taken for thousands of years?

Answers in nineteenth-century America ranged from increasing bible production and distribution to adapting the Bible to take the forms of its most successful competitors. Both these strategies were successful in attracting readers to the biblical narrative, but they also had their own unforeseen consequences, such as fragmenting the bible market and blurring divine inspiration with human invention. It became quickly apparent that there would be no easy answers to keeping the Bible the central written text in American culture.

While the Bible may have moved from the center of the country's print culture by the 1880s, it would be inaccurate to say that widespread interest in the Bible no longer existed.[11] The Bible did not disappear from America's publishing marketplace; it simply no longer towered over it.

Perhaps most striking in the attempt to understand the Bible's changing role is how it forces one to reconsider the precious Protestant value of *sola scriptura* (the Bible alone). Most often applied to scriptural interpretation, this clarion call to foreground the words of Scripture frequently ignores the fact that God's word is never truly alone when it reaches its readers on a printed page. Even if not constrained by doctrine and clergy, Scripture is constrained by its own materiality: how it is set in type, formatted, commented upon in marginalia, illustrated, bound, and distributed. If the story of nineteenth-century publishing teaches us anything, it is that bible packaging, content, and distribution all inseparably work together to give the Book meaning. A book *is* judged by its cover, as well as by all aspects of its content and method of conveyance—a precious lesson worth remembering in any attempt to interpret the meaning and influence of the Word once it becomes words.

Appendixes

An Overview of Bible Production in
the United States, 1777-1880

Mark A. Noll and Nathan O. Hatch, religious historians who have paid serious attention to the role of the Bible in American culture, have noted that "the history of the printing and distribution of the Bible and biblical materials is an immense, yet vastly neglected topic."[1] In fact, so little work has been done on even the most basic contours of American bible publishing in the eighteenth and nineteenth centuries that it is helpful to paint with broad brush strokes the nature of bible production and distribution during the first century following the Revolutionary War.

As Figure 46 shows, according to the data collected in Margaret Hills's *The English Bible in America*, the number of cities with printers who published bibles between 1777 to 1880 form a rough bell-shaped curve peaking in the 1830s. The number of separate editions peak in the 1840s.[2] As with all statistics, these need explanation. While "Cities" may be a fairly straightforward category, "Editions" is a category that quickly leads to confusion. In the bibliographic sense of the word, "edition" delineates all copies of a book that are reproduced from a single set of type plates or a single act of composition.[3] For the most part, Figure 46 records specific acts of composition from a certain set of plates. There are important exceptions, however, to this way of counting bible editions.

Hills recorded not only every edition of the English Bible published in America, but different printings as well. Here enters some confusion. Hills sometimes lists separate printings made from the same plates, as in the case of Mathew Carey's standing type bible plates. At other times, Hills fails to list the separate printings (often numbering in the hundreds) of a bible produced by the American Bible Society.[4] One can only guess at the reasons for this difference. The obvious answer would be that the sheer number of printings produced by publishers (such as the American Bible Society) from a single set of plates was so large, and the difference among the books was so small, that Hills did not think it necessary to list the many editions/printings of certain American Bible Society volumes. Simply put, the 14th edition and the 114th edition of an ABS quarto brevier bible did not differ enough to warrant separate entries.

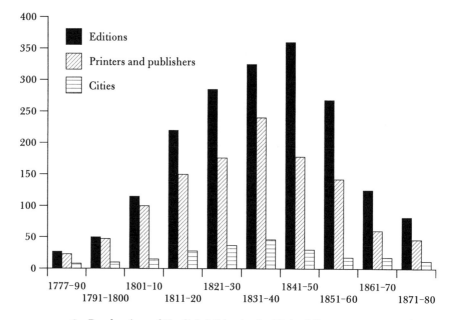

FIGURE 46. Production of English bibles in the United States, 1777–1880. (Data taken from Hills, *The English Bible*, pp. 1–293)

Because there are few instances in which multiple printings were made from single plates, I have taken Hills's list in its entirety rather than seeking to weed out listings for separate editions/printings made from the same plates by the same publishing enterprise. Thus, with some slight deviations, the use of a set of plates by one publisher would amount to one edition in the above figure. (If these plates were used by another publisher, their bible was then counted as another edition.)

Because Hills does not list all the printings of a bible printed from a single set of plates, it is easy to misread the bell-shaped curve of editions portrayed in Figure 46 to imply that bible production was decreasing as the century wore on. In reality, bible production remained strong up through 1880 and beyond. Publishing practices and matters of economics simply made it more common for fewer publishers to print larger and larger press runs of bibles. For example, by the 1850s, the American Bible Society was regularly printing well over 100 editions of a bible from a single set of plates. Thus, what looks like a single edition of the Bible in the Hills bibliography was often several hundred printings of that edition, which translates into hundred of thousands of volumes. Consequently, the decrease in editions before 1880 indicates that fewer sets of plates may have been involved in bible production, but the number of volumes printed in each edition probably rose.

The actual number of bibles printed in a given year is extremely difficult, if not impossible, to ascertain. The loss of records, coupled with the large number of firms involved in printing the Bible during this period, make a determination of the numbers of bibles printed in these years a daunting research project. Thus, no attempt has been made to determine the total number of bibles printed by a given firm or produced during a given year.

One notable exception is the American Bible Society, which kept both public and private records for many years on the number of volumes they printed. My belief that the production volume of bibles did not decrease noticeably before 1880 is based on the fact that the American Bible Society—and sister organizations such as the American and Foreign Bible Society—more than compensated in their large volume of production for the declining number of publishers producing bibles.

The category of "Printers and publishers" in Figure 46 also requires definition. Where "printing" crosses over the line into "publishing" in the nineteenth century is not entirely clear. Up to 1815, printers most often served the multilayered functions of a publisher by obtaining the copy, directing the production, and handling the advertising and distribution. During these years, the imprint "published by" seems to mean largely the same thing as "printed by." Up to 1830, J. & J. Harper was still putting the words "printed by" on their title pages, even though the company was clearly serving in the role of publisher.[5]

Compounding the confusion between the terms "publisher" and "printer" is the fact that publishing enterprises often joined together to produce a bible. For instance, Hills lists over 800 publishing enterprises active in producing bibles in this period. This number is deceptive because it does not offer any idea of the constant realignment and name changes that publishing enterprises underwent during this period. For example, the New York publisher Evert A. Duyckinck was involved in producing sixteen different bibles or New Testaments between 1810 and 1830, but he did this under the name of three different publishing firms: E. Duyckinck, E. Duyckinck & P. A. Mesier, and Duyckinck & Miller. To add to the confusion, Peter Mesier—his partner in several of these bible ventures—also was involved in bible printings that carried his name separate from Duyckinck's, as well as bible printings that he helped finance but that do not carry his name at all on their title pages.[6]

Another possible reason for confusion between printer and publisher is that bibles were published in installments. Ezra Sargeant began publishing a bible in 1811; it would take thirty-seven installments and fifteen years to complete the entire volume. Six publishing firms would be involved in the edition, including Ezra Sargeant (1811–12); James Eastburn (1812);

183

• *1–5 bible editions*
New Haven, CT
Wilmington, DE
Boston, MA
Newburyport, MA
Exeter, NH
Elizabethtown, NJ
Lancaster, PA

◻ *6–15 bible editions*
Worcester, MA
Trenton, NJ
New York, NY

▲ *over 15 bible editions*
Philadelphia, PA

☐ State
▨ Territory

FIGURE 47. American bible publishers, 1777–1800. (Data taken from Hills, *The English Bible*, pp. 1–14)

Eastburn, Kirk & Co. (1813–16); Daniel Hitt and Abraham Paul (1817–22); Abraham Paul (1823–25); N. Bangs and J. Emory (1825–26).[7] Consequently, it quickly becomes apparent how difficult it is to determine the exact associations between printers and their levels of involvement in various bible editions.

What is clear, however, is that before the 1820s, bible production was most often a group project for publishers. There was a pronounced tendency for several printers and booksellers to band together in order to produce an edition of the Bible. Sometimes there was simply strength (and capital) in numbers, while at other times publishers would take over the bible editions of publishers who had died or gone out of business.

More established printers like Isaiah Thomas and Mathew Carey could finance the printing of bibles out of their own resources, with a single firm listed on their title pages. Smaller printers often joined together for bible projects. For example, in 1805 T. Kirk of Brooklyn printed a New Testament for the firms of Campbell and Mitchell, Sage and Thompson, D. Smith and B. Dornin, and S. Stansbury.[8] This practice of cooperative printing among companies would continue through the decade beginning in 1810, at the end of which it became more commonly the practice of af-

• *1–5 bible editions*

Mobile, AL	Claremont, NH
Tuscaloosa, AL	Dover, NH
Tuscumbia, AL	Exeter, NH
Bridgeport, CT	Keene, NH
Middlebury, CT	Sandbornton, NH
Middletown, CT	Elizabethtown, NJ
New Haven, CT	Newark, NJ
Brunswick, ME	Trenton, NJ
Portland, ME	Buffalo, NY
Amherst, MA	Saratoga Springs, NY
Andover, MA	Utica, NY
Boston, MA	Cincinnati, OH
Lunenburg, MA	Zanesville, OH
Newburyport, MA	Harrisburg, PA
Northampton, MA	Pittsburgh, PA
Salem, MA	Charleston, SC
Springfield, MA	Bellows Fall, VT
St. Louis, MO	Bethany, VA

▲ *over 15 bible editions*

□ *6–15 bible editions*

Hartford, CT

Baltimore, MD	New York, NY
Cooperstown, NY	Philadelphia, PA
Woodstock, VT	Brattleboro, VT

□ State
▨ Territory

FIGURE 48. American bible publishers, 1831–40. (Data taken from Hills, *The English Bible*, pp. 109–164)

fluent publishing enterprises to hire printers to produce bibles solely for their firms, which would then either sell these bibles themselves through their own network of agents, or sell the bibles to other booksellers.[9]

As specialization came to characterize the industry, publishing came to take on its modern connotations of responsibility for many aspects of producing a book while printing came to delineate only the physical production of the book. With this in mind, Figure 46 can be said to show that as the volume of bible production increased before 1880, fewer publishers, in fewer cities, using fewer sets of plates produced those volumes.

In considering the location of American bible production, certain trends appear between 1777 and 1880 (Figures 47, 48, and 49). The three great early American publishing centers of Boston, Philadelphia, and New York produce the vast majority of bibles throughout this century. Boston is the only one of these three centers that significantly recedes from bible production after the 1820s. After this decade, Boston is primarily known for the more eccentric and specialized versions of the English Bible (such as Unitarian and Universalist translations) it produces.

Philadelphia, on the other hand, is the first great publishing center of the English Bible in America and remains a center of bible publishing activ-

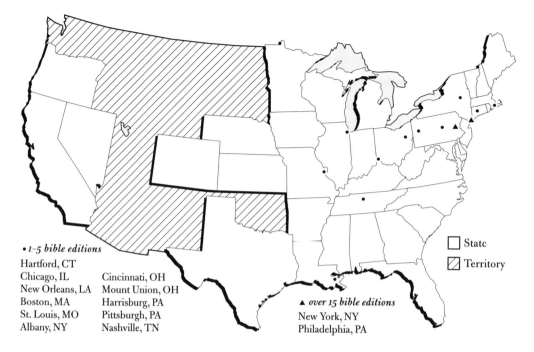

• *1–5 bible editions*
Hartford, CT
Chicago, IL
New Orleans, LA
Boston, MA
St. Louis, MO
Albany, NY

Cincinnati, OH
Mount Union, OH
Harrisburg, PA
Pittsburgh, PA
Nashville, TN

▲ *over 15 bible editions*
New York, NY
Philadelphia, PA

☐ State
▨ Territory

FIGURE 49. American bible publishers, 1871–80. (Data taken from Hills, *The English Bible*, pp. 278–293)

ity throughout this period. New York becomes a significant center for bible production beginning in the 1790s. It replaces Philadelphia as the chief center of English bible publishing in the decade beginning in 1810. Not surprisingly, the Northeastern states dominate bible publishing throughout these years. States south of Kentucky and Virginia produced only twelve editions of the English Bible in this period, five of which appeared during the Civil War. Finally, several western cities produced bibles during this period. Cincinnati, Ohio, was the most important western bible publishing center; Muscatine, Iowa, was the westernmost city to publish a bible edition. Other cities little known today for their role in American publishing played a significant role in producing English bibles during this period. These cities include Brattleboro, Vermont; Hartford, Connecticut; Lunenburg, Massachusetts; and Cooperstown, New York.

American Bible Society (ABS) Production and Distribution, 1818-1880

The following figures were collected from two sources. For the years 1818 to 1848, the data was collected from W. P. Strickland's *History of the American Bible Society* (New York: Harper & Brothers, 1849). For the years 1849 to 1880, the data came from the 33rd to the 65th Annual Reports of the American Bible Society. In 1849, the Society no longer recorded in its annual reports how many bibles it printed; it simply noted the number of bibles it distributed from its depository. These production and distribution figures broadly define the term "bible" to include both bibles and New Testaments.

TABLE 1

Year	English Bibles Printed	Bibles Issued from Depository	Year	English Bibles Printed	Bibles Issued from Depository
1818	20,400	17,594	1838	142,000	58,000
1819	71,320	31,118	1839	114,000	134,937
1820	64,482	41,513	1840	139,000	157,261
1821	59,800	68,177	1841	166,875	150,202
1822	36,625	54,806	1842	275,000	257,067
1823	53,600	54,805	1843	220,000	216,605
1824	77,575	60,439	1844	293,000	314,582
1825	48,550	63,851	1845	417,350	429,092
1826	81,000	67,134	1846	482,000	483,073
1827	67,734	71,621	1847	671,500	627,764
1828	118,750	134,607	1848	760,900	655,066
1829	360,000	200,583	1849		560,219
1830	308,000	238,583	1850		551,546
1831	270,000	242,000	1851		519,190
1832	156,000	115,802	1852		571,946
1833	0	91,168	1853		733,042
1834	149,375	100,832	1854		672,372
1835	34,000	123,236	1855		615,480
1836	194,000	221,236	1856		548,013
1837	228,000	206,240	1857		635,264

TABLE 1 *(continued)*

Year	English Bibles Printed	Bibles Issued from Depository	Year	English Bibles Printed	Bibles Issued from Depository
1858		585,673	1870		1,012,710
1859		599,017	1871		924,096
1860		628,697	1872		902,442
1861		711,125	1873		917,608
1862		1,082,974	1874		804,489
1863		1,252,260	1875		712,390
1864		1,417,371	1876		663,926
1865		1,516,375	1877		589,145
1866		943,986	1878		643,669
1867		1,004,818	1879		915,294
1868		984,854	1880		1,083,860
1869		1,020,630			

Total number of bibles and New Testaments issued from the ABS depository from 1818 to 1880 = 32,023,475

Prices for the Cheapest Editions of
American Bibles in the Nineteenth Century

Price lists for the American Bible Society have been meticulously preserved. The same cannot be said for non-Bible Society editions. The table below is pieced together from a number of sources to track the cheapest bible prices advertised at various points throughout the nineteenth century. All prices are in dollars and cents.

TABLE 2

Publisher	1801	1807	1814	1819	1831	1838	1841	1844	1854	1858	1880	1897
Carey Bible[1]	5	3.5	—	—	—	—	—	—	—	—	—	—
Folsom Bible[2]	—	—	1.125	—	—	—	—	—	—	—	—	—
Wood Bible[3]	—	—	—	—	—	—	1.125	.6	—	—	—	—
ABS Bible[4]	—	—	—	.64	.7	.5	—	.45	.3	.3	.3	.2
Merriam Bible[5]	—	—	—	—	—	—	1	—	—	—	—	—
Jenks Bible[6]	—	—	—	—	—	—	—	.75	—	—	—	—
Sears Bible[7]	—	—	—	—	—	—	—	—	—	—	—	1.4
ABS NT[8]	—	—	—	—	.12	.1	—	.06	.08	.07	.05	.05
Jenks NT[9]	—	—	—	—	—	—	—	.125	—	—	—	—
Sears NT[10]	—	—	—	—	—	—	—	—	—	—	—	.18

[1]Skeel, *Mason Locke Weems* 2:136. Carey, *Plans and Terms*, pp. 3–7.

[2]The account book records of George McKean Folsom (a retail bookseller, not a publisher) are located at the Massachusetts Historical Society. Bible prices in entries for April 2 and May 7, 1814, account book, 1813–1814; Bradford and Read, Boston, Massachusetts.

[3]Price lists found in the Broadsides Collection of the American Antiquarian Society.

[4]All American Bible Society bible prices are found in price lists included in the Society's Annual Report for that given year.

[5]Price located in the G. & C. Merriam collection at the American Antiquarian Society.

[6]Bible price, entry of B.B. Mussey for August 1, 1844, Jenks and Palmer account book, 1841–1846, Boston, Massachusetts. Massachusetts Historical Society.

[7]*Sears Roebuck Catalogue* (1897), p. 348.

[8]All American Bible Society testament prices are found in price lists included in the Society's Annual Report for that given year.

[9]New Testament price, entry of James Loring for August 27, 1844, Jenks and Palmer account book, 1841–1846, Boston, Massachusetts. Massachusetts Historical Society.

[10]*Sears Roebuck Catalogue* (1897), p. 348.

Survey of Bible Bindings from the
American Bible Society (1,238-edition sample)

Because it is simply too difficult to determine how a rebound volume was originally bound, all rebound editions have been subtracted from the statistical percentages presented here (see Figure 50), which are taken from the table following the figure. Data combines bound bibles and New Testaments.

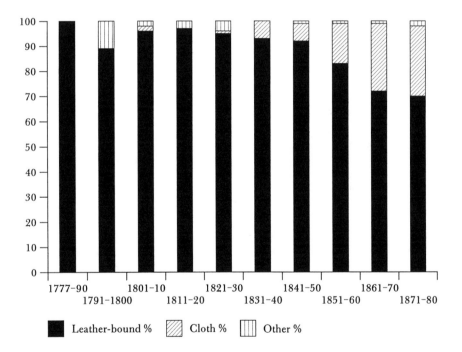

FIGURE 50. Percentages of bible binding types, 1777–1880. (Data taken from a survey of the bible collection of the American Bible Society, New York)

TABLE 3

	1777–90	1791–1800	1801–10	1811–20	1821–30	1831–40	1841–50	1851–60	1861–70	1871–80
Leather	3	16	54	122	185	210	267	268	196	124
Cloth	0	0	1	0	3	16	19	54	74	49
Other/Sheets/ Boards	0	2	1	4	7	0	4	2	4	4
Rebound	0	1	9	27	27	31	26	42	20	3
Total Minus Rebound	3	18	56	126	195	226	290	324	274	177
Percentage Leather	100%	89%	96%	97%	95%	93%	92%	83%	72%	70%
Percentage Cloth	0%	0%	2%	0%	1%	7%	7%	16%	27%	28%
Percentage Other	0%	11%	2%	3%	4%	0%	1%	1%	1%	2%

New Translations of the English Bible in
the United States, 1808-1880

The importance of denominational alignment for translators differed. For instance, Noah Webster was careful not to make any sectarian overtures in his translation because he wanted it to enjoy the widest readership possible, while Spencer Cone felt it absolutely necessary to make his version reflect his Baptist views. When known, the denominational affiliations of American translators are listed below:

TABLE 4

Year	Translator	Denomination	Scripture
1808	Charles Thomson	non-aligned	Bible
1815	Charles Thomson	non-aligned	Gospels
1823	Abner Kneeland	Universalist	N.T.
1826	Alexander Campbell	Baptist/Disciple	N.T.
1827	George R. Noyes	Unitarian	Job
1828	John Gorham Palfrey	Unitarian	N.T.
1830	Egbert Benson		Epistles
1833	Noah Webster	Episcopal	Bible
1833	Rodolphus Dickinson	Episcopal	N.T.
1833–37	George R. Noyes	Unitarian	Prophets
1842	A. C. Kendrick	Baptist	Bible
1845	Isaac Leeser	Jewish	O.T.
1848	Jonathan Morgan	Universalist	N.T.
1849	Nathan Whiting	Adventist	N.T.
1849	Francis Patrick Kenrick	Catholic	Gospels
1850	Spencer Cone & Wm. Wyckoff	Baptist	N.T.
1851	James Murdock	Congregational	N.T.
1851	Francis Patrick Kenrick	Catholic	Acts, Epistles, Apocalypse
1852	Hezekiah Woodruff		N.T.
1855	Andrews Norton	Unitarian	Gospels
1857	Francis Patrick Kenrick	Catholic	Psalms, Wisdom Lit.

TABLE 4 (*continued*)

Year	Translator	Denomination	Scripture
1858	Leicester Sawyer	Unitarian	N.T.
1859	Francis Patrick Kenrick	Catholic	Job, Prophets
1860	Francis Patrick Kenrick	Catholic	Pentateuch, Historical books
1861	Leicester Sawyer	Unitarian	Prophets
1861	Leonard Thorn		N.T.
1862–64	American Bible Union	Baptist et al.	Partial N.T.
1864	Leicester Sawyer	Christian Rationalist	Daniel, Apocrypha
1864	H. T. Anderson	Disciple of Christ	N.T.
1865	Benjamin Wilson		N.T.
1867	Joseph Smith Jr.	Mormon	Bible
1868	George R. Noyes	Unitarian	N.T.
1869	Nathaniel S. Folsom	Unitarian	Gospels
1876	Julia E. Smith		Bible
1878	John B. Rotherham	Wesleyan/Baptist/ Disciple of Christ	N.T.

Production of Catholic Bibles in English
in the United States, 1790-1880

Figure 51 below gives some idea of the growth of Catholic bible production, but the number of editions listed gives little indication of the actual number of volumes produced.

After significant growth in the number of publishers producing Catholic bibles in the 1850s and the number of editions produced, an expected consolidation of Catholic bible production took place after the Civil War.[1] From the many publishers who had entered the Bible market, by the 1860s certain firms had established themselves as strong enough to remain.

From the data available for the period after the Civil War, two informative trends emerge: First, Catholic bible production was highly centralized, spreading to only as many as six cities in this period (see Figure 52). The cities that produced at least one copy of the Catholic scriptures in-

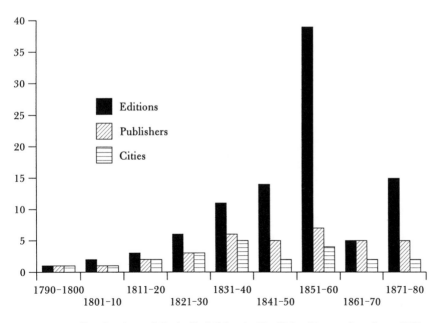

FIGURE 51. Production of Catholic bibles in English. (Data taken from Hills, *The English Bible*, pp. 4-293)

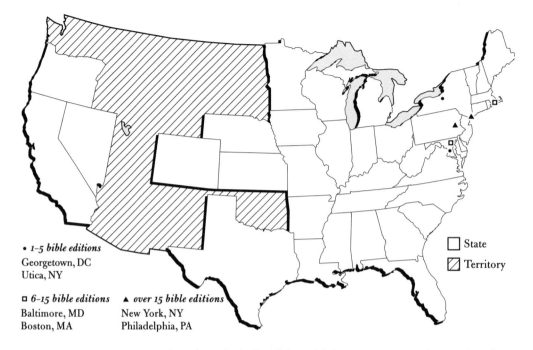

FIGURE 52. American Catholic bible publishers, 1790–1880. (Data taken from Hills, *The English Bible*, pp. 4–293)

clude New York (sixty editions), Philadelphia (seventeen editions), Baltimore (ten editions), Boston (seven editions), Utica (three editions) and Georgetown (one edition).

At first, Philadelphia dominated the field of Catholic bible production, but by the 1870s, New York became dominant. Baltimore, with its long history of Catholicism, produced the third-largest number of Catholic bible editions prior to 1880.

If one counts the various evolution of firms (such as Edward Dunigan to Edw. Dunigan and Brother) as one entity, there were only twenty-one publishers who produced Catholic bibles in this period. The most dominant firm in the period was Edward Dunigan (and Brother) of New York City who produced twenty-seven editions between 1844 and 1862. The Dunigans were so successful that Edward followed in the footsteps of Mathew Carey and hired out his bible production to another printer.[2]

Next to Edw. Dunigan and Brother, the most prolific firm was that of D. J. Sadlier, which produced twenty-one editions between 1842 and 1880 in both Boston and New York City. One other significant publisher of the period was Eugene Cummiskey of Philadelphia who dominated the early period of Catholic bible production. Cummiskey produced ten editions in Philadelphia between 1824 and 1858.

Reference Material

Notes

PREFACE

1. For a sampling of scholarship that denominates early Americans as such, see Bozeman, *To Live Ancient Lives*, p. 13; Gaer and Siegel, *The Puritan Heritage*; Baird, *Religion in America*, p. 59; and Stein, "America's Bibles," p. 184.

2. "Popular Reasons for Studying the Scriptures," p. 3.

3. For a concise overview of the importance of the Bible in antebellum America, see Barlow, *Mormons and the Bible*, pp. 3–10.

4. Everett, *Orations and Speeches*, 2:664. Hirsch, *The Dictionary of Cultural Literacy*, pp. 1–26. See also Bloom, *The Closing of the American Mind*, pp. 56–57.

5. Cremin, *American Education: The Colonial Experience*, pp. 40–41, 185, 191, 362; Cremin, *American Education: The National Experience*, pp. 61–62, 66–67; Kaestle, *Pillars of the Republic*, pp. 51, 98; Warner, *The Letters of the Republic*, p. 14; Carter, *A Culture of Disbelief*, p. 11.

6. Hills, *The English Bible*, pp. 109–164; Carvajal, "The Bible," pp. D1, D10.

7. Noll, "Review Essay," p. 496.

8. Wacker, "The Demise of Biblical Civilization," in Hatch and Noll, *The Bible in America*, p. 122. Although bible sales have recently slackened, it is far too early to determine whether this will be a long-term trend.

9. Wacker, "The Demise of Biblical Civilization," in Hatch and Noll, *The Bible in America*, p. 124.

10. "The Book of Books," p. 325; "Popular Reasons," p. 3. See also Zboray and Zboray, "Books, Reading," p. 587.

11. The phrase "classic preeminence" is found in "Bible Revision," p. 185; see also "The Book of Books," p. 325; "Popular Reasons," p. 3.

12. Goodwin, "The Bible as a Book of Education," p. 252. See also Cmiel, *Democratic Eloquence*, p. 223.

13. The early 1980s saw the beginning of a new wave of scholarship on the Bible's place in American culture. Whereas scholars such as John Wright, Paris Marion Simms, E. B. O'Callaghan, and Margaret Hills paid attention to the bibliographic characteristics of the Bible, this new wave focused on the Bible as an agent of influence. Prominent among this scholarship stands a six-volume project (published between 1982 and 1988) sponsored by the Centennial Publications Program of the Society of Biblical Literature entitled "The Bible in American Culture Series," a series whose task is to "search out the way in which the Bible permeates, subtly or powerfully, the very fabric of life within the United States" (Frerichs, *The Bible and Bibles in America*, p. ix).

Simultaneous with the appearance of the first volume of this series in 1982, the religious historians Nathan Hatch and Mark Noll edited a collection of essays entitled *The Bible in America: Essays in Cultural History*. The best overview of recent scholarship on the Bible in America is Noll, "Review Essay," pp. 493–509.

14. Notable exceptions to a monolithic view of the Bible in American history include Stout, "Word and Order in Colonial New England," and Fogarty, "The Quest for a Catholic Vernacular Bible in America," in Hatch and Noll, *The Bible in America*, pp. 19–38, 163–180; and McDannell, *Material Christianity*, pp. 67–102.

15. Figures taken from Hills, *The English Bible*, pp. 1–293.

16. "Popular Reasons," p. 3.

17. Finke, Roger, and Rodney Stark, *The Churching of America*, p. 113.

18. Hatch and Noll, *The Bible in America*, p. 4.

19. Alden, "The Bible as Printed Word," in Frerichs, *The Bible and Bibles in America*, p. 14.

20. As early as 1835, Americans could obtain bible editions in almost a dozen different languages, and new efforts were being made to translate the Bible in the language of several Native American tribes (Dwight, *The Centennial History*, 1:131).

21. This percentage is derived from the editions listed in Hills, *The English Bible*, pp. 1–293. I define the Northeast region of the United States as including Connecticut, Delaware, Maine, Maryland, Massachusetts, New Hampshire, New Jersey, New York, Pennsylvania, Rhode Island, and Vermont.

22. For a glancing reference to bible importation in this period, see Hills, "American Bible Society Historical Essay #18," 3:36, American Bible Society Archives.

CHAPTER 1 Production

1. North, "American Bible Society Historical Essay #201," 1: 68, letter from Elias Boudinot to Rev. John B. Romeyn, Burlington, June 5, 1816, American Bible Society Archives.

2. Madison, Hamilton, and Jay,. *The Federalist Papers*, p. 343.

3. Hall, *The Organization of American Culture*, pp. 79–94, 125–150. Concerning the Federalist tensions with Jeffersonian thinking, see Fischer, *The Revolution of American Conservatism*; Wood, *The Radicalism of the American Revolution*, pp. 305–369; Elkins and McKitrick, *The Age of Federalism*, pp. 643–754; Quist, "Slaveholding Operatives," p. 481.

4. North, "American Bible Society Historical Essay #201," 1:46–47, letter from Elias Boudinot to William Jay, Burlington, April 4, 1816, American Bible Society Archives.

5. Warner, *The Letters of the Republic*; Bailyn, *The Ideological Origins*; Berger, *Broadsides & Bayonets*; Smith, *Printers and Press Freedom*; Ferguson, *The American Enlightenment*.

6. Cmiel, *Democratic Eloquence*, p. 50.

7. Keane, *Tom Paine*, pp. 307–308, 331–333, 389–399.

8. Paine, *Collected Writings*, p. 677.

9. Boudinot, *The Age of Revelation*, p. xx.

10. For the publishing history and cultural impact of Paine's *The Age of Reason*, see Keane, *Tom Paine*, pp. 389–399.

11. For a wonderful treatment of the appearance of the American Bible Society, see Wosh, *Spreading the Word*, pp. 1–16.

12. Strickland, *History of the American Bible Society*, pp. 28–29.

13. North, "American Bible Society Historical Essay #201," 1:32, Elias Boudinot to William Jay, Burlington, April 4, 1816; 1:46, Elias Boudinot to Joshua M. Wallace, May 3, 1816; 1:72, Elias Boudinot to John B. Romyen, Burlington, July 5, 1816; Boudinot, *A Star in the West*, p. 298, American Bible Society Archives.

14. Goodrich, *Recollections of a Lifetime*, p. 757.

15. *New York Daily Times*, Sept. 28, 1855; Bailyn, *The Ideological Origins*, p. 1; Hudson, *Journalism in the United States*, p. 771; Hatch, "Elias Smith," in Joyce, *Printing and Society*, pp. 250–251.

16. Zboray, *A Fictive People*, pp. 3–11, 213.

17. Gaskell, *A New Introduction*, p. 253.

18. Wroth, *The Colonial Printer*, p. 93.

19. Hamilton, *The Country Printer*, p. 79.

20. Thomas, *The History of Printing*, p. 33; Gaskell, *A New Introduction*, pp. 207–213; Steinberg, *Five Hundred Years of Printing*, p. 201.

21. Silver, *The American Printer*, p. 91; Zboray, *A Fictive People*, p. 10.

22. *American Dictionary of Printing*, p. 208.

23. Nord, "The Evangelical Origins," pp. 11–12.

24. Nord, "The Evangelical Origins," p. 12; Zboray, *A Fictive People*, p. 11. For an excellent treatment of the changing nature of the papermaking industry in the United States, see McGaw, *Most Wonderful Machine*.

25. For discussions of this centralization, see Zboray, *A Fictive People*, pp. 6–9; Wosh, *Spreading the Word*, pp. 7–34.

26. French, *Bookbinding in Early America*, p. 56.

27. Sellers, *The Market Revolution*, p. 370.

28. Gaskell, *A New Introduction*, pp. 231–249.

29. Zboray, *A Fictive People*, p. 11; Groves, "Judging Literary Books by Their Covers," in Moylan and Stiles, *Reading Books*, pp. 75–100.

30. For the most complete discussion of transportation in the antebellum period, see Taylor, *The Transportation Revolution*. See also Dilts, *The Great Road*.

31. Sheehan, *This Was Publishing*, pp. 144–168, 190–195, 240–244.

32. Zboray, *A Fictive People*, 11–12. See also Sheehan, *This Was Publishing*, p. 217; *Dictionary of Literary Biography*, vol. 49, pt. 2, pp. 591–652. For an extended discussion of cheaper fiction in this period, see Denning, *Mechanic Accents*, pp. 9–46.

33. For a thoughtful discussion of the growth and influence of libraries in early nineteenth-century America, see Yeatman, "Literary Culture and the Role of Libraries," pp. 345–367. See also Davidson, *Revolution and the Word*, pp. 27–29.

34. Exman, *The Brothers Harper*, pp. 383–387.

35. Zboray, *A Fictive People*, pp. 196–201; Soltow and Stevens, *The Rise of Literacy*, 53, 56, 155–176, 189; Vinovskis and Bernard, "Beyond Catharine Beecher," p. 863; Isaac, *The Transformation of Virginia*, p. 122. If the northern population is considered as a whole, taking into account especially the high rate of illiterate immigrants and poorly educated African Americans who increasingly populated this region, estimates of literacy can drop down to 75–80 percent (Folger and Nam, *Education of the American Population*, pp. 112–113). Soltow and Stevens place the illiteracy rate for nonwhites in the early nineteenth century at 75 percent (*The Rise of Literacy*, p. 51). Janet Cornelius puts the literacy rate for African Americans in the antebellum South at around 10 percent (Cornelius, *When I Can Read My Title Clear*, pp. 8–9).

36. Smith, *American Reading Instruction*, pp. 10–35; Lockridge, *Literacy in Colonial New England*, pp. 4–5; and Hall, *Worlds of Wonder*, p. 18.

37. Cremin, *American Education: The Colonial Experience*, p. 181.

38. Soltow and Stevens, *The Rise of Literacy*, p. 55.

39. Boylan, *Sunday School*, pp. 22–59.

40. Perhaps the best discussion of the connection between reading and religion in the antebellum period is found in Nord, "Religious Reading and Readers in Antebellum America," pp. 241–272. See also Moorhead, "The Millennium and the Media," and Nord, "Systematic Benevolence," in Sweet, *Communication & Change*, pp. 216–269.

41. Smith, *Printers and Press Freedom*; Schudson, *Discovering the News*, pp. 12–60.

42. De Witt Clinton, Message to the New York Legislature, 1826, in Welter, *American Writings on Popular Education*, p. 24.

43. Soltow and Stevens, *The Rise of Literacy*, pp. 96–114. For discussions of gender, education, and republican ideology in this period, see Linda Kerber, *Women of the Republic*, p. 229; and Gilmore, *Reading Becomes a Necessity of Life*, p. 42.

44. For an excellent treatment of the rise of common schools in this period, see Kaestle, *Pillars of the Republic*. See also Cremin, *American Education: The National Experience*, pp. 103–245.

45. Gilmore, *Reading Becomes a Necessity of Life*, pp. 127–128. See also Soltow and Stevens, *The Rise of Literacy*, p. 25.

46. Blumin, *The Emergence of the Middle Class*, p. 71.

47. Brown, "From Cohesion to Competition," in Joyce, *Printing and Society*, pp. 304–305.

48. Harry Stout points out that in colonial America a minister's prestige and position were often reflected in the size of his library. Stout, *New England Soul*, p. 32. See also Brown, *Knowledge Is Power*, p. 73.

49. For an excellent discussion concerning the moral and genteel connotations of various types of reading material before the Civil War, see Lehuu, "Changes in the Word," pp. xi–xiii, 207–281.

50. The connection between the classics and the wealthier, more educated

segments of society is noted by several scholars. See Isaac, *The Transformation of Virginia*, p. 246; Brown, *Knowledge Is Power*, pp. 47, 89; and Soltow and Stevens, *The Rise of Literacy*, pp. 50, 79, 87–88.

51. Hart, *The Popular Book*, p. 88. See also Kasson, *Rudeness and Civility*, pp. 34–69. Numerous literary scholars and historians have argued that the emulation of genteel behavior did not stop with advice manuals, but reached into the fiction of the day as well. Sentimental novels, for instance, not only allowed flights of the imagination, but also taught proper behaviors and reinforced various genteel values. See Bushman, *The Refinement of America*, pp. 280–312, and Tompkins, *Sensational Designs*, pp. 122–146.

52. Kasson, *Rudeness and Civility*, p. 43.

53. For good overviews of American reading tastes during this period and the movement of reading toward a more recreational activity, see Hart, *The Popular Book*, pp. 3–125, and Reynolds, *Beneath the American Renaissance*.

54. Clark, "The Diary of an Apprentice Cabinetmaker," p. 316.

55. Journal of Rebecca Amory Lowell, vol. 4, 1830, Rebecca Loring Lowell Papers, Massachusetts Historical Society.

56. As quoted in Zboray and Zboray, "Books, Reading, and the World of Goods," p. 587.

57. *Annual Reports*, 1830, pp. 530–531.

58. The years for the other General Supplies were: second, 1856–1860; third, 1866–1870; and fourth, 1882–1890. For treatments of the American Bible Society's first General Supply, see Nord, "The Evangelical Origins," pp. 18–21; Strickland, *History of the American Bible Society*, pp. 114–116; Wosh, *Spreading the Word*, p. 118.

59. For thoughts on the moral efficacy of bible distribution, see *Annual Reports*, 1830, p. 531; population figure as given in American Bible Society, Board of Managers Minutes, March 27, 1856, American Bible Society Archives.

60. The entire petition is reprinted in Gaines, "The Continental Congress Considers the Publication of a Bible," pp. 275–276.

61. Gaines, "The Continental Congress Considers the Publication of a Bible," p. 280.

62. McColloch, "Additional Memoranda," p. 105.

63. There is some dispute on whether or not Aitken's New Testament was the first bible edition printed in America. Isaiah Thomas notes that the first English Bible in America was produced by the firm of Kneeland and Green principally for Daniel Henchman. Because it was produced outside of the royal copyright, it was carried through the press in secret and printed with a fake London imprint on its title page (*The History of Printing in America*, pp. 103, 121). The scholarship on this particular edition of the Bible is vexed since no copy has ever been located. See Lydenberg, "The Problem of the Pre-1776 Bible," pp. 183–194.

64. Hills, *The English Bible*, pp. 1–2.

65. Holmgren, "A 'Pious and Laudable Undertaking,'" p. 17.

66. Maser, "The Day America Needed Bibles," p. 142. For a picture of an ornamented edition, see Wroth, *The Colonial Printer*, p. 212.

67. For a longer discussion of distribution practices common to colonial print-ers, see Reilly, "The Wages of Piety," in Joyce, *Printing and Society*, pp. 83–131.

68. Aitken Account Book, Library Company of Philadelphia, entries for the years 1782–1785. One good example of the trouble Aitken had selling his bible appears in a 1782 entry, where he notes of the 242 bibles he had sent to a Mr. Wm. Hutchinson, 202 of them had been returned (Aitken Account Book, p. 377).

69. For a discussion of how publishers banded together to produce bibles, see Appendix 1.

70. Holmgren, "A 'Pious and Laudable Undertaking,'" p. 17.

71. For all of Mathew Carey's importance, little scholarship has been done on him. The two largest biographical treatments of him include Bradsher, *Mathew Carey*, and Green, *Mathew Carey*. For information on Carey's firm after he turned it over to his son and son-in-law in 1817, see Kaser, *Messrs. Carey & Lea of Philadelphia*.

72. Clarkin, *Mathew Carey*, p. 9. Eventually, he would publish two more edi-tions of the complete Douay Bible, both in 1805.

73. For the number of Carey editions in this period, see Hills, *The English Bible in America*, pp. 15–77. For further comment on Carey's success in, and commitment to, the American Bible market, see Green, *Mathew Carey*, pp. 18–20.

74. Skeel, *Mason Locke Weems*, 2:7–8, April 1, 1796. Emily Ellsworth Skeel published a three-volume set that serves as the standard primary document source on Mason Weems. Other helpful works on Weems include Wills, "Mason Weems, Bibliopolist," pp. 66–69; Zboray, *A Fictive People*, pp. 37–54; Leary, *The Book-Peddling Parson*; and Green, *Mathew Carey*, pp. 10–17. For letters bear-ing on Weems's role in interesting Carey in bible publishing, see Skeel, *Mason Locke Weems*, 3:210, December 5, 1801; 3:359, January 28, 1825. For a letter bear-ing on Carey hiring Weems, see Skeel, *Mason Locke Weems*, 2:7–8, April 1, 1796.

75. Skeel, *Mason Locke Weems*, 2:xiii.

76. Skeel, *Mason Locke Weems*, 2:109, November 19, 1798.

77. Skeel, *Mason Locke Weems*, 2:139–140, August 22, 1800.

78. Skeel, *Mason Locke Weems*, 2:137, August 13, 1800.

79. Skeel, *Mason Locke Weems*, 2:147, October 20, 1800.

80. Skeel, *Mason Locke Weems*, 2:143, September 15, 1800; Skeel, *Mason Locke Weems*, 2:153, November 27, 1800.

81. Skeel, *Mason Locke Weems*, 2:151, November 15, 1800.

82. Skeel, *Mason Locke Weems*, 2:156–159, December 11, 1800, December 18, 1800.

83. Green, *Mathew Carey*, p. 19.

84. Skeel, *Mason Locke Weems*, 2:190, May 10, 1801.

85. Green, "From Printer to Publisher," p. 30.

86. Skeel, *Mason Locke Weems*, 2:206, November 27, 1801.

87. Skeel, *Mason Locke Weems*, 3:75, July 19, 1812; Skeel, *Mason Locke Weems*, 3:148, January 6, 1816.

88. Skeel, *Mason Locke Weems*, 2:228, February 10, 1802.

89. Skeel, *Mason Locke Weems*, 3:148, January 6, 1816.

90. Carey, *Plans and Terms*, pp. 3–7.

91. Skeel, *Mason Locke Weems*, 2:200, Sept. 28, 1801.

92. Skeel, *Mason Locke Weems*, 2:204, November 25, 1801.

93. Skeel, *Mason Locke Weems*, 3:251, November 1, 1802.

94. Skeel, *Mason Locke Weems*, 2:206–7, November 27, 1801.

95. Skeel, *Mason Locke Weems*, 2:207, December 5, 1801.

96. Skeel, *Mason Locke Weems*, 3:54, December 18, 1811.

97. For the extreme profitability of Carey's 1801 quarto bible, see Green, "From Printer to Publisher," p. 40.

98. Carey, *Plans and Terms*.

99. Carey, *Plans and Terms*, p. 3.

100. Carey, *Plans and Terms*, pp. 3–8.

101. Dwight, *The Centennial History*, p. 8. The British and Foreign Bible Society, the inspiration and model for the many bible societies that were founded in the United States in the first twenty years of the nineteenth century, was founded in 1804.

102. For Mathew Carey's involvement with the Philadelphia Bible Society, see *The First Report of the Bible Society Established at Philadelphia*, p. 30; and *The Second Report of the Bible Society Established at Philadelphia*, p. 33. The Philadelphia Bible Society kept ordering bibles from Carey through 1812 until it could get its own printing operation in place. See *The Third Report of the Bible Society Established at Philadelphia*, pp. 7, 18; *The Fifth Report of the Bible Society Established at Philadelphia*, p. 11; *The Sixth Report of the Bible Society Established at Philadelphia*, p. 13.

103. Carey was still a major presence in the American bible market even after the establishment of bible societies such as the one in Philadelphia, evidenced by another circular Carey distributed in 1814 listing the contents of his "Bible Warehouse." The circular was titled "To the Booksellers throughout the United States: Bible Warehouse." This one-page advertisement continues to list terms of credit and a vast array of bibles for sale ranging in price from $1.25 to $12.50.

It is interesting to note that Carey did not publish all the bibles he advertised in his warehouse. He carried several pocket bibles printed by fellow Philadelphian William Woodward. In his sales strategy of offering customers the widest range of bibles possible, Carey looked to acquire bible editions produced by other publishers.

104. Skeel, *Mason Locke Weems*, 3:117, February 16, 1815.

105. Hills, *The English Bible*, p. 37. Kubler ignores this bible edition as the first stereotyped book produced in America in favor of John Watts's "The Larger Catechism" (1813). Kubler may have made this choice because Watts produced his plates in the United States, while the first edition of the Bible to be printed from stereotype plates was printed from plates that had been imported from England (Kubler, *A New History*, p. 148).

106. Hills, *The English Bible*, p. 46.

107. According to Hills's bibliography (pp. 1–293), the figures for bibles and testaments that positioned themselves on their title pages as stereotype editions:

Years	Number of bibles and testaments
1811–20	54
1821–30	58
1831–40	99
1841–50	28
1851–60	2
1861–70	6
1871–80	2

It is difficult to know exactly what drew publishers to advertise so avidly their bibles as stereotyped editions, but it was most likely a combination of the selling point of something new coupled with the fact that stereotyped editions had the capability of being more error-free than a hand-set edition. By the 1850s, advertising the stereotyped status of a bible edition significantly decreased, but this trend should not be taken to mean a decline in bible stereotyping. Probably, just the reverse was happening: the increasingly common practice of stereotyping no longer made it a sales point for new bible editions.

108. "Constitution," in *Annual Reports*, p. 10.

109. "To the People of the United States," in *Annual Reports*, p. 14.

110. In 1817, the Society lent plates to the Kentucky Bible Society located in Lexington (Hills, *The English Bible*, p. 50). The quality of the Kentucky imprints was low, and the Society was worried that it would not be able to control the quality of the bible production if it did not centralize its printing practices (Board of Managers Minutes, July 15, 1819). See also Board of Managers Minutes, February 1, 1821.

111. Hills, *The English Bible*, pp. 50–51. See also Standing Committee Minutes, March 5, 1817, American Bible Society Archives.

112. "An Appeal to the Christians of America," in *Annual Reports*, p. 8.

113. Exman, *The Brothers Harper*, p. 20.

114. Perhaps the best overview of the American Bible Society's penchant for new technology is found in Nord, "The Evangelical Origins," pp. 7–13. Fanshaw would serve as the Society's printer from 1817 to 1845 (with the exception of a five-year hiatus in the 1820s when he worked for the American Tract Society), playing a key role in the American Bible Society's early forays in bible printing. Operating as an independent printer, Fanshaw rented space from the Bible Society, owned much of his own equipment, and devoted almost all his time and resources to the printing demands of the American Bible Society. Not until 1845 would the Society actually take over its own printing processes by releasing Fanshaw (Hills, "American Bible Society Historical Essay #18," 3:65–76A).

115. American Bible Society Archives, *Annual Reports*, p. 24; Hills, "American Bible Society Historical Essay #18," 2:60, American Bible Society Archives.

116. Hills, "American Bible Society Historical Essay #18," 3:32, American Bible Society Archives. See also the detailed fourteen-page report of Messrs. Woolley, Peet, and Walsh on American Bible Society binding practices, Committee on Publications, January 28, 1848, American Bible Society Archives.

117. For an example of the early practice of distributing bibles in sheets, see Board of Managers Minutes, March 5, 1817, American Bible Society Archives. For quality control issues, see Board of Managers Minutes, September 3, 1818; September 25, 1818; and October 1, 1818, American Bible Society Archives.

118. Standing Committee Minutes, March 3, 1818, and March 10, 1818, American Bible Society Archives.

119. Standing Committee Minutes, September 25, 1818, American Bible Society Archives. As Margaret Hills summarizes the report of Woolley, Peet, and Walsh: "The beginnings of the Society's contracts with Mr. Starr [the person in charge of ABS binding for three decades] from early 1818 on had led to the increase in 'hands' from 15 in 1818 to 230 in 1848; the amount of binding in the first year of the Society was $1,157 and for the present year [1848] nearly $100,000" ("American Bible Society Historical Essay #18," 3:32, American Bible Society Archives).

120. American Bible Society, *Second Annual Report*, 1818, Appendix, p. 57.

121. Dwight, *The Centennial History*, p. 164.

122. For an excellent discussion of how the loosely formed auxiliary and agent program eventually developed into a highly organized and administrated professional bureaucracy, see Wosh, *Spreading the Word*, pp. 62–88, 175–199.

123. *Annual Reports*, p. 10.

124. Board of Managers Minutes, January 15, 1817, American Bible Society Archives. This 5 percent addition to the cost of the book remained remarkably stable throughout this period with only slight increases charged in the 1830s for more expensive leather-bound bibles in order to help keep down the price of plainer books (Hills, "American Bible Society Historical Essay #18," 3:2, American Bible Society Archives).

125. Board of Managers Minutes, April 2, 1829, 4:90–91, American Bible Society Archives.

126. Nord, "The Evangelical Origins," p. 18.

127. The most extensive discussion of the charitable giving practices of the American Bible Society is found in Nord, "Free Books."

128. Board of Managers Minutes, October 7, 1880, American Bible Society Archives.

129. North and Compagno, "American Bible Society Historical Essay #14, Part VI-B-5," pp. 23–24, American Bible Society Archives.

130. North and Compagno, "American Bible Society Historical Essay #14, Part VI-B-5," p. 27, American Bible Society Archives.

131. North and Compagno, "American Bible Society Historical Essay #14, Part VI-B-5," pp. 45–46, American Bible Society Archives.

132. North and Compagno, "American Bible Society Historical Essay #14, Part VI-B-5," p. B-7-6, American Bible Society Archives.

133. *American Bible Society. Extracts of Correspondence, &c. New Series,* June 1830, p. 355 (hereafter cited as *Extracts*). Chauncy Goodrich (1790–1860) is actually misnamed in the *Extracts* as "Professor Goodspeed."

134. *Extracts,* June 1830, p. 355.

135. A Member, *An Expose.* See also Wosh, *Spreading the Word,* pp. 125–126.

136. A Member, *An Expose,* pp. 17–18.

137. A Member, *An Expose,* p. 5.

138. A Member, *An Expose,* p. 21.

139. See Appendix 3 for price data on the cheapest scripture editions available in nineteenth-century America.

140. For discussions of book pricing during this period, see Zboray, *A Fictive People,* pp. 11–12; Charvat, *The Profession of Authorship,* pp. 44–45, 75, 285–286; Barnes, *Authors, Publishers, and Politicians,* p. 4; Winship, *Ticknor and Fields,* p. 19.

141. Letter from Thomas K. Whitearsh to Messrs. G. & C. Merriam, Chicago, November 29, 1844, G. & C. Merriam Collection, American Antiquarian Society, Worcester, Mass.

142. I define illustrated bibles here as any bible containing maps, frontispieces, or pictures. These percentage figures—as the percentages for the bible editions containing major commentaries—are derived from Hills, *The English Bible,* 1–293.

143. Major commentary is defined here as bibles that included the notes of scholars such as Clarke, Scott, Henry, Bagster, or Canne.

144. For evidence of this trend, see Hills, *The English Bible,* pp. 207–293.

CHAPTER 2 Packaging

1. Quincy, *Memoir of the Life,* p. 52.

2. Quincy, *Memoir of the Life,* p. 52.

3. Quincy, *Memoir of the Life,* p. 51.

4. For descriptions of Washington's inauguration, see *The American Museum,* May 1789, 5:505; Bowen, *The History of the Centennial Celebration,* pp. 30–54; *Presidential Inaugural Bibles,* pp. 9–12; Wright, *Historical Bibles in America,* 177–179; and Abbot, *The Papers of George Washington,* pp. 152–158.

5. This practice was especially common for pulpit bibles and dates back at least to the mid-sixteenth century in America. Cressy, "Books as Totems," p. 92.

6. For an overview of the role of the Bible in the taking of oaths, see *Presidential Inaugural Bibles,* p. 6.

7. Cressy, "Books as Totems," p. 98. See also Enoch Lewis, *A Dissertation on Oaths.*

8. Cressy, "Books as Totems," p. 101.

9. For a glimpse of widespread practice of randomly picking scripture verses, see Henry, *Letters to an Anxious Inquirer,* pp. 205–206.

10. McDannell, *Material Christianity,* p. 68.

11. Stoddard, "Morphology and the Book," p. 4. For additional thoughts on the elasticity of the term "reading," see Mukerji and Schudson, *Rethinking Popular Culture*, p. 11.

12. For examples of how people, even nonreaders, "read" bibles as purely physical objects in the antebellum period, see Nord, "Religious Reading and Readers," p. 260.

13. Stout, *New England Soul*, p. 32; Brown, *Knowledge Is Power*, pp. 97–99; Bushman, *The Refinement of America*, p. 282.

14. Zboray, *A Fictive People*, p. 143. Walker, *The Art of Book-Binding*, pp. 21–25.

15. Walker, *The Art of Book-Binding*, pp. 60–61. See also Wolf, *From Gothic Windows to Peacocks*, p. 17.

16. Zboray, *A Fictive People*, p. 153.

17. Howsam, *Cheap Bibles*, p. 131.

18. Gaskell, *A New Introduction*, pp. 231–249.

19. The American Bible Society's library includes an unmatched collection of English bibles produced in America before 1880. Added to this advantage is the fact that the American Bible Society actively collected various editions of the Bible as they were released. This point is particularly important in considering leather-bound books, which have greater durability than their cloth counterparts. One might be able to argue that a larger number of leather bibles exist in this collection simply because they were able to stand the test of time. The American Bible Society's policy of collecting bibles as they were released mitigates this objection. Thus, this collection promises a more accurate representation of the Bible market as it evolved, rather than how it was later preserved.

20. I do not mean to suggest here that bibles were the only books still bound in leather by the 1850s. The works of classical authors and expensive editions of more contemporary works continued to enjoy leather bindings throughout the nineteenth century.

21. See Appendix 4.

22. Wolf, *From Gothic Windows to Peacocks*, p. 11.

23. Wolf, *From Gothic Windows to Peacocks*, pp. 8–25.

24. The special collections of the Van Pelt Library (University of Pennsylvania, Philadelphia) holds a copy of the New Testament published by Jacob Johnson & Co., 1804, with the following inscription: "The Cover of this Book is part of the Skin of a Favourite Dog which belonged to my Brother John Wallace during my Apprenticeship, and was Bound in the Year 1804—by myself-."

25. The cultural anthropologist James Deetz has argued that a culture's religious artifacts are among the slowest to change in their production processes, appearance, and usage (Deetz, *In Small Things Forgotten*, pp. 50–51, 88). See also Binford, "Archaeology as Anthropology," pp. 217–225.

26. An additional reason for the persistence of leather in bible binding was the material's durability. Leather wore better than cloth, making it the binding of choice for publishers such as the American Bible Society, which was interested in producing bibles that would last.

27. For a discussion of the prominent display of large bibles in family parlors,

see McDannell, *The Christian Home*, pp. 83–85; McDannell, *Material Christianity*, p. 68. See also Wosh, *Spreading the Word*, p. 20.

28. Halttunen, *Confidence Men*, pp. 59–60. See also Lehuu, "Changes in the Word," pp. 134–138.

29. McDannell, *Material Christianity*, p. 98.

30. Phillips, *The Christian Home*, p. 89.

31. Beecher and Stowe, *The American Woman's Home*, pp. 456–457. See also McDannell, *The Christian Home*, p. xiii.

32. For examples of how bibles were displayed in family parlors, see Williams and Jones, *Beautiful Homes*, pp. 200–202; McDannell, *Material Christianity*, pp. 96–97. See also Grier, *Culture & Comfort*, pp. 10, 14–15.

33. The phrase "moral growth" in connection to home decoration is found in Beecher and Stowe, *The American Woman's Home*, p. 84. Phrases such as "moral sensibility," "moral growth," and "moral uplift" appear throughout the domestic advice literature of the nineteenth century (Clapper, "Thousands of Happy Children: Sentimental Chromolithographs of the 1870s and 1880s"). Clapper argues that central to the activity of home decoration in this period was the desire to create a place of moral nurture for all who entered the home.

34. Jones, "The Influence of European Ideas in Nineteenth-Century America," p. 251; Peterson, "Scottish Common Sense in America," p. 1. See also Hughes and Allen, *Illusions of Innocence*, pp. 153–154; Marsden, "Everyone One's Own Interpreter," in Hatch and Noll, *The Bible in America*, pp. 79–100; and Meyer, *The Instructed Conscience*, pp. vii–11.

35. Notable exceptions to an understanding of Scottish Common Sense's relationship to notions of sentimentality appear in Kaplan's *Sacred Tears* and, to a lesser extent, Todd's *Sensibility*.

36. Beecher, *A Treatise on Domestic Economy*, p. 36.

37. Wills, *Inventing America*, pp. 149–255; Hatch, *The Democratization of American Christianity*, p. 129.

38. Peterson, "Scottish Common Sense," 1–19. See also Sher and Smitten, *Scotland and America*.

39. Peterson, "Scottish Common Sense," pp. 20–46; Kaplan, *Sacred Tears*, pp. 20–32; McCosh, *The Scottish Philosophy*, pp. 29–36, 49–86; Norton, "From Moral Sense to Common Sense."

40. Reid, *Essays on the Intellectual Powers* in *Philosophical Works*, 1:219–338. See also Martin, *The Instructed Vision*, p. 3; Taylor, *Sources of the Self*, pp. 248–265.

41. For the phrase "moral sense" and its uses, see Reid, *Essays on the Active Powers* in *Philosophical Works*, 2:670–679, and Smith, *The Theory of Moral Sentiments* in *Adam Smith's Moral and Political Philosophy*, pp. 7–8. See also Shaftesbury, "Treatise I, 'A Letter Concerning Enthusiasm'" and "The Moralists, A Philosophical Rhapsody," in *Characteristics*, 1:5–39, 2:3–153; Hutcheson, *A Short Introduction*, pp. 1–71, and *A System of Moral Philosophy*, pp. 1–78, 100–115, 227–251.

42. Samuels, *The Culture of Sentiment*, p. 4.

43. The lack of attention paid to the connection between Scottish Common Sense philosophy and sentimentalism can be explained, in part, by an inattention

in serious scholarly works to defining the terms "sentimentalism," "sentimentality," and "sentiment." For the best historical analysis of the terms "sentiment" and "sentimentality," see Kaplan, *Sacred Tears*, pp. 11–20.

44. Beecher, *Royal Truths*, p. 25. See also McLoughlin, *The Meaning of Henry Ward Beecher*, p. 105, and Grier, *Culture and Comfort*, pp. 5–8.

45. Kerber, *Women of the Republic*, pp. 189–231, and Douglas, *The Feminization of American Culture*. See also McDannell, *Material Christianity*, p. 80.

46. Epstein, *The Politics of Domesticity*, pp. 82–83; Jensen, *Loosening the Bonds*, pp. 145–166.

47. McDannell, *The Christian Home*, pp. 77–107, 127–149.

48. Biographical material on Isaiah Thomas (1749–1831) can be found in Shipton, *Isaiah Thomas*; Thomas, *Memoir of Isaiah Thomas*; Thomas, *Three Autobiographical Fragments*; and Thomas, "The Diary of Isaiah Thomas, 1805–1828." For discussions of the influence of various strains of Enlightenment thought on notions of refinement and cultural formation, see Bushman, *The Refinement of America*, pp. 3–206; Brown, *Knowledge Is Power*, pp. 42–64.

49. Nichols, *Bibliography of Worcester*, p. viii.

50. Nichols, *Bibliography of Worcester*, p. ix.

51. The engravers included Joseph H. Seymour of Philadelphia, Amos Doolittle of New Haven, Samuel Hill, and H. Norman (Nichols, *Bibliography of Worcester*, p. 37).

52. For an overview of the technical considerations involved in producing illustrations within books, see Gaskell, *A New Introduction*, pp. 154–158; Gascoigne, *How to Identify Prints*, 12c. For a good—if broad—overview of the history of illustrated books, see Bland, *A History of Book Illustration*. For the most complete listing of illustrations in early American Bibles, see Slee, "A Summary of the English Editions."

53. For comments on the special nature of paper used for copperplate illustrations, see E. T. Andrews to Isaiah Thomas, Boston, June 15 and July 9, 1791, Isaiah Thomas Papers, Box 1, Folder 9, American Antiquarian Society.

54. Park, *The Idea of Rococo*, p. 42. See also Heckscher, *American Rococo*, p. 4. Along with Park's and Heckshcher's works, good treatments of the rococo style in the eighteenth and nineteenth centuries include Starobinski, *Revolution in Fashion*; Zafran, *The Rococo Age*; and Levey, *Rococo to Revolution*.

55. For a good discussion of the role of feeling in the midst of eighteenth-century Enlightenment thought, see Schama, *Citizens*, pp. 145–162.

56. For an informative treatment of breasts in seventeenth- and eighteenth-century politics, art, and literature, see Yalom, *A History of the Breast*, pp. 105–123, and Hart and Stevenson, *Heaven and the Flesh*, pp. 74–91. See also Zafran, *The Rococo Age*, p. 12.

57. E. T. Andrews to Isaiah Thomas, Boston, May 26, 1791, Isaiah Thomas Papers, Box 1, Folder 9, American Antiquarian Society.

58. Davis, "Printing and the People," in Mukerji and Schudson, *Rethinking Popular Culture*, pp. 83–84.

59. The best recent scholarly discussions on the interplay between juxta-

posed visual and verbal texts include Mitchell, *Iconology*, and Miller, *Illustration*. For a pathbreaking study on popular religious imagery found both inside and outside of written texts, see Morgan, *Visual Piety*.

60. Burgess, *Old Prints*, pp. 66–79.

61. For the most comprehensive history of Brattleboro in this period, see *Annals of Brattleboro*.

62. *Annals of Brattleboro*, pp. 231–234; Tebbel, *A History of Book Publishing*, 1:455–456.

63. Hills, *The English Bible*, pp. 48, 116, 135.

64. Wilson, *Signs & Wonders*, pp. 1–43. See also Irwin, *American Hieroglyphics*.

65. Nir, *The Bible and the Image*; Shepherd, *Zealous Intruders*, pp. 1–106; Davis, *The Landscape of Belief*; and Vogel, *To See a Promised Land*, pp. 1–93.

66. This is not to say that Scottish Common Sense philosophy and its influence on American theology were entirely responsible for American Protestants' interest in the Holy Land. For example, certain strains of Protestant theology believed that the region of Palestine must first be evangelized before Christ would return. This belief led several denominations and mission organizations to send missionaries to this region, and to a demand for news about the state of such evangelizing efforts. For a fuller discussion of millennial thought and its connection to American perceptions of, and interest in, the Holy Land, see Feldman, *Dual Destinies*, pp. 1–107; Shepherd, *Zealous Intruders*, pp. 228–257; Vogel, *To See a Promised Land*, pp. 95–124; Priest, *A View of the Expected*; Parsons, L. "The Dereliction and Restoration"; and Stuart, *Sermon at the Ordination of the Rev. William G. Schauffler*.

67. Instructive discussions of the developments in nineteenth-century American biblical criticism include Grant, *A Short History of the Interpretation of the Bible*, pp. 139–164; Bozeman, *Protestants in an Age of Science*; Giltner, *Moses Stuart*, pp. 45–88; Brown, *The Rise of Biblical Criticism*; Cashdollar, *The Transformation of Theology*; Turner, *Without God, Without Creed*, pp. 143–150; Livingstone, *Darwin's Forgotten Defenders*.

68. Rowe, *History of Andover Theological Seminary*; Williams, *The Andover Liberals*, pp. 1–7; and Williams, *The Harvard Divinity School*, pp. 21–77.

69. Although her claim is impossible to prove, Naomi Shepherd has called Thomson's book the best-selling volume between Stowe's *Uncle Tom's Cabin* and Wallace's *Ben-Hur* (Shepherd, *Zealous Intruders*, p. 90). Whether this claim is accurate or not, the book's popularity is testified to by the fact that it went through eighteen printings, remaining in print for thirty years.

70. Thomson, *The Land and the Book*, 1:1.

71. Brown, *The Rise of Biblical Criticism*, pp. 111–124.

72. Robinson, *Biblical Researches*, 1:viii–xii, 251–257.

73. For an excellent introduction to the philological debates in theology in the early nineteenth century, see Gura, *The Wisdom of Words*, pp. 15–71.

74. Shepherd, *Zealous Intruders*, pp. 170–192.

75. Morris, *Freemasonry in the Holy Land*, p. 14; Hackett, *Illustrations of Scripture*, p. 73.

76. Hovenkamp, *Science and Religion*, pp. 147–164. See also Handy, *The Holy Land in American Protestant Life*, pp. 3–40; Ingraham, *An Historical Map of Palestine*; and "Palestine, a Perpetual Witness for the Bible," pp. 192–223.

77. *The English Version of the Polyglott Bible*, 1837, advertisement at the end of the volume.

78. For treatments of the nineteenth-century American interest in travel literature, see Exman, *The Brothers Harper*, p. 94; Goodrich, *Recollections of a Lifetime*, pp. 759, 762; Exman, *The House of Harper*, p. 21; and Zboray, *A Fictive People*, pp. 162–163. For comments on the absolute "avalanche of books on the Holy Land" in this period, see Shepherd, *Zealous Intruders*, pp. 78–79.

79. *The English Version of the Polyglott Bible*, 1837, advertisement at the end of the volume.

80. So popular were the illustrations of all aspects of the biblical text that Fessenden & Co. released its bible illustrations under a separate cover for fifty cents in 1836. This packet of illustrations could then be viewed separately from a bible or bound into any royal octavo bible edition (*Pictorial Illustrations of the Bible*).

81. *The English Version of the Polyglott Bible*, 1837, "A New Geographical and Historical Index," p. 14.

82. *The English Version of the Polyglott Bible*, 1837, advertisement at the end of the Bible.

83. It should be noted that Carey's bibles stand at a liminal moment in biblical cartography. While Carey included this foldout map that emphasized the narrative content of the biblical drama, he also included more "scientific" maps that would foreshadow later nineteenth-century bible editions.

84. *The English Version of the Polyglott Bible*, 1837.

85. McDannell, *Material Christianity*, pp. 87–102.

86. *Catalogue of Books Published by Harper & Brothers, 1845*, p. 13. See also O'Callagahn, *A List of Editions*, pp. 288–289.

87. Weitenkempf, "American Bible Illustration," p. 155; Exman, *The House of Harper*, p. 80; *American Dictionary of Printing*, p. 8; and Bland, *A History of Book Illustration*, p. 303.

88. Exman, *The House of Harper*, p. 24; Spann, *The New Metropolis*, p. 409.

89. Exman, *The House of Harper*, pp. 34–35. See also *American Dictionary of Printing*, pp. 157–166; and Gascoigne, *How to Identify Prints*, 33b, 72.

90. Derby, *Fifty Years Among Authors*, p. 95; O'Callaghan, *A List of Editions*, pp. 288–289.

91. Harper and Brothers Collection, Columbia University, *Contract Book* (New York: Chadwyck-Healy), Reel A1, 75–77.

92. Exman, *The House of Harper*, p. 35. For an extended discussion of Harper and Brothers advertising strategies, see Zboray, *A Fictive People*, pp. 56–68.

93. Harper and Brothers Collection, *Contract Book* (New York: Chadwyck-Healy), Reel A1, 330–331. See also Simms, *The Bible in America*, p. 266; Exman, *The House of Harper*, p. 80.

94. Copies of the *Illuminated Bible* with pictures of New York churches

on their covers can be found in the collections of the American Antiquarian Society.

95. The classic discussions of the rising importance of women in antebellum religious life are Welter, "The Feminization of American Religion," in Hartman and Banner, *Clio's Consciousness Raised*, pp. 137–157, and Douglas, *The Feminization of American Culture*, pp. 17–117. See also Hardesty, *Your Daughters Shall Prophesy*; Ginzberg, *Women and the Work of Benevolence*; James, *Women in American Religion*, pp. 89–125; Finke and Stark, *The Churching of America*, pp. 33–35; and Johnson and Wilentz, *The Kingdom of Matthias*, pp. 7, 22–24.

96. Calhoun, *A Social History of the Family*, 2:51–77; Wishy, *The Child and the Republic*, pp. 3–78; Greven, *The Protestant Temperament*, pp. 21–43, 151–191, 265–295; and Hoffert, *Private Matters*, pp. 142–192.

97. Dunn, *What Happened to Religious Education?* pp. 110–111.

98. An unbound copy of the *Illuminated Bible* in sheets is located in the Special Collections of the Columbia University Library.

99. *Illuminated Bible*, thirty-sixth installment of printed sheets, back cover.

100. The term "emotionalism" in the context of antebellum religious culture is taken from Thomas, *Revivalism and Cultural Change*, p. 67.

101. Miller, *Illustration*, pp. 67–70.

102. Although they have paid no attention to the role of pictures in the process, numerous scholars have noted a move away from logic-based argumentation in antebellum religious rhetoric and thought. Examples include Reynolds, "From Doctrine to Narrative," pp. 479–498; Douglas, *The Feminization of American Culture*, pp. 121–164; and Moore, *Selling God*, pp. 12–39. See also Billington, *The Protestant Crusade*, p. 67.

103. Hill, *Mark Twain and Elisha Bliss*, p. 5. See also Sheehan, *This Was Publishing*, pp. 189–192.

104. Sheehan, *This Was Publishing*, p. 192.

105. For a wonderful discussion of subscription publishing, see Hill, *Mark Twain and Elisha Bliss*, pp. 1–20. See also Sheehan, *This Was Publishing*, pp. 190–195; and Arbour, *Canvassing Books*, Figures 5.1 and 5.2.

106. Tebbel, *A History of Book Publishing*, 2:534.

107. Hills, *The English Bible*, p. 293.

108. The best collection of bible canvassing books is located in the private collections of Michael Zinman. See Arbour, *Canvassing Books*, pp. 34–42.

109. *The Devotional and Practical Pictorial Family Bible*, price page.

110. *The Holy Bible*, M. R. Gately & Co., 1880.

CHAPTER 3 Purity

1. Detailed treatments of this conflict include "Report of the Special Committee of Nine," the Board of Managers Minutes (Submitted January 14, 1858) 2369–2399. American Bible Society Archives (Coxe, *Apology for the Common English Bible*).

2. Bruce, *The English Bible*, pp. 108–109.

3. Board of Managers Minutes, January 14, 1858, 2368, American Bible Society Archives.

4. *The Holy Bible*, Thomas 1791 Royal quarto, pp. 3–4.

5. *The Holy Bible*, Thomas 1791 Royal quarto, p. 4.

6. Hixon, *Isaac Collins*, pp. 137–157; Hills, *The English Bible*, p. 7. For an example of the adoption of the Collins Bible as a standard of textual accuracy, see *The Holy Bible*, 1804 Carey quarto, t.p.

7. *The Holy Bible*, Carey, 1801, pp. 1–2.

8. *The Holy Bible*, Sleight, 1828, t.p.; see also *The Holy Bible*, White, Gallaher, and White, 1831; and *The Holy Bible*, Holbrook and Fessenden, 1831.

9. A representative example of this sentiment is found in James, *The Anxious Inquirer*, pp. 1–2.

10. Representative arguments surrounding a new translation of the Bible include "Revision Movement," pp. 493–519; "Bible Revision," pp. 184–210; "Dr. Curtis on a Standard English Bible," pp. 136–144; "Revision of the English Bible," pp. 144–163; "Does the Bible Need Retranslating?" pp. 15–34; Trench, *On the Authorized Version*.

11. Kingsley, "Revision of the English Bible," p. 155. See also Nord, "Religious Reading," p. 256.

12. See Appendix 5.

13. Efficacy was a common argument to prove the divine nature of the scriptures. See *Holy Bible*, Carey quarto, 1803, p. 1075.

14. Trench, *On the Authorized Version*, pp. 174–175.

15. Bruce, *The English Bible*, pp. 12–14. Wycliffe died in 1384, but the animosity toward his bible was so great that in 1428 his bones were dug from his grave and burned.

16. For a longer discussion of the emergence of English translations of the Bible, see Greenslade, *The Cambridge History*, 3:141–174; and Bruce, *The English Bible*, pp. 1–113.

17. Guppy, *A Brief Sketch*, p. 55.

18. The popularity of the Geneva Bible can be seen in the fact that 160 editions of it were produced between 1560 and 1640 (Stout, "Word and Order," in Hatch and Noll, *The Bible in America*, p. 35). See also Alden, "The Bible as Printed Word," in Frerichs, *The Bible and Bibles*, pp. 11–12.

19. As quoted in Greenslade, *The Cambridge History*, 3:164.

20. Bruce, *The English Bible*, p. 97; Stout, "Word and Order," in Hatch and Noll, *The Bible in America*, p. 21; Craig, "The Geneva Bible as a Political Document," pp. 40–49.

21. Bruce, *The English Bible*, pp. 98–99. See also *The Holy Bible*, Robert Barker 1617, "To the Reader."

22. Schaff, *A Companion*, pp. 325–330; Bruce, *The English Bible*, p. 107; Lewis, *The English Bible*, pp. 29–31.

23. Stout, "Word and Order," in Hatch and Noll, *The Bible in America*, pp. 19–26. See also Shea, "The Bible in American History," p. 135.

24. Stout, "Word and Order," in Hatch and Noll, *The Bible in America*, p. 26.

25. Early Americans did produce a new translation of a portion of the scriptures in 1640 when they published their first book, *The Psalms in Metre* (Thomas, *Printing in America*, pp. 53–54).

26. Thomson, *A Synopsis of the Four Evangelists*, p. iii. See also Rush, *Autobiography*, pp. 289–290.

27. The best scholarly biography of Charles Thomson is Schlenther, *Charles Thomson*.

28. Adams, *The Works of John Adams*, 2:358.

29. Schlenther, *Charles Thomson*, p. 194.

30. Hendricks, *Charles Thomson*, p. 173.

31. Rush, *Autobiography*, p. 290.

32. Hendricks, *Charles Thomson*, p. 170.

33. Harley, *The Life of Charles Thomson*, p. 163.

34. Harley, *The Life of Charles Thomson*, p. 168.

35. Schlenther, *Charles Thomson*, p. 210.

36. *The Philadelphia Universalist*, 1:6, 190–191.

37. See Appendix 5.

38. Although Kneeland was a Universalist, it should be remembered that Unitarianism (of which Universalism was an offshoot) was first a theological stance, then a denomination. Kneeland had a Unitarian view of Christ and morality, but differed from many of his Unitarian colleagues in his notion of eternal punishment. So, although Kneeland was a Universalist when he published his Bible in 1823, he was also closely allied with many of the Unitarians' theological concerns. For a longer discussion of the similarities and differences between Unitarians and Universalists, see Robinson, *The Unitarians and the Universalists*, pp. 9–73. See also Wright, *American Unitarianism, 1805–1865*, pp. 3–30, and Wilbur, *A History of Unitarianism*, 2:379–466.

39. Burnap, *Popular Objections to Unitarian Christianity*, pp. 51–74.

40. King and Dewey, *The New Discussion of the Trinity*, p. 51.

41. Norton, *A Statement of Reasons*, p. 40.

42. Burnap, *Popular Objections*, p. 52.

43. Burnap, *Popular Objections*, p. 53.

44. Wright, *American Unitarianism*, p. 3.

45. In 1809, the London firm of Thomas B. Wait and Company printed Belsham's *The New Testament: in an Improved Version* for sale and distribution by W. Wells of Boston. In 1820, the Massachusetts firm of Hilliard and Metcalf published Wakefield's *A Translation of the New Testament*.

46. For a wonderful treatment of the first publication of Griesbach's New Testament in the United States see Jackson, "The Two Worlds of William Wells," chapter 3, pp. 13–18.

47. Brown, *The Rise of Biblical Criticism*, p. 38.

48. The best synthesis and overview of the work and influence of Johann Griesbach (1745–1812) on biblical criticism is found in Orchard and Longstaff, *J. J. Griesbach*.

49. The "Received Text" or *Textus receptus* in the purest sense was not a single, static text but a series of different Greek editions that had begun with the work of Erasmus in 1516 and continued for the next three centuries through the work of scholars such as Calvin's coworker Theodore Beza (1519–1605). For longer discussions of the "Received Text" and Griesbach's work, see Everett, "Novem Testamentum Graece," pp. 460–486, and Palfrey, "Griesbach's New Testament," pp. 267–275.

50. Hills, *The English Bible*, p. 30.

51. Kneeland, *H KAINH ΔIAΘHKH*, p. vi.

52. Kneeland, *The Philadelphia Universalist*, 1:148.

53. Kneeland, *H KAINH ΔIAΘHKH*, I John 5:7.

54. Kneeland, *H KAINH ΔIAΘHKH*, p. ix.

55. *Report of the Arguments*, and Kneeland, *An Introduction to the Defence*.

56. Brief treatments of Kneeland's bible can be found in Simms, *The Bible in America*, pp. 139, 152–153; Frerichs, *The Bible and Bibles in America*, pp. 46–47; and Orlinsky and Bratcher, *A History of Bible Translation*, pp. 55–56.

57. Metzger, *The Text of the New Testament*, pp. 95–146.

58. Campbell, *The Sacred Writings*, 1826, pp. 6–7.

59. Griesbach as quoted in Delling, "Johann Jakob Griesbach," in Orchard, *J. J. Griesbach*, p. 10.

60. Peters, *Sprinkling the Only Mode of Baptism*, pp. 41–43.

61. Of course, depending on the denomination, there were different shadings within this baptismal spectrum. For treatments of the extensive arguments on baptism in this period, see *A Debate Between Rev. A. Campbell and Rev. N. L. Rice*; Peters, *Sprinkling the Only Mode of Baptism*; and Hibbard, *Christian Baptism*.

62. The best treatment of the emergence, different editions, and influence of Alexander Campbell's New Testament is Thomas, *Alexander Campbell*.

63. In 1851, Campbell published his most comprehensive work on baptism, a volume of over four hundred pages, titled *Christian Baptism*.

64. Kellems, *Alexander Campbell*, pp. 47–131, and Richardson, "Alexander Campbell as an Advocate of Christian Unity," in Seale, *Lectures in Honor of the Alexander Campbell*, pp. 101–126.

65. Richardson, *Memoirs of Alexander Campbell*, 2:40–41.

66. Campbell, *The Christian System*, p. 6. See also Harrell, *Quest for a Christian America*, p. 27.

67. Richardson, *Memoirs of Alexander Campbell*, 1:352.

68. Stout, *Dictionary of Christianity in America*, p. 214.

69. *The Christian Baptist*, 1823, 1:94.

70. Campbell, *The Sacred Writings*, 1828, p. vi. See also Thomas, *Alexander Campbell*, pp. 171–172.

71. *The Christian Baptist*, March 5, 1827, p. 167.

72. Richardson, *Memoirs of Alexander Campbell*, 2:144–145, and Thomas, *Alexander Campbell and His New Version*, pp. 17–43.

73. *A Debate Between Rev. A. Campbell and Rev. N. L. Rice*, p. 67.

74. Locke, *A Paraphrase and Notes on the Epistles of St. Paul.*

75. Thomas, *Alexander Campbell*, pp. 26–27, 49–52, 56–64.

76. Campbell, *The Sacred Writings*, 1828, p. xxxvii.

77. Campbell, *The Sacred Writings*, 1828, p. iii.

78. Campbell, *The Sacred Writings*, 1828, pp. iv–v. See also *A Debate Between Rev. A. Campbell and Rev. N. L. Rice*, pp. 66–67.

79. Campbell, *The Sacred Writings*, 1828, pp. 449–450. See also Thomas, *Alexander Campbell*, p. 47.

80. Noah Webster, *The Holy Bible*, p. iii.

81. *The Millennial Harbinger*, 1834, 5:150ff, 204ff, 274ff, 296ff, 350ff.

82. Campbell, *The Sacred Writings*, 1828, p. xiii.

83. *The Millennial Harbinger*, 4:576.

84. Thomas, *Alexander Campbell and His New Version*, p. 62.

85. "The Burman Translation of the Bible," 1:116–136.

86. "American Bible Society," 2:299–301. See also *First Annual Report of the American and Foreign Bible Society*, 1838, p. 52.

87. Winter and Winter, *The Claims of the American & Foreign Bible Society*, pp. 9–23.

88. "American Bible Society," 2:309.

89. "American Bible Society," 2:310–311. For a discussion of Baptists that did not support national Bible societies at all, see Lambert, *The Rise of the Anti-Mission Baptists.*

90. *First Annual Report of the American and Foreign Bible Society*, 1838, p. 10.

91. *First Annual Report of the American and Foreign Bible Society*, 1838, p. 9.

92. *First Annual Report of the American and Foreign Bible Society*, 1838, p. 13.

93. Winter, *The Claims*, pp. 26–40.

94. Wyckoff and Buckbee, *Documentary History*, 1:342–343; Wyckoff, *A Sketch of the Origin and Some Particulars*, pp. 68–77.

95. Wyckoff and Buckbee, *Documentary History*, 1:343.

96. Cone, *Some Account of the Life of Spencer Houghton Cone*, pp. 369–370.

97. Cone, *Some Account of the Life of Spencer Houghton Cone*, p. 373. The term "Pedo-Baptist" refers to Christians found in a wide range of denominations (including Presbyterian, Episcopalian, and Congregational) who believed in baptizing infants.

98. Wyckoff and Buckbee, *Documentary History*, 1:18–19.

99. "Revision Movement," p. 494; Wyckoff and Buckbee, *Documentary History*, 1:13.

100. Cmiel, "Democratic Eloquence," pp. 159–164.

101. Webster, *The Holy Bible*, p. xvi.

102. "Revision of the English Bible," p. 155. See also *An Argument Sustaining the Common English Version.*

103. "Bible Revision," p. 185.

104. Cmiel, "Democratic Eloquence," 1986, pp. 183–184.

105. For the most complete treatments of the development of the Revised Ver-

sion, see Schaff, *A Companion*; Hemphill, *A History of the Revised Version*; and *Historical Account of the Work*.

106. Schaff, *A Companion*, pp. 380–398; Bruce, *The English Bible*, pp. 138–147.

107. Cmiel, *Democratic Eloquence*, pp. 216–217.

108. Hills, *The English Bible*, p. 295.

109. Cmiel, *Democratic Eloquence*, p. 219.

110. Thuesen, "Some Scripture Is Inspired by God," pp. 609–610.

111. *Where the Old and the New Versions Differ*. See also *The Parallel Bible*. On the belief that the Bible was America's primary text, see Bell and Edmunds, *Discussion on Revision*, p. 26; Everett, "The Bible," in *Orations and Speeches* 2:664–673; "Bible Revision," p. 185; Cmiel, "Democratic Eloquence," 1986, p. 164.

112. *New York Times*, November 13, 1881.

113. By the time the Revised Standard Version (the Revised Version's replacement) appeared in 1952, fifty-two new translations had been printed in the United States (Hills, *The English Bible*, pp. 294–413).

114. Westcott and Hort, *The New Testament* vii.

CHAPTER 4 Pedagogy

1. Billington, *The Protestant Crusade*, pp. 233–234.

2. Billington, *The Protestant Crusade*, pp. 193–194.

3. Bourne, *History of the Public School Society*, pp. 246–247.

4. Finke and Stark, *The Churching of America*, p. 113.

5. Spann, *The New Metropolis*, p. 23; Kaestle, *Pillars of the Republic*, p. 163. See also Shaw, *Dagger John*, p. 141.

6. *New-York Observer*, August 16, 1834; Billington, *The Protestant Crusade*, pp. 74–75, 195–198.

7. *A Full and Complete Account*.

8. Billington, *The Protestant Crusade*, p. 221.

9. *New-York Observer*, March 16, 1844.

10. *The New York Herald*, May 8, 1844; Dunn, *What Happened to Religious Education?* p. 272.

11. *American Republican*, May 7–10, 1844.

12. *The New York Herald*, May 9, 1844; Billington, *The Protestant Crusade*, pp. 225–229.

13. Hassard, *Life of the Most Reverend John Hughes*, p. 276.

14. *American Republican*, June 17, 1844.

15. Kaestle, *Pillars of the Republic*, p. 3.

16. Dunn, *What Happened to Religious Education?* p. 15.

17. Johnson, *Old-Time Schools*, p. 19.

18. Barnard, "Schools as They Were Sixty Years Ago," p. 123. See also Kaestle, *Pillars of the Republic*, p. 31.

19. The best treatment of the popularity of Webster's spellers is found in Monaghan, *A Common Heritage*. See also Johnson, *Old-Time Schools*, pp. 185–186.

20. Barnard, "Schools as They Were Sixty Years Ago," p. 131.

21. Cmiel, *Democratic Eloquence*, pp. 74–75.

22. Cremin, *American Education: The National Experience*, p. 69.

23. Mann, *Lectures and Annual Reports*, p. 395.

24. Mann, *Lectures and Annual Reports*, p. 395. Robinson, *Two Centuries*, pp. 1–39; Nietz, "Some Findings," p. 82. See also Dunn, *What Happened to Religious Education?* pp. 76–89.

25. Kaestle, *Pillars of the Republic*, p. 17.

26. The best biographical treatment of Horace Mann remains Messerli, *Horace Mann*.

27. Dunn, *What Happened to Religious Education?* p. 306.

28. Dunn, *What Happened to Religious Education?* pp. 136, 141, 181. See also Messerli, *Horace Mann*, pp. 433–435.

29. Lannie, *Public Money and Parochial Education*, p. ix; Boles, *The Bible, Religion, and the Public Schools*, p. 24.

30. Purcell, "Report 'On the Expediency'," p. 119; Seelye, "The Bible in Schools," p. 735.

31. McCluskey, *Public Schools and Moral Education*, p. 97.

32. Lannie, *Public Money and Parochial Education*, pp. 1–7.

33. The standard biographical treatments of Hughes are Hassard, *Life of the Most Reverend John Hughes*, and Shaw, *Dagger John*.

34. Lannie, *Public Money and Parochial Education*, p. 39.

35. Shaw, *Dagger John*, p. 142.

36. Lannie, *Public Money and Parochial Education*, p. 6.

37. Kehoe, *The Complete Works*, 1:85

38. Elson, *Guardians of Tradition*, pp. 47–54; Jorgenson, *The State and the Non-Public School*, pp. 60–67; Guilday, *A History of the Councils of Baltimore*, pp. 94–95; Bourne, *History of the Public School Society*, p. 251. See also Lannie, *Public Money and Parochial Education*, pp. 103–112; Stokes, *Church and State* 2:572–580.

39. *New-York Observer*, September 5, 1840; *Christian Advocate and Journal*, April 24, 1840.

40. Bourne, *History of the Public School Society*, p. 250.

41. Bond's speech is quoted at length in Bourne, *History of the Public School Society*, pp. 253–268.

42. *The New Testament* (New York: Leavitt, 1834). See also Parsons, "First American Editions of Catholic Bibles," p. 92.

43. Bourne, *History of the Public School Society*, p. 259.

44. Lannie, *Public Money and Parochial Education*, p. 211.

45. Shaw, *Dagger John*, pp. 186–187.

46. Dunn, *What Happened to Religious Education?* pp. 271–274; Jorgenson, *The State and the Non-Public School*, pp. 90–97.

47. Billington, *The Protestant Crusade*, pp. 380–436.

48. For the best single account of the influence of Know-Nothing politics on American education, see Jorgenson, *The State and the Non-Public School*, pp. 69–110.

49. For a partial list of states that had some sort of nonsectarian textbook law by the turn of the twentieth century, see Dunn, *What Happened to Religious Education?* p. 242.

50. Lannie, *Public Money and Parochial Education*, pp. 254–255.

51. Dunn, *What Happened to Religious Education?* p. 254.

52. Exman, *The Brothers Harper*, pp. 183–210; Exman, *The House of Harper*, p. 24.

53. Exman, *The Brothers Harper*, p. 190.

54. Guilday, *A History of the Councils of Baltimore*, pp. 94–95; Dunn, *What Happened to Religious Education?* pp. 208–210.

55. Carey, "To the Roman Catholics"; Shaw, *Dagger John*, p. 47; Hills, *The English Bible*, pp. 4–5; Clarkin, *Mathew Carey*, p. 9.

56. See Appendix 6.

57. Fogarty, "The Quest for a Catholic Vernacular Bible," in Hatch and Noll, *The Bible in America*, pp. 164–165.

58. American Bible Society, Board of Managers Minutes, September 3, 1818, and September 25, 1818, American Bible Society Archives.

59. Greenslade, *The Cambridge History*, 3:161–163.

60. *The Holy Bible*, D. J. Sadlier, 1845, Luke 1:48.

61. *The Holy Bible*, D. J. Sadlier, 1845; *The Holy Bible*, D. J. Sadlier, 1852; *The Holy Bible*, D. J. Sadlier, 1853.

62. Fogarty, "The Quest for a Catholic Vernacular Bible," in Hatch and Noll, *The Bible in America*, pp. 169–170. The best biographical treatment of Bishop Kenrick is Nolan's *The Most Reverend Francis Patrick Kenrick*.

63. Kenrick, *The New Testament*, pp. iii–v, ix–x.

64. Fogarty, "American Catholic Translations," in Frerichs, *The Bible and Bibles in America*, pp. 120–121.

65. Jackson, "The Two Worlds of William Wells," p. 13. See also Hills, *The English Bible*, pp. 20–21.

66. Nolan, *The Most Reverend Francis Patrick Kenrick*, pp. 394–395.

67. Nolan, *Pastoral Letters*, pp. 228–229.

68. Guilday, *A History of the Councils of Baltimore*, pp. 94–95, 179, 211, 237–239; Burns, *The Growth and Development*, pp. 181–196.

69. Gabel, *Public Funds for Church and Private Schools*, pp. 487–493.

70. Stokes, *Church and State*, p. 395.

71. Stokes, *Church and State*, p. 395.

72. *Harpers Weekly*, October 1, 1870.

73. Jorgenson, *The State and the Non-Public School*, p. 112–114.

74. Stokes, *Church and State*, pp. 727–728.

75. Stokes, *Church and State*, pp. 722–723.

76. Burns, *The Growth and Development*, p. 188.

77. Kaestle, "Moral Education and Common Schools in America," p. 105.

78. McCloskey, *The Bible in the Public Schools*, p. vii.

79. A complete record of the legal trial of *Minor v. the Board of Education of the City of Cincinnati*, along with a helpful introduction, is found in McCloskey, *The Bible in the Public Schools*.

80. Keesecker, *Legal Status of Bible Reading*, pp. 2–3.

81. Boles, *The Bible, Religion, and the Public Schools*, pp. 58–99.

82. Boles, *The Bible, Religion, and the Public Schools*, p. 112.

83. Boles, *The Bible, Religion, and the Public Schools*, p. 118.

84. Brown, *The Secularization of American Education*, p. 147.

85. McCloskey, *The Bible in the Public Schools*, pp. vii–viii.

86. *The Norton Anthology of American Literature*, 1:1573, 2001.

87. For good analysis of early American sentiment against novel reading, see Davidson, *Revolution and the Word*, pp. 38–54.

CHAPTER 5 Popularity

1. The Cutting bible (New York: Harper and Brothers, 1846) is located in the collections of the American Bible Society.

2. James Blakely's bible (Boston: West and Richardson, 1817) is located in the collections of the American Antiquarian Society.

3. James Griffith's bible (Philadelphia: William Young, 1802) is located in the collections of the American Antiquarian Society.

4. Abigail Torr's bible (Boston: Greenough and Stebbins, 1812) is located in the collections of the American Antiquarian Society.

5. For a discussion of the prominent place enjoyed by "family bibles" in nineteenth-century Christian homes, see Phillips, *The Christian Home*, pp. 82–91.

6. *The Holy Bible . . . with a Perpetual Genealogical Family Register* (Nashville: Southern Methodist Publishing House, 1859).

7. Revelation 13:8, 17:8, 20:12, 20:17.

8. Scott, *The Gospel Restored*, p. 9.

9. Campbell, *The Sacred Writings*, 1828, p. xxxvii.

10. The relationship between American Protestantism and fiction writing is complex in the opening decades of the nineteenth century. Levels of Protestant acceptance of fiction depended on several factors, including readers' denominational sympathies, ages, level of education, and geographic location. Baym, *Novels, Readers, and Reviewers*, pp. 13–14; Reynolds, *Faith in Fiction*, pp. 73–144; Zboray, *A Fictive People*, p. 92; *Instructions of the Executive Committee*, pp. 8–9; Romeyn, *Plea for the Evangelical Press*; Nord, "Religious Reading and Readers," pp. 250–253; and Phillips, *The Christian Home*, pp. 89–90.

11. Fliegelman, "Anthologizing the Situation of American Literature," p. 337. See also Birney, *The Literary Lives of Jesus*; Pals, *The Victorian "Lives" of Jesus*; and Williams, "Recent Lives of Christ."

12. "Novel Reading," p. 16.

13. Allibone, *A Critical Dictionary*, 3:2862; Wright, *The New and Complete Life*, 1795, t.p.

14. Wright, *The New and Complete Life*, 1795, t.p., p. iii.

15. Wright, *The New and Complete Life*, 1795, p. iv.

16. Wright, *The New and Complete Life*, 1795, t.p.

17. Wright, *The New and Complete Life*, 1795, p. iv.

18. Examples of such quasi-biblical folio editions exist in the collections of both the American Antiquarian Society and the Library Company of Philadelphia.

19. Wright, *The New and Complete Life*, 1803. See also Silver, *The American Printer*, p. 166.

20. Wright, *The New and Complete Life*, 1795, p. iv.

21. Wright, *The New and Complete Life*, 1795, p. 135.

22. Wright, *The New and Complete Life*, 1795, p. iv.

23. Reynolds, *Faith in Fiction*, p. 135.

24. Brodie, *No Man Knows*, pp. 67–68.

25. Numerous biographies have been written on Joseph Smith, Jr. The information collated here derives from material found in three of these books: Hill, *Joseph Smith*; Brodie, *No Man Knows My History*; and Bushman, *Joseph Smith*.

26. Brown, *Historical Atlas of Mormonism*, pp. 6–7.

27. For good treatments of treasure hunting, American revivalism, and their relationship to Joseph Smith, Jr., see Quinn, *Early Mormonism*; Brooke, *The Refiner's Fire*; Cross, *The Burned-over District*; De Pillis, "The Social Sources of Mormonism," pp. 50–79; Hill, "The Rise of Mormonism," pp. 411–430; Taylor, "The Early Republic's Supernatural Economy," pp. 6–34.

28. Smith, *History of the Church*, 1:6. See also Shipps, *Mormonism*, pp. 25–30; Hill, *Joseph Smith*, pp. 50–53; Allen, "Emergence of a Fundamental."

29. Mulder and Mortenson, *Among the Mormons*, pp. 42, 45–46. See also Gutjahr, "The Golden Bible."

30. Hills, American Bible Society Historical Essay #18, 3:8, American Bible Society Archives.

31. "Revision of the English Bible," pp. 159–160; "Does the Bible Need Re-Translating?" pp. 20–25; "The New Testament, Translated from the Original Greek," pp. 588–593; and "Revision Movement," pp. 517–519.

32. Warren Foote journal, Early LDS Journals and Writings, in *LDS Collectors Library*, p. 2.

33. *Messenger and Advocate*, Oct. 1834. See also Luman Shurtliff journal, Early LDS Journals and Writings, in *LDS Collectors Library*, p. 22.

34. Examples of good scholarship historicizing *The Book of Mormon* in antebellum America include Vogel, "Anti-Universalist Rhetoric in the Book of Mormon," in Metcalfe, *New Approaches*, pp. 21–52; Bushman, "The Book of Mormon and the American Revolution," pp. 3–20; Smith, "The Book of Mormon in a Biblical Culture," pp. 3–22; Hatch, *The Democratization of American Christianity*, pp. 113–122; Marquardt, *Early Nineteenth Century Events*, pp. 114–135; Brooke, *The Refiner's Fire*, pp. 149–183; and perhaps most interestingly, Rick Grunder, *Mormon Parallels*.

35. "New Jerusalem: Letter from Independence," in Mulder and Mortenson, *Among the Mormons*, p. 74.

36. Adair, *The History of the American Indians*; Smith, *View of the Hebrews*; Priest, *The Wonders of Nature* and *American Antiquities*.

37. Boudinot, *A Star in the West*, pp. 279–280.

38. Andrew, *The Early Temples of the Mormons*, pp. 8–9; and Brooke, *The Refiner's Fire*, pp. 198–199.

39. *Doctrine and Covenants*, 78:15.

40. Hill, *Joseph Smith*, pp. 205–243; and Brodie, *No Man Knows My History*, pp. 208–224.

41. For a good overview of early Mormonism in Missouri, see LeSueur, *The 1838 Mormon War*, pp. 8–53.

42. *Doctrine and Covenants*, 107:53–56, 116:1, 117:8; and Hill, *Joseph Smith*, pp. 222–223.

43. For the best overall treatment of eschatology and millennialism in early Mormonism, see Underwood, *The Millenarian World*. See also McConkie, *The Millennial Messiah*, 578–588.

44. Smith, *The Book of Mormon*, p. 514.

45. Smith, *History of the Church*, 1:15–16, 183–185; Sorenson, *An Ancient American Setting*. See also Persuitte, *Joseph Smith*, pp. 163–167.

46. Smith, *The Book of Mormon*, pp. 471–474.

47. Smith, *The Book of Mormon*, pp. 476–477.

48. Smith, *The Book of Mormon*, p. 479. Smith would later modify his teaching on the Trinity (Charles, "Book of Mormon Christology," in Metcalfe, *New Approaches*, pp. 81–114).

49. Smith, *The Book of Mormon*, pp. 477–478.

50. Representative examples include Smith, *The Book of Mormon*, pp. 476, 479, 485, 486, 497.

51. Smith, *The Book of Mormon*, pp. 490, 492, 493, 503, 507.

52. Campbell, *Delusions*, p. 9; Brodie, *No Man Knows My History*, pp. 67–82; O'Dea, *The Mormons*, pp. 22–40; and Vogel, *Religious Seekers*, pp. 67–96. For one of the few rhetorical examinations of *The Book of Mormon*, see Hatch, *The Democratization of American Christianity*, pp. 115–120.

53. Smith, *The Book of Mormon*, p. 490.

54. Smith, *The Book of Mormon*, p. 489.

55. Peters, "Bowels of Mercy," p. 11.

56. Smith, *The Book of Mormon*, pp. 479–485. See also Larson, "The Historicity of the Matthean Sermon on the Mount," in Metcalfe, *New Approaches to the Book of Mormon*, pp. 115–163.

57. Smith, *The Book of Mormon*, p. 496.

58. Stocks, "The Book of Mormon"; and Stocks, "The Book of Mormon in English," pp. 85–107.

59. Shipps, *Mormonism*, pp. 25–39; Underwood, "Book of Mormon Usage"; Price, "The Mormon Missionary," pp. 304–392.

60. Smith, *The Book of Mormon*, p. 491.

61. Hart, *The Popular Book*, pp. 95, 111; Cummins, *The Lamplighter*, p. ix.

62. Tompkins, *Sensational Designs*, pp. 148–149.

63. Moore, *Selling God*, pp. 12–39. See also Hedrick, *Harriet Beecher Stowe*, pp. 133–134.

64. Bode, *The Anatomy of American Popular Culture*, p. 146.

65. The most complete biographical treatment of Joseph Holt Ingraham is Weathersby, *J. H. Ingraham*. See also Derby, *Fifty Years Among Authors*, p. 238.

66. Hart, *The Popular Book*, pp. 98–99. See also Bode, *The Anatomy of American Popular Culture*, p. 145.

67. Bode, *The Anatomy of American Popular Culture*, p. 146.

68. Weathersby, *J. H. Ingraham*, p. 109.

69. Ingraham, *The Prince of the House of David*, p. v.

70. Ingraham, *The Prince*, p. vii; French, "A Hundred Years of a Religious Bestseller," pp. 45–54.

71. Ingraham, *The Prince*, pp. v–vi.

72. Ingraham, *The Prince*, t.p.

73. Ingraham, *The Prince*, t.p., p. v.

74. Ingraham, *The Prince*, p. vi.

75. Ingraham, *The Prince*, p. vii.

76. Ingraham, *The Prince*, pp. 200–201.

77. Ingraham, *The Prince*, pp. 175, 202.

78. Ingraham, *The Prince*, pp. 175–176.

79. As quoted in Smith-Rosenberg, "The Female Animal," p. 334.

80. For another study of a feminized treatment of Christ, see Emery, "The Feminization of Christ."

81. Smith-Rosenberg, "The Female Animal," p. 338.

82. Douglas, *The Feminization of American Culture*, pp. 80–164.

83. Douglas, *The Feminization of American Culture*, p. 110.

84. Ginzberg, *Women and the Work of Benevolence*.

85. Mansfield, *The Legal Rights*, p. 19.

86. Hale, *Woman's Record*, p. xxxix.

87. See also McIntosh, *Woman in America*; James, *Changing Ideas About Women in the United States*, pp. 121–276; and Ryan, *The Empire of the Mother*, pp. 97–142.

88. Ingraham, *The Prince*, dedication page.

89. Ingraham, *The Prince*, p. 99.

90. For an excellent discussion of the increased commingling of biblical and fictional written discourse in this period, see Buell, *New England Literary Culture*, pp. 166–190.

91. Van Doren, *The American Novel*, pp. 113–114. See also Reynolds, *Faith in Fiction*, pp. 197–215; and Tompkins, *Sensational Designs*, pp. 147–160.

92. McKee, *"Ben-Hur" Wallace*, p. 143; Wallace, *Autobiography*, p. 927. For the best treatment of the novel's origin, see Theisen, "My God," pp. 33–34.

93. Carter, *The Spiritual Crisis*, p. 67. See also Theisen, "My God," pp. 35–36; and Gutjahr, "To the Heart of Solid Puritans."

94. Hart, *The Popular Book*, p. 164.

95. Phy, "Lew Wallace and *Ben-Hur*," p. 9; and Theisen, "My God," p. 39. See also "The Head of Medusa," p. 711.

96. Wallace, *Ben-Hur*, p. 71.

97. Tebbel, *The American Magazine*, p. 71.

98. Livingstone, *Darwin's Forgotten Defenders*, p. 48.

99. Livingstone, *Darwin's Forgotten Defenders*, p. 35.

100. Cashdollar, *The Transformation of Theology*, p. 13.

101. Cashdollar, *The Transformation of Theology*, p. 11.

102. Brown, *The Rise of Biblical Criticism*, pp. 94–139.

103. Marsden, *Fundamentalism and American Culture*, pp. 20–21.

104. Marsden, *Fundamentalism and American Culture*, pp. 16–17.

105. Marsden, *Fundamentalism and American Culture*, pp. 20–21.

106. Callcott, *History in the United States*, pp. 163–164.

107. Wallace, *Ben-Hur*, p. 35.

108. Wallace, *Autobiography*, p. 932.

109. *The Nation*, p. 149.

110. As quoted in Marsden, *Fundamentalism and American Culture*, p. 21.

111. Wallace, *Ben-Hur*, p. 35.

112. *The Nation*, p. 149.

113. Andrews, *Religious Novels*, p. 5.

114. Andrews, *Religious Novels*, pp. 24–25.

115. Andrews, *Religious Novels*, pp. 32–33.

POSTSCRIPT

1. Winthrop, "September Meeting," p. 445. Good biographical material on George Livermore (1809–1865) is contained in "September Meeting," pp. 442–462.

2. George Livermore's library remained largely intact until 1894 when it was sold at auction in Boston. There does exist a catalogue of this sale that reveals the magnificent nature of Livermore's private library, a quarter of which was biblical material (*Catalogue of the Valuable Private Library*).

3. The best treatment of J. Pierpont Morgan (1837–1913) in relation to his book collecting is Satterlee, *J. Pierpont Morgan*. See also Taylor, *Pierpont Morgan*.

4. Cannon, *American Book Collecting*, p. 287.

5. *In August Company*, p. 115.

6. A brief, engagingly written history of the early English Bible can be found in Wilson, *The People and the Book*.

7. "The Bible in Sunday Schools," p. 147.

8. Wacker, "The Demise of Biblical Civilization," in Hatch and Noll, *The Bible in America*, pp. 121–138. Another notable exception is Turner, *Without God, Without Creed*, pp. 143–150. A small sampling of books in which one might expect some treatment of the bible's declining role in the country's print culture, but

have no such discussion, include Hart, *The Popular Book*; Mott, *Golden Multitudes*; Cremin, *American Education: The National Experience*; Phy, *The Bible and Popular Culture*; Sweet, *Communication and Change*; Marty, *Pilgrims in Their Own Land*; Pay and Donaldson, *Downfall*; Hadden and Shupe, *Secularization and Fundamentalism*; and Bruce, *A House Divided*.

9. Coxe, *An Apology for the Common English Bible*, p. 15. See also Cmiel, *Democratic Eloquence*, 106. The idea that mass production lessens the value of the item reproduced resonates with Walter Benjamin's thoughts on art in the age of mechanical reproduction. Benjamin (*Illuminations*, p. 221) argues that a piece of art loses what he calls its "aura"—"the quality of its presence" or "unique existence"—when it is mass produced and dislodged from "the domain of tradition" (a set of cultural codes that give the original piece of art its uniqueness).

10. *The Holy Bible*, Philadelphia: William W. Woodward, p. xv.

11. Cmiel, *Democratic Eloquence*, p. 223. As late as the mid-1980s, Gallup Poll results reported that forty-seven percent of Americans said they read the Bible regularly. Noll, *A History of Christianity*, p. 408. See also Balmer, *Mine Eyes Have Seen*, pp. 196–199; Duke, *Religious Publishing*, pp. 79–102.

APPENDIX 1

1. Hatch and Noll, *The Bible in America*, p. 6.

2. The statistical data for Figure 47 are taken from Hills, *The English Bible*, pp. 1–293. It should be noted that these are approximate figures. Exact numbers concerning the cities involved in bible production in a given period, along with numbers on printers and editions are difficult to ascertain because many bible editions were printed over a number of years, by different publishers, in different locations. Also, many bibles were published without publishing dates on their title pages.

3. For a longer discussion of the term "edition," see Gaskell, *A New Introduction*, pp. 314–315.

4. Hills, *The English Bible*, pp. 19, 22.

5. Boynton, *Annals of American Bookselling*, p. 157.

6. Hills, *The English Bible*, p. 23.

7. The installment sheets for this bible are located in the collections of the Library Company of Philadelphia.

8. Hills, *The English Bible*, p. 23.

9. Hills, *The English Bible*, pp. 57, 61, 63, 66.

APPENDIX 6

1. Statistical data for Figure 49 are taken from Hills, *The English Bible*, pp. 4–293.

2. Hills, *The English Bible*, p. 249.

.

Bibliography

MANUSCRIPT SOURCES

Robert Aitken Account Book, 1777–1798. Philadelphia: Library Company of Philadelphia.

American Bible Society Papers, 1816–1997. New York: American Bible Society.

Book Trades Collection, 1726–1939. Worcester, Mass.: American Antiquarian Society.

Bradford and Read Collection, George Folsom account book, 1813–1814. Boston: Massachusetts Historical Society.

Broadsides Collection, n.d. Worcester, Mass.: American Antiquarian Society.

Harper and Brothers Collection, 1817–1973. New York: Columbia University.

Jenks & Palmer Account Book, 1841–1846. Boston: Massachusetts Historical Society.

Rebecca Loring Lowell Papers, 1813–1854. Boston: Massachusetts Historical Society.

G. & C. Merriam Company Papers, 1818–1860. Worcester, Mass.: American Antiquarian Society.

Isaiah Thomas Papers, 1748–1874. Worcester, Mass.: American Antiquarian Society.

NEWSPAPERS

American Bible Society. Extracts of Correspondence, &c. New Series (New York)

American Museum (Philadelphia)

American Republican (New York)

Christian Advocate and Journal (New York)

Messenger and Advocate (Kirtland, Ohio)

New York Daily Times (New York)

New York Herald (New York)

New-York Observer (New York)

New York Times (New York)

The Philadelphia Universalist Magazine and Christian Messenger (Philadelphia)

PRIMARY AND SECONDARY SOURCES

Abbot, W. W., ed. *The Papers of George Washington*. Charlottesville: University Press of Virginia, 1987.

Adair, James. *The History of the American Indians*. London: Edward and Charles Dilly, 1775.

Adams, John. *The Works of John Adams*. Edited by Charles Francis Adams. 2 vols. Boston: Charles C. Little and James Brown, 1850.

Allen, James B. "Emergence of a Fundamental: The Expanding Role of Joseph Smith's First Vision in Mormon Religious Thought." *Journal of Mormon History* 7 (1980): 43–61.

Allibone, S. Austin. *A Critical Dictionary of English Literature*. 3 vols. Philadelphia: J. B. Lippincott & Co., 1876.

"American Bible Society." *The Christian Review* 2 (June 1836): 299–313.

American Bible Society. *Second Annual Report 1818*. New York: Daniel Fanshaw, 1819.

American Dictionary of Printing and Bookmaking. New York: Howard Lockwood & Co., 1894.

Anderson, H. T. *The New Testament*. Cincinnati: Published for the Author, 1864.

Andrew, Laurel B. *The Early Temples of the Mormons: The Architecture of the Millennial Kingdom in the American West*. Albany: State University of New York Press, 1978.

Andrews, Charles Wesley. *Religious Novels: An Argument Against Their Use*. 2nd rev. ed. New York: Anson D. F. Randolf, 1856.

Annals of Brattleboro, 1681–1895. Brattleboro, Vt.: E. L. Hildreth, 1921.

Annual Reports of the American Bible Society. Vol. 1. New York: Daniel Fanshaw, 1838.

Arbour, Keith. *Canvassing Books, Sample Books, and Subscription Publishers' Ephemera, 1833–1951, in the Collection of Michael Zinman*. Ardsley, New York: The Haydn Foundation for the Cultural Arts, 1996.

An Argument Sustaining the Common English Version of the Bible. New York: J. A. Gray, 1850.

Bailyn, Bernard. *The Ideological Origins of the American Revolution*. Cambridge: Harvard University Press, 1967.

Baird, Robert. *Religion in America: The Origin, Progress, Relation to the State, and Present Condition of the Evangelical Churches in the United States*. New York: Harper & Brothers, 1844.

Balmer, Randall. *Mine Eyes Have Seen the Glory: A Journey into the Evangelical Subculture in America*. New York: Oxford University Press, 1993.

Barlow, Philip L. *Mormons and the Bible: The Place of the Latter-day Saints in American Religion*. New York: Oxford University Press, 1991.

Barnard, Henry. "Schools as They Were Sixty Years Ago." *American Journal of Education* 3:13 (1863): 123–144.

Barnes, James J. *Authors, Publishers and Politicians: The Quest for an Anglo-American Copyright Agreement, 1815–1854*. Columbus: Ohio State University Press, 1974.

Baym, Nina. *Novels, Readers, and Reviewers: Responses to Fiction in Antebellum America*. Ithaca, N.Y.: Cornell University Press, 1984.

Beecher, Catharine. *A Treatise on Domestic Economy*. Rev. ed. New York: Harper and Brothers, 1855.

Beecher, Catharine, and Harriet Beecher Stowe. *The American Woman's Home*. New York: J. B. Ford & Co., 1869.

Beecher, Henry Ward. *Royal Truths*. Boston: Ticknor and Fields, 1866.

Bell, T. S., and James Edmunds. *Discussion on Revision of the Holy Oracles*. Louisville, Ky.: Morton and Griswold, 1856.

Benjamin, Walter. *Illuminations*. Translated by Harry Zohn. New York: Schocken Books, 1969.

Berger, Carl. *Broadsides & Bayonets: The Propaganda War of the American Revolution*. Rev. ed. San Rafael, Calif.: Presidio Press, 1976.

"The Bible in Sunday Schools." *Century Magazine* 29 (November 1884): 146–148.

"Bible Revision." *The North American Review* 88 (January 1859): 184–210.

Billington, Ray Allen. *The Protestant Crusade, 1800–1860: A Study in the Origins of American Nativism*. New York: Macmillan, 1938.

Binford, Lewis. "Archaeology as Anthropology." *American Antiquity* 28:2 (October 1962): 217–225.

Birney, Alice L. *The Literary Lives of Jesus*. New York: Garland Publishing, 1989.

Bland, David. *A History of Book Illustration: The Illuminated Manuscript and the Printed Book*. 2nd rev. ed. Berkeley: University of California Press, 1969.

Bloom, Allan. *The Closing of the American Mind*. New York, Simon and Schuster, 1987.

Blumin, Stuart M. *The Emergence of the Middle Class: Social Experience in the American City, 1760–1900*. New York: Cambridge University Press, 1989.

Bode, Carl. *The Anatomy of American Popular Culture*. Westport, Conn.: Greenwood, 1959.

Boles, Donald E. *The Bible, Religion, and the Public Schools*. Ames: Iowa State University Press, 1961.

"The Book of Books." *The Bible Union Quarterly* 8 (May 1852): 325–327.

Boudinot, Elias. *The Age of Revelation, or The Age of Reason Shewn to Be an Age of Infidelity*. Philadelphia: Asbury Dickins, 1801.

———. *A Star in the West; or, A Humble Attempt to Discover the Long Lost Ten Tribes of Israel*. Trenton, N.J.: D. Fenton, S. Hutchinson, and J. Dunham, 1816.

Bourne, William Oland. *History of the Public School Society of the City of New York*. New York: Wm. Wood, 1870.

Bowen, Clarence Winthrop, ed. *The History of the Centennial Celebration of the Inauguration of George Washington as First President of the United States*. New York: D. Appleton, 1892.

Boylan, Anne. *Sunday School: The Formation of an American Institution*. New Haven, Conn.: Yale University Press, 1988.

Boynton, Henry Walcott. *Annals of American Bookselling 1638–1850*. New York: John Wiley & Sons, 1932.

Bozeman, Theodore Dwight. *Protestants in an Age of Science: The Baconian Ideal and Antebellum American Religious Thought.* Chapel Hill: University of North Carolina Press, 1977.

————. *To Live Ancient Lives: The Primitivist Dimension in Puritanism.* Chapel Hill: University of North Carolina Press, 1988.

Bradford, Alden. *Evangelical History: or, a Narrative of the Life, Doctrines, and Miracles of Jesus Christ.* Boston: Bradford and Read, 1813.

Bradsher, Earl Lockridge. *Mathew Carey: Editor, Author and Publisher.* 1912; New York: AMS, 1966.

Brodie, Fawn M. *No Man Knows My History.* 2nd rev. ed. New York: Alfred A. Knopf, 1971.

Brooke, John L. *The Refiner's Fire: The Making of Mormon Cosmology, 1644–1844.* New York: Cambridge University Press, 1994.

Brown, Jerry Wayne. *The Rise of Biblical Criticism in America, 1800–1870.* Middletown, Conn.: Wesleyan University Press, 1969.

Brown, Richard D. *Knowledge Is Power: The Diffusion of Information in Early America, 1700–1865.* New York: Oxford University Press, 1989.

Brown, S. Kent, Donald Q. Cannon, and Richard H. Jackson, eds. *Historical Atlas of Mormonism.* New York: Simon & Schuster, 1994.

Brown, Samuel Windsor. *The Secularization of American Education.* New York: Teachers College, Columbia University, 1912.

Bruce, F. F. *The English Bible: A History of Translations from the Earliest English Versions to the New English Bible.* New York: Oxford University Press, 1970.

Bruce, Steve. *A House Divided: Protestantism, Schism, and Secularization.* New York: Routledge, 1990.

Buell, Lawrence. *New England Literary Culture: From Revolution through Renaissance.* New York: Cambridge University Press, 1986.

Burgess, Fred W. *Old Prints and Engravings.* New York: Tudor, 1937.

"The Burman Translation of the Bible." *The Christian Review* 1 (March 1836): 116–136.

Burnap, George W. *Popular Objections to Unitarian Christianity.* Boston: William Crosby and H. P. Nichols, 1848.

Burns, J. A. *The Growth and Development of the Catholic School System in the United States.* New York: Benziger Brothers, 1912.

Bushman, Richard L. "The Book of Mormon and the American Revolution." *Brigham Young University Studies* 17 (1976): 3–20.

————. *Joseph Smith and the Beginnings of Mormonism.* Chicago: University of Illinois Press, 1984.

————. *The Refinement of America: Persons, Houses, Cities.* New York: Alfred A. Knopf, 1992.

Calhoun, Arthur W. *A Social History of the Family from the Colonial Times to the Present.* 3 vols. Cleveland, Ohio: Arthur H. Clark, 1918.

Callcott, George H. *History in the United States 1800–1860: Its Practice and Purpose.* Baltimore: The Johns Hopkins University Press, 1970.

Campbell, Alexander. *Christian Baptism: With Its Antecedents and Consequents.* Bethany, Va.: Alexander Campbell, 1851.

———. *The Christian System*. 4th ed. Cincinnati: H. S. Bosworth, 1866.

———. *Delusions. An Analysis of the Book of Mormon*. Boston: Benjamin H. Greene, 1832.

———, ed. *The Sacred Writings of the Apostles and Evangelists of Jesus Christ Commonly Styled the New Testament*. Buffaloe, Va.: Alexander Campbell, 1826.

———, ed. *The Sacred Writings of the Apostles and Evangelists of Jesus Christ Commonly styled the New Testament*. 2nd ed. Bethany, Va.: Alexander Campbell, 1828.

Campbell, George. *The Four Gospels, Translated from the Greek*. Philadelphia: Thomas Dobson, 1796.

Cannon, Carl L. *American Book Collecting and Collectors*. New York: The H. W. Wilson Co., 1941.

Carey, Mathew. *Plans and Terms of Supplying the Booksellers Throughout the Union, with School and Quarto Bibles*. Philadelphia: Mathew Carey, 1807.

———. "To the Booksellers throughout the United States: Bible Warehouse." Philadelphia: Mathew Carey, June 8, 1814.

———. "To the Roman Catholics of America." Philadelphia: Mathew Carey, 1789.

Carter, Paul A. *The Spiritual Crisis of the Gilded Age*. DeKalb: Northern Illinois University Press, 1971.

Carter, Stephen. *A Culture of Disbelief*. New York: Basic Books, 1993.

Carvajal, Doreen. "The Bible, a Perennial, Runs into Sales Resistance." *New York Times*, October 28, 1996: D1+.

Cashdollar, Charles. *The Transformation of Theology, 1830–1890*. Princeton, N.J.: Princeton University Press, 1989.

Catalogue of Books Published by Harper & Brothers, 1845. New York: Harper & Brothers, 1845.

Catalogue of the Valuable Private Library of the Late George Livermore, Esq. Boston: C. F. Libbie, 1894.

Charvat, William. *Literary Publishing in America, 1790–1850*. Amherst, Mass.: University of Massachusetts Press, 1959.

———. *The Profession of Authorship in America, 1800–1870*. Columbus: Ohio State University Press, 1968.

The Christian Baptist. Buffaloe, Va.: Alexander Campbell, 1823–1830.

Clapper, Michael. "Thousands of Happy Children: Sentimental Chromolithographs of the 1870s and 1880s." Unpublished paper given at the 1993 American Studies Association Meeting, Boston.

Clark, Christopher. "The Diary of an Apprentice Cabinetmaker: Edward Jenner Carpenter's 'Journal' 1844–45," *Proceedings of the American Antiquarian Society* 98:2 (1988): 303–394.

Clarkin, William. *Mathew Carey: A Bibliography of His Publications, 1785–1825*. New York: Garland, 1984.

Cmiel, Kenneth. *Democratic Eloquence: The Fight over Popular Speech in Nineteenth-Century America*. New York: William Murrow, 1990.

———. "Democratic Eloquence: Language, Education and Authority in Nineteenth-Century America." Diss., University of Chicago, 1986.

Cone, Edward W., and Spencer W. Cone. *Some Account of the Life of Spencer Houghton Cone*. New York: Livermore & Rudd, 1856.

Cornelius, Janet Duitsman. *When I Can Read My Title Clear: Literacy, Slavery and Religion in the Antebellum South*. Columbia: University of South Carolina Press, 1991.

Coxe, Arthur Cleveland. *An Apology for the Common English Bible*. Baltimore: J. Robinson, 1857.

Craig, Hardin, Jr. "The Geneva Bible as a Political Document." *The Pacific Historical Review* 7 (1938): 40–49.

Cremin, Lawrence. *American Education: The Colonial Experience, 1607–1783*. New York: Harper & Row, 1970.

———. *American Education: The National Experience, 1783–1876*. New York: Harper & Row, 1980.

Cressy, David. "Books as Totems in Seventeenth-Century England and New England." *The Journal of Library History*, 21:1 (Winter 1986): 92–106.

Cross, Whitney. *The Burned-over District*. Ithaca, N.Y.: Cornell University Press, 1950.

Cummins, Maria Susanna. *The Lamplighter*. 1850; New Brunswick, N.J.: Rutgers University Press, 1988.

Davidson, Cathy N. *Revolution and the Word: The Rise of the Novel in America*. New York: Oxford University Press, 1986.

Davis, John. *The Landscape of Belief: Encountering the Holy Land in Nineteenth-Century American Art and Culture*. Princeton, N.J.: Princeton University Press, 1996.

A Debate Between Rev. A. Campbell and Rev. N. L. Rice, on the Action, Subject, Design and Administrator of Christian Baptism, reported by Marcus T. C. Gould. Lexington, Ky.: A. T. Skillman & Son, 1844.

Deetz, James. *In Small Things Forgotten: The Archaeology of Early Life*. New York: Doubleday, 1977.

Denning, Michael. *Mechanic Accents: Dime Novels and Working-Class Culture in America*. New York: Verso, 1987.

De Pillis, Mario. "The Social Sources of Mormonism." *Church History* 37 (March 1968): 50–79.

Derby, James C. *Fifty Years Among Authors, Books and Publishers*. New York: G. W. Carleton, 1884.

Dickinson, Rodolphus. *A New and Corrected Version of the New Testament*. Boston: Lilly Wait, Colman, & Holden, 1833.

Dictionary of Literary Biography, Volume 49, Parts 1 and 2. Edited by Peter Dzwonkoski. Detroit, Mich.: Bruccoli Clark, 1986.

Dilts, James D. *The Great Road: The Building of the Baltimore & Ohio, the Nation's First Railroad, 1828–1853*. Stanford, Calif.: Stanford University Press, 1993.

Doctrine and Covenants. Salt Lake City, Utah: Church of Jesus Christ of Latter-day Saints, 1981.

"Does the Bible Need Retranslating?" *The Church Review and Ecclesiastical Register* 10 (April 1857): 15–34.

Douglas, Ann. *The Feminization of American Culture.* New York: Anchor Books, 1977.

"Dr. Curtis on a Standard English Bible." *The Southern Presbyterian Review* 11 (1859): 136–144.

Duke, Judith S. *Religious Publishing and Communications.* White Plains, N.Y.: Knowledge Industry Publications, 1981.

Dunn, William Kailer. *What Happened to Religious Education?* Baltimore: The Johns Hopkins University Press, 1958.

Dwight, Henry Otis. *The Centennial History of the American Bible Society.* New York: Macmillan, 1916.

Eliot, John. *The Holy Bible.* Cambridge, Mass.: Samuel Green and Marmaduke Johnson, 1663.

Elkins, Stanley, and Eric McKitrick. *The Age of Federalism: The Early American Republic, 1788–1800.* New York: Oxford University Press, 1993.

Elson, Ruth Miller. *Guardians of Tradition: American Schoolbooks of the Nineteenth Century.* Lincoln: University of Nebraska Press, 1964.

Emery, Linda Sue Miller. "The Feminization of Christ: Harriet Beecher Stowe's Use of the Bible." Diss., Washington State University, 1992.

The English Version of the Polyglott Bible. Brattleboro, Vt.: Brattleboro Typographic Co., 1837.

The English Version of the Polyglott Bible. Brattleboro, Vt.: Fessenden, 1836.

Epstein, Barbara Leslie. *The Politics of Domesticity: Women, Evangelism, and Temperance in Nineteenth-Century America.* Middletown, Conn.: Wesleyan University Press, 1981.

Everett, Edward. *Orations and Speeches.* 3 vols. Boston: Little, Brown, 1883.

Everett, Oliver. "Novem Testamentum Graece, ex recensione J. Jac. Griesbachii." *North American Review* 15 (1822): 460–486.

Exman, Eugene. *The Brothers Harper.* New York: Harper & Row, 1965.

———. *The House of Harper: One Hundred and Fifty Years of Publishing.* New York: Harper & Row, 1967.

Feldman, Egal. *Dual Destinies: The Jewish Encounter with Protestant America.* Chicago: University of Illinois Press, 1990.

Ferguson, Robert A. *The American Enlightenment, 1750–1820.* Cambridge: Harvard University Press, 1997.

The Fifth Report of the Bible Society Established at Philadelphia. Philadelphia: Fry and Kammerer, 1813.

Finke, Roger, and Rodney Stark. *The Churching of America 1776–1990.* New Brunswick, N.J.: Rutgers University Press, 1992.

The First Report of the Bible Society Established at Philadelphia. Philadelphia: Fry and Kammerer, 1809.

Fischer, David H. *The Revolution of American Conservatism: The Federalist Party in the Era of Jeffersonian Democracy.* New York: Harper & Row, 1965.

Fliegelman, Jay. "Anthologizing the Situation of American Literature." *American Literature* 65:2 (June 1993): 334–338.

Folger, John K., and Charles B. Nam. *Education of the American Population.* Washington, D.C.: U.S. Government Printing Office, 1967.

French, Hannah D. *Bookbinding in Early America*. Worcester, Mass.: American Antiquarian Society, 1986.

French, Warren G. "A Hundred Years of a Religious Bestseller." *Western Humanities Review* 10:1 (Winter 1955–56): 45–54.

Frerichs, Ernest S. *The Bible and Bibles in America*. Atlanta: Scholars Press, 1988.

A Full and Complete Account of the Late Awful Riots in Philadelphia. Philadelphia: John Perry, 1844.

Gabel, Richard J. *Public Funds for Church and Private Schools*. Washington, D.C.: Murray & Heister, 1937.

Gaer, Joseph, and Ben Siegel. *The Puritan Heritage: America's Roots in the Bible*. New York: New American Library, 1964.

Gaines, William H., Jr. "The Continental Congress Considers the Publication of a Bible, 1777." *Studies in Bibliography* 3 (1950–51): 274–281.

Gascoigne, Bamber. *How to Identify Prints*. London: Thames and Hudson, 1986.

Gaskell, Philip. *A New Introduction to Bibliography*. New York: Oxford University Press, 1972.

Gilmore, William. *Reading Becomes a Necessity of Life: Material and Cultural Life in Rural New England, 1780–1835*. Knoxville: The University of Tennessee Press, 1989.

Giltner, John H. *Moses Stuart: The Father of Biblical Science in America*. Atlanta: Scholars Press, 1988.

Ginzberg, Lori D. *Women and the Work of Benevolence: Morality, Politics, and Class in the Nineteenth-Century United States*. New Haven, Conn.: Yale University Press, 1990.

Goodrich, Samuel. *Recollections of a Lifetime*. New York: Arundel Print, 1856.

Goodwin, H. M. "The Bible as a Book of Education," *The New Englander* 43 (1883): 252–272.

Grant, Robert M. *A Short History of the Interpretation of the Bible*. Rev. ed. New York: Macmillan, 1963.

Green, James N. "From Printer to Publisher: Mathew Carey and the Origins of Nineteenth-Century Book Publishing." In *Getting the Books Out: Papers of the Chicago Conference on the Book in 19th-Century America*. Edited by Michael Hackenberg. Washington, D.C.: The Center for the Book, Library of Congress, 1987.

———. *Mathew Carey: Publisher and Patriot*. Philadelphia: The Library Company of Philadelphia, 1985.

Greenslade, S. L., ed. *The Cambridge History of the Bible: The West from the Reformation to the Present Day*, Vol. 3. London: Cambridge University Press, 1963.

Greven, Philip. *The Protestant Temperament: Patterns of Child-Rearing, Religious Experience, and the Self in Early America*. New York: Alfred A. Knopf, 1977.

Grier, Katherine C. *Culture and Comfort: People, Parlors, and Upholstery, 1850–1930*. Rochester, N.Y.: The Strong Museum and the University of Massachusetts Press, 1988.

Grunder, Rick. *Mormon Parallels*. Ithaca, N.Y.: Rick Grunder Books, 1987.

Guilday, Peter. *A History of the Councils of Baltimore, 1791–1884.* New York: Macmillan, 1932.

Guppy, Henry. *A Brief Sketch of the History of the Transmission of the Bible Down to the Revised English Version of 1881–1895.* Manchester, England: The Manchester University Press, 1926.

Gura, Philip F. *The Wisdom of Words: Language, Theology, and Literature in the New England Renaissance.* Middletown, Conn.: Wesleyan University Press, 1981.

Gutjahr, Paul. "The Golden Bible in the Bible's Golden Age: *The Book of Mormon* and Antebellum Print Culture." *ATQ* New Series 12:4 (December 1998).

———. "'To the Heart of Solid Puritans': Historicizing the Popularity of *Ben-Hur*." *Mosaic* 26:3 (Summer 1993): 53–67.

Hackett, Horatio B. *Illustrations of Scripture: Suggested by a Tour of the Holy Land.* Boston: William Heath, 1857.

Hadden, Jeffrey K., and Anson Shupe. *Secularization and Fundamentalism Reconsidered.* New York: Paragon House, 1989.

Hale, Sarah Josepha. *The Woman's Record.* New York: Harper & Brothers, 1855.

Hall, David D. *Worlds of Wonder, Days of Judgment: Popular Religious Beliefs in Early New England.* Cambridge: Harvard University Press, 1989.

Hall, Peter D. *The Organization of American Culture, 1700–1900: Private Institutions, Elites, and the Origins of American Nationality.* New York: New York University Press, 1982.

Halttunen, Karen. *Confidence Men and Painted Women: A Study of Middle-Class Culture in America, 1830–1870.* New Haven, Conn.: Yale University Press, 1982.

Hamilton, Milton W. *The Country Printer.* New York: Columbia University Press, 1936.

Handy, Robert T. *The Holy Land in American Protestant Life, 1800–1948: A Documentary History.* New York: Arno, 1981.

Hardesty, Nancy A. *Your Daughters Shall Prophesy: Revivalism and Feminism in the Age of Finney.* Brooklyn, N.Y.: Carlson Publishing, 1991.

Harley, Lewis R. *The Life of Charles Thomson.* Philadelphia: George W. Jacobs, 1900.

Harpers Weekly. New York: Harper and Brothers, 1870–1872.

Harrell, David Edwin, Jr. *Quest for a Christian America: The Disciples of Christ and American Society to 1866.* Nashville, Tenn.: Disciples of Christ Historical Society, 1966.

Hart, Clive, and Kay Gilliland Stevenson. *Heaven and the Flesh: Imagery of Desire from the Renaissance to the Rococo.* New York: Cambridge University Press, 1995.

Hart, James D. *The Popular Book: A History of America's Literary Taste.* Berkeley: University of California Press, 1963.

Hartman, Mary S., and Lois Banner, eds. *Clio's Consciousness Raised: New Perspectives on the History of Women.* New York: Harper, 1974.

Hassard, John R. G. *Life of the Most Reverend John Hughes, D. D.* New York: D. Appleton, 1866.

Hatch, Nathan O. *The Democratization of American Christianity*. New Haven, Conn.: Yale University Press, 1989.

Hatch, Nathan O., and Mark A. Noll, eds. *The Bible in America: Essays in Cultural History*. New York: Oxford University Press, 1982.

"The Head of Medusa, and Other Novels." *The Atlantic Monthly* (May 1881): 710–714.

Heckscher, Morrion H., and Leslie Greene Bowman. *American Rococo, 1750–1775: Elegance in Ornament*. New York: The Metropolitan Museum of Art, 1992.

Hedrick, Joan D. *Harriet Beecher Stowe: A Life*. New York: Oxford University Press, 1994.

Hemphill, Samuel. *The History of the Revised Version of the New Testament*. London: Elliot Stock, 1906.

Hendricks, James Edwin. *Charles Thomson and the Making of a New Nation, 1729–1824*. Madison, Wisc.: Fairleigh Dickinson University Press, 1979.

Henry, T. Charlton. *Letters to an Anxious Inquirer*. 4th ed. Philadelphia: Presbyterian Board of Publication, 1840.

Hibbard, F. G. *Christian Baptism*. New York: Phillips & Hunt, 1841.

Hill, Donna. *Joseph Smith: The First Mormon*. Garden City, N.Y.: Doubleday, 1977.

Hill, Hamlin. *Mark Twain and Elisha Bliss*. Columbia, Mo.: University of Missouri Press, 1964.

Hill, Marvin. "The Rise of Mormonism." *New York History* 61 (1980): 411–430.

Hills, Margaret T. "American Bible Society Historical Essay #18, Part 2: The Production and Supply of Scriptures 1821–1830." Typescript. New York: American Bible Society, 1964.

———. "American Bible Society Historical Essay #18, Part 3: Production & Supply of Scriptures 1831–1860." Typescript. New York: American Bible Society, 1964.

———. *The English Bible in America: A Bibliography of Editions of the Bible & the New Testament Published in America 1777–1957*. New York: American Bible Society, 1962.

Hirsch, E. D. Jr., Joseph F. Kett, James Trefil. *The Dictionary of Cultural Literacy*. Boston: Houghton Mifflin, 1988.

Historical Account of the Work of the American Committee of Revision of the Authorized English Version of the Bible. New York: Charles Scribner's Sons, 1885.

Hixon, Richard F. *Isaac Collins: A Quaker Printer in the 18th Century*. New Brunswick, N.J.: Rutgers University Press, 1968.

Hoffert, Sylvia D. *Private Matters: American Attitudes Toward Childbearing and Infant Nurture in the Urban North, 1800–1860*. Chicago: University of Illinois Press, 1989.

Holmgren, Laton E. "A 'Pious and Laudable Undertaking': The Bible of the Revolution." *American History* 10:6 (Oct. 1975): 12–17.

The Holy Bible. 6 vols. Notes by Thomas Scott. Boston: Samuel T. Armstrong, 1832.

The Holy Bible. Boston: Greenough and Stebbins, 1812.

The Holy Bible. Boston: West and Richardson, 1817.

The Holy Bible. Brattleboro, Vt.: Holbrook and Fessenden, 1824.

The Holy Bible. Brattleboro, Vt.: Holbrook and Fessenden, 1831.

The Holy Bible. Brattleboro, Vt.: J. Holbrook's Stereotype Copy, 1816.

The Holy Bible. Brattleboro, Vt.: J. Holbrook's Stereotype Copy, 1818.

The Holy Bible. London: Robert Barker, 1611.

The Holy Bible. London: Robert Barker, 1617.

The Holy Bible. Minion edition. New York: American Bible Society, 1829.

The Holy Bible. Nashville, Tenn.: Southern Methodist Publishing House, 1859.

The Holy Bible. New York: Henry C. Sleight, 1828.

The Holy Bible. New York: M. R. Gately, 1880.

The Holy Bible. New York: The New-York Bible Society, 1816.

The Holy Bible. New York: D. J. Sadlier, 1845.

The Holy Bible. New York: D. J. Sadlier, 1852.

The Holy Bible. New York: D. J. Sadlier, 1853.

The Holy Bible. New York: White, Gallaher and White, 1831.

The Holy Bible. Nonpariel edition. New York: American Bible Society, 1830.

The Holy Bible. Translated from Latin Vulgate. Philadelphia: Carey, Stewart, 1790.

The Holy Bible. Philadelphia: Mathew Carey, 1801.

The Holy Bible. Philadelphia: Mathew Carey, 1803.

The Holy Bible. Philadelphia: Mathew Carey, 1804.

The Holy Bible. Translated from Latin Vulgate. Philadelphia: Mathew Carey, 1805.

The Holy Bible. Philadelphia: R. Aitken, 1782.

The Holy Bible. Philadelphia: William W. Woodward, 1814.

The Holy Bible. Philadelphia: William Young, 1802.

The Holy Bible. Trenton, N.J.: Isaac Collins, 1791.

The Holy Bible. Folio edition. Worcester, Mass.: Isaiah Thomas, 1791.

The Holy Bible. Royal quarto edition. Worcester, Mass.: Isaiah Thomas, 1791.

Hovenkamp, Herbert. *Science and Religion in America, 1800–1860.* Philadelphia: University of Pennsylvania Press, 1978.

Howe, Samuel Storrs. "The Dangerous Prevalence of Fiction." *Annals of Iowa* 3:2 (April 1884): 49–58.

Howsam, Leslie. *Cheap Bibles: Nineteenth-Century Publishing and the British and Foreign Bible Society.* New York: Cambridge University Press, 1991.

Hudson, Frederic. *Journalism in the United States from 1690 to 1872.* New York: Haskell House Publishers, 1968.

Hughes, Richard T., and Leonard C. Allen. *Illusions of Innocence: Protestant Primitivism in America, 1630–1875.* Chicago: University of Chicago Press, 1988.

Hutcheson, Francis. *A Short Introduction to Moral Philosophy.* Glasgow: Robert Foulis, 1747.

———. *A System of Moral Philosophy.* Glasgow: R. and A. Foulis, 1755.

The Illuminated Bible. New York: Harper & Brothers, 1846.

In August Company: The Collections of the Pierpont Morgan Library. New York: The Pierpont Morgan Library, 1993.

Ingraham, Joseph Holt. *The Pillar of Fire; or, Israel in Bondage*. New York: Pudney & Russell, 1859.

———. *The Prince of the House of David*. New York: Pudney & Russell, 1855.

———. *The Throne of David*. Philadelphia: G. G. Evans, 1860.

Ingraham, Joseph Wentworth. *An Historical Map of Palestine, or the Holy Land*. Boston: Thomas B. Wait and Joseph W. Ingraham, 1828.

Instructions of the Executive Committee of the American Tract Society. New York: American Tract Society, 1868.

Irwin, John T. *American Hieroglyphics: The Symbol of the Egyptian Hieroglyphics in the American Renaissance*. Baltimore: The Johns Hopkins University Press, 1980.

Isaac, Rhys. *The Transformation of Virginia, 1740–1790*. Chapel Hill: University of North Carolina Press, 1982.

Jackson, Leon. "The Two Worlds of William Wells: Ideology and Economy in the Early American Republic of Letters." Ph.D. diss., Oxford University, 1994.

James, Janet Wilson. *Changing Ideas About Women in the United States, 1776–1825*. New York: Garland, 1981.

———, ed. *Women in American Religion*. Philadelphia: University of Pennsylvania Press, 1980.

James, John Angell. *The Anxious Inquirer after Salvation*. New York: American Tract Society, D. Fanshaw, n.d.

Jensen, Joan M. *Loosening the Bonds: Mid-Atlantic Farm Women, 1750–1850*. New Haven, Conn.: Yale University Press, 1986.

Johnson, Clifton. *Old-Time Schools and School-books*. New York: Dover, 1963.

Johnson, Paul, and Sean Wilentz. *The Kingdom of Matthias*. New York: Oxford University Press, 1994.

Jones, Howard Mumford. "The Influence of European Ideas in Nineteenth-Century America." *American Literature* 7 (1935): 241–273.

Jorgenson, Lloyd P. *The State and the Non-Public School, 1825–1925*. Columbia, Mo.: University of Missouri Press, 1987.

Joyce, William L., David D. Hall, Richard D. Brown, and John B. Hench, eds. *Printing and Society in Early America*. Worcester, Mass.: American Antiquarian Society, 1983.

Kaestle, Carl F. "Moral Education and Common Schools in America: A Historian's View." *Journal of Moral Education* 13:2 (May 1984): 101–111.

———. *Pillars of the Republic: Common Schools and American Society*. New York: Hill and Wang, 1983.

Kaplan, Fred. *Sacred Tears: Sentimentality in Victorian Literature*. Princeton, N.J.: Princeton University Press, 1987.

Kasson, John F. *Rudeness and Civility: Manners in Nineteenth-Century Urban America*. New York: Hill and Wang, The Noonday Press, 1990.

Keane, John. *Tom Paine*. Boston: Little, Brown, 1995.

Keesecker, Ward W. *Legal Status of Bible Reading and Religious Instruction in Public Schools*. Washington, D.C.: U.S. Department of the Interior, Bulletin 14, 1930.

Kehoe, Laurence, ed. *The Complete Works of the Most Rev. John Hughes, D. D.* 2 vols. New York: The American News Company, 1864.

Kellems, Jesse R. *Alexander Campbell and the Disciples.* New York: Richard R. Smith, 1930.

Kenrick, Francis Patrick. *The New Testament.* 2nd ed. Baltimore: Kelly, Hedian & Piet, 1862.

Kerber, Linda K. *Women of the Republic: Intellect & Ideology in Revolutionary America.* New York: W. W. Norton, 1980.

King, Thomas Starr, and Orville Dewey. *The New Discussion of the Trinity.* Boston: Walker, Wise, 1860.

Kneeland, Abner. *An Introduction to the Defence of Abner Kneeland Charged with Blasphemy.* Boston: Abner Kneeland, 1834.

———, trans. *Η ΚΑΙΝΗ ΔΙΑΘΗΚΗ, The New Testament in Greek and English.* Philadelphia: Abner Kneeland, 1823.

———, trans. *The New Testament; Being the English Only of the Greek and English Testament.* Philadelphia: Abner Kneeland, 1823.

Kubler, George Adolf. *A New History of Stereotyping.* New York: J. J. Little & Ives, 1941.

Lambert, Byron Cecil. *The Rise of the Anti-Mission Baptists: Sources and Leaders, 1800–1840.* New York: Arno, 1980.

Lannie, Vincent P. *Public Money and Parochial Education: Bishop Hughes, Governor Seward, and the New York School Controversy.* Cleveland: Press of Case Western Reserve University, 1968.

LDS Collectors Library, 1995 Edition. CD-ROM. Provo, Utah: Infobases, 1995.

Leary, Lewis. *The Book-Peddling Parson.* Chapel Hill, N.C.: Algonquin Books, 1984.

Lehuu, Isabelle. "Changes in the Word: Reading Practices in Antebellum America." Diss., Cornell University, 1992.

LeSueur, Stephen C. *The 1838 Mormon War in Missouri.* Columbia: University of Missouri Press, 1987.

Levey, Michael. *Rococo to Revolution: Major Trends in Eighteenth-Century Painting.* New York: Thames and Hudson, 1966.

Lewis, Enoch. *A Dissertation on Oaths.* N.p.: Uriah Hunt, 1838.

Lewis, Jack P. *The English Bible from KJV to NIV: A History and Evaluation.* 2nd ed. Grand Rapids, Mich.: Baker Book House, 1991.

Livingstone, David N. *Darwin's Forgotten Defenders: The Encounter Between Evangelical Theology and Evolutionary Thought.* Grand Rapids, Mich.: W. B. Eerdmans, 1987.

Locke, John. *A Paraphrase and Notes on the Epistles of St. Paul to the Galations, 1 and 2 Corinthians, Romans, Ephesians.* 2 vols. Edited by Arthur W. Wainwright. Oxford: Clarendon, 1987.

Lockridge, Kenneth. *Literacy in Colonial New England.* New York: W. W. Norton, 1974.

Lydenberg, Harry Miller. "The Problem of the Pre-1776 Bible." *The Papers of the Bibliographical Society of America* 48 (1954): 183–194.

Madison, James, Alexander Hamilton, and John Jay. *The Federalist Papers*. New York: Penguin Books, 1987.

Mann, Horace. *Lectures and Annual Reports on Education*. Cambridge, Mass.: Published for the Editor, 1867.

Mansfield, Edward. *The Legal Rights, Liabilities and Duties of Women*. Boston: John P. Jewett, 1845.

Marquardt, H. Michael. *Early Nineteenth-Century Events Reflected in the Book of Mormon*. Salt Lake City, Utah: Utah Lighthouse Ministry, 1979.

Marsden, George M. *Fundamentalism and American Culture: The Shaping of Twentieth-Century Evangelicalism*. New York: Oxford University Press, 1980.

Martin, Terence. *The Instructed Vision: Scottish Common Sense Philosophy and the Origins of American Fiction*. Bloomington: Indiana University Press, 1961.

Marty, Martin. *Pilgrims in Their Own Land: 500 Years of Religion in America*. New York: Penguin Books, 1984.

Maser, Frederick E. "The Day America Needed Bibles." *Religion in Life* 45:2 (Summer 1976): 138–145.

McCloskey, Robert G. Introduction to *The Bible in the Public Schools*. New York: Da Capo, 1967.

McCluskey, Neil Gerard. *Public Schools and Moral Education: The Influence of Horace Mann, William Torrey Harris and John Dewey*. New York: Columbia University Press, 1958.

McColluch, William. "Additional Memoranda for the History of Printing by Isaiah Thomas Communicated by Wm. McColluch, Philadelphia." *Proceedings of the American Antiquarian Society* 93:2 (1922): 100–247.

McConkie, Bruce R. *The Millennial Messiah: The Second Coming of the Son of Man*. Salt Lake City, Utah: Deseret Book, 1982.

McCosh, James. *The Scottish Philosophy: Biographical, Expository, Critical, from Hutcheson to Hamilton*. New York: Scribner, 1890.

McDannell, Colleen. *The Christian Home in Victorian America, 1840–1900*. Bloomington: Indiana University Press, 1986.

———. *Material Christianity: Religion and Popular Culture in America*. New Haven: Yale University Press, 1995.

McGaw, Judith A. *Most Wonderful Machine: Mechanization and Social Change in Berkshire Paper Making, 1801–1885*. Princeton, N.J.: Princeton University Press, 1987.

McIntosh, Maria Jane. *Woman in America*. New York: D. Appleton, 1850.

McKee, Irving. *"Ben-Hur" Wallace*. Berkeley: University of California Press, 1947.

McLoughlin, William G. *The Meaning of Henry Ward Beecher*. New York: Alfred A. Knopf, 1970.

A Member. *An Expose of the Rise and Proceedings of the American Bible Society During the Thirteen Years of Its Existence*. New York: n.p., 1830.

Messerli, Jonathan. *Horace Mann: A Biography*. New York: Alfred A. Knopf, 1972.

Metcalfe, Brent Lee, ed. *New Approaches to the Book of Mormon: Explorations in Critical Methodology*. Salt Lake City, Utah: Signature Books, 1993.

Metzger, Bruce M. *The Text of the New Testament: Its Transmission, Corruption, and Restoration*, 2nd ed. New York: Oxford University Press, 1968.

Meyer, D. H. *The Instructed Conscience*. Philadelphia: University of Pennsylvania Press, 1972.

The Millennial Harbinger. Bethany, Va.: Alexander Campbell, 1830–1866.

Miller, J. Hillis. *Illustration*. Cambridge: Harvard University Press, 1992.

Mitchell, W. J. T., ed. *Iconology: Image, Text, Ideology*. Chicago: University of Chicago Press, 1987.

Monaghan, E. Jennifer. *A Common Heritage: Noah Webster's Blue-Black Speller*. Hamden, Conn.: Archon Books, 1983.

Moore, R. Laurence. *Selling God: American Religion in the Marketplace of Culture*. New York: Oxford University Press, 1994.

Morgan, David. *Visual Piety: A History and Theory of Popular Religious Images*. Berkeley: University of California Press, 1998.

Morris, Robert. *Freemasonry in the Holy Land*. New York: Masonic Publishing, 1872.

Mott, Frank Luther. *Golden Multitudes: The Story of Best Sellers in the United States*. New York: Macmillan, 1947.

Moylan, Michele, and Lane Stiles, eds. *Reading Books: Essays on the Material Text and Literature in America*. Amherst, Mass.: University of Massachusetts Press, 1996.

Mukerji, Chandra, and Michael Schudson, eds. *Rethinking Popular Culture: Contemporary Perspectives in Cultural Studies*. Berkeley: University of California Press, 1991.

Mulder, William, and Russell A. Mortenson, eds. *Among the Mormons: Historic Accounts by Contemporary Observers*. Lincoln: Univesity of Nebraska Press, 1973.

The Nation. 80:2069 (February 23, 1905): 148–149.

New Devotional and Practical Pictorial Family Bible subscription book. Philadelphia: National Publishing, 187?.

New Illustrated Devotional and Practical Polyglot Family Bible subscription book. N.p.: National Publishing, 187?.

The New Testament. New York: Leavitt, 1834.

The New Testament. Translated from Latin Vulgate. Philadelphia: Mathew Carey, 1805.

The New Testament. Translated from Latin Vulgate. Philadelphia: Mathew Carey, 1811.

The New Testament. Translated from Latin Vulgate. Philadelphia: Mathew Carey, 1816.

The New Testament. Philadelphia: R. Aitken, 1777.

The New Testament. Philadelphia: R. Aitken, 1778.

The New Testament. Philadelphia: R. Aitken, 1779.

The New Testament. Philadelphia: R. Aitken, 1781.

"The New Testament, Translated from the Original Greek." *The British and Foreign Evangelical Review* 29 (July 1859): 579–598.

Nichols, Charles Lemuel. *Bibliography of Worcester from 1775–1848*. Worcester, Mass.: Printed privately, 1899.

Nietz, John A. "Some Findings from Analyses of Old Textbooks." *History of Education Journal* 3:3 (Spring 1952): 79–87.

Nir, Yeshayahu. *The Bible and the Image*. Philadelphia: University of Pennsylvania Press, 1985.

Nolan, Hugh J. *The Most Reverend Francis Patrick Kenrick Third Bishop of Philadelphia, 1830–1851*. Washington, D.C.: The Catholic Universities of America Press, 1948.

———, ed. *The Pastoral Letters of the United States Catholic Bishops*. Vol. 1. Washington, D.C.: United States Catholic Conference, 1984.

Noll, Mark A. *A History of Christianity in the United States and Canada*. Grand Rapids, Mich.: William B. Eerdmans, 1992.

———. "Review Essay: The Bible in America," *Journal of Biblical Literature* 106:3 (Sept. 1987): 493–509.

Nord, David Paul. "The Evangelical Origins of Mass Media in America, 1815–1835." *Journalism Monographs* 88 (May 1984).

———. "Free Books, Free Grace, Free Riders: The Economics of Religious Publishing in Early Nineteenth-Century America." *Proceedings of the American Antiquarian Society* 106:2 (Oct. 1996): 241–272.

———. "Religious Reading and Readers in Antebellum America." *Journal of the Early Republic* 15:2 (Summer 1995): 241–272.

North, Eric M. "American Bible Society Historical Essay #201: The Correspondence, etc., of Elias Boudinot with the American Bible Society." 2 vols. Transcript. New York: American Bible Society, 1965.

———. "American Bible Society Historical Essay #18: The Production and Supply of Scriptures, Part I, 1816–1820." Transcript. New York: American Bible Society, 1963.

North, Eric M., and Rebecca Bromley. "American Bible Society Historical Essay #14: Distribution of the Scriptures in the U.S.A. 1861–1900." Transcript. New York: American Bible Society, 1965.

North, Eric M., and Dorothy U. Compagno. "American Bible Society Historical Essay #14: Part 4, Scripture Distribution in the U.S.A., 1851–1860." Transcript. New York: American Bible Society, 1964.

Norton, Andrews. *Translation of the Gospels with Notes*. 8th ed. 2 vols. Cambridge, Mass.: John Wilson and Son, 1888.

———. *A Statement of Reasons for Not Believing the Doctrine of Trinitarians*. 3rd. ed. Boston: American Unitarian Association, 1867.

The Norton Anthology of American Literature. Vol. 1, 4th ed. New York: W. W. Norton, 1994.

Norton, David Fate. "From Moral Sense to Common Sense: An Essay on the Development of Scottish Common Sense Philosophy, 1700–1765," Diss., University of California, San Diego, 1966.

"Novel Reading," Tract 515. *Tracts of the American Tract Society* 12. New York: American Tract Society, n.d.

O'Callaghan, Edward. *A List of Editions of the Holy Scriptures and Parts Thereof.* Albany, N.Y.: Munsell & Rowland, 1861.

O'Dea, Thomas F. *The Mormons.* Chicago: University of Chicago Press, 1957.

Orchard, Bernard, and Thomas R. W. Longstaff, eds. *J. J. Griesbach: Synoptic and Text-Critical Studies 1776–1976.* New York: Cambridge University Press, 1978.

Orlinsky, Harry M., and Robert G. Bratcher. *A History of Bible Translation and the North American Contribution.* Atlanta: Scholars Press, 1991.

Packard, Joseph. "Sacred Theology." *Bibliotheca Sacra* 110 (April 1858): 289–300.

Paine, Thomas. *Collected Writings.* New York: The Library of America, 1995.

"Palestine, a Perpetual Witness for the Bible." *The New Englander* 42 (1859): 192–223.

Palfrey, John Gorham. *The New Testament in the Common Version.* Boston: Gray and Bowen, 1830.

Pals, Daniel L. *The Victorian "Lives" of Jesus.* San Antonio, Tex.: Trinity University Press, 1982.

The Parallel Bible. Cambridge: C. J. Clay and Son, 1885.

Park, William. *The Idea of Rococo.* Newark, N.J.: University of Delaware Press, 1992.

Parsons, Levi. "The Dereliction and Restoration of the Jews: A Sermon, Preached in Park-Street Church Boston, Sabbath, Oct. 31, 1819, just before the Departure of the Palestine Mission." Boston: Samuel T. Armstrong, 1819.

Parsons, Wilfrid. "First American Editions of Catholic Bibles." *Historical Records and Studies* 27 (1937): 89–98.

Pay, Marty, and Hal Donaldson. *Downfall: Secularization of a Christian Nation.* Green Forest, Ark.: New Leaf, 1991.

Persuitte, David. *Joseph Smith and the Origins of The Book of Mormon.* Jefferson, N.C.: McFarland, 1985.

Peters, Absolom. *Sprinkling the Only Mode of Baptism.* Albany, N.Y.: E. H. Pease, 1848.

Peters, John Durham. "Bowels of Mercy." Unpublished paper, 1994.

Peterson, Richard J. "Scottish Common Sense in America, 1768–1850: An Evaluation of Its Influence." Diss., American University, 1963.

Phillips, S. *The Christian Home, as it is in the Sphere of Nature and the Church.* New York: Gurdon Bill, 1862.

Phy, Allene Stuart, ed. *The Bible and Popular Culture in America.* Philadelphia: Fortress, 1985.

———. "Lew Wallace and *Ben-Hur*." In *The Romanticist*, 6–8. Nashville: The F. Marion Crawford Memorial Society, 1986.

Pictorial Illustrations of the Bible. Brattleboro, Vt.: Fessenden, 1836.

"Popular Reasons for Studying the Scriptures." *The Christian Disciple* 6 (1817): 3–6.

Presidential Inaugural Bibles: Catalogue of an Exhibition, November 17, 1968, through February 23, 1969. Washington Cathedral: The Rare Book Library.

Price, Rex Thomas, Jr. "The Mormon Missionary of the Nineteenth Century." Diss., University of Wisconsin, Madison, 1991.

Priest, Josiah. *American Antiquities, and Discoveries in the West*. 2nd rev. ed. Albany, N.Y.: Hoffman and White, 1833.

———. *A View of the Expected Christian Millennium*. Albany: Loomis, 1827.

———. *The Wonders of Nature and Providence Displayed*. Albany, N.Y.: Josiah Priest, 1825.

The Psalms in Metre, Faithfully translated for the Use, Edification, and Comfort of the Saints in Publick and Private, especially in New England. Cambridge, Mass.: Stephen Daye, 1640.

Purcell, J. B. "Report 'On the Expediency of Introducing Selections from the Bible'." *Transactions of the Seventh Annual Meeting of the Western Literary Institute*. Cincinnati, Ohio: James R. Allbach, 1838, 118–120.

Quincy, Eliza Susan Morton. *Memoir of the Life of Eliza S. M. Quincy*. Boston: J. Wilson and Son, 1861.

Quinn, D. Michael. *Early Mormonism and the Magic World View*. Salt Lake City, Utah: Signature Books, 1987.

Quist, John W. "Slaveholding Operatives of the Benevolent Empire: Bible, Tract, and Sunday School Societies in Antebellum Tuscaloosa County, Alabama." *The Journal of Southern History* 62:3 (August 1996): 481–526.

Reid, Thomas. *Philosophical Works*. 2 vols. Edited by Harry M. Bracken. Hildesheim, Germany: George Olms Verlagsbuchhandlung, 1967.

Report of the Arguments of the Attorney of the Commonwealth, at the Trials of Abner Kneeland. Boston: Beals, Homer, 1834.

"Revision Movement." *The Southern Presbyterian Review* 10 (Jan 1858): 493–519.

"Revision of the English Bible." *The New Englander* 18 (1859): 144–163.

Reynolds, David S. *Beneath the American Renaissance: The Subversive Imagination in the Age of Emerson and Melville*. Cambridge: Harvard University Press, 1988.

———. *Faith in Fiction: The Emergence of Religious Literature in America*. Cambridge: Harvard University Press, 1981.

———. "From Doctrine to Narrative: The Rise of Pulpit Storytelling in America." *American Quarterly* 32:5 (Winter 1980): 479–498.

Richardson, Robertson. *Memoirs of Alexander Campbell*. 2 vols. Philadelphia: J. B. Lippincott, 1868.

Robinson, David. *The Unitarians and the Universalists*. Westport, Conn.: Greenwood, 1985.

Robinson, Edward. *Biblical Researches in Palestine and Later Biblical Researches in Palestine*. 3 vols. Boston: Crocker and Brewster, 1856.

Robinson, R. R. *Two Centuries of Change in the Content of School Readers*. Nashville, Tenn.: George Peabody College for Teachers, 1930.

Romeyn, James. *Plea for the Evangelical Press: A Discourse Delivered in the Broadway Tabernacle*. New York: American Tract Society, 1843.

Rowe, Henry K. *History of Andover Theological Seminary*. Newton, Mass.: Thomas Todd Company, 1933.

Rush, Benjamin. *Autobiography of Benjamin Rush*. Edited by George W. Corner. Princeton, N.J.: Princeton University Press, 1948.

Ryan, Mary P. *The Empire of the Mother*. New York: The Institute for Research in History and the Haworth Press, 1982.

Samuels, Shirley, ed. *The Culture of Sentiment: Race, Gender, and Sentimentality in 19th Century America*. New York: Oxford University Press, 1992.

Satterlee, Herbert L. *J. Pierpont Morgan: An Intimate Portrait*. New York: Macmillan, 1939.

Sawyer, Leicester Ambrose. *The New Testament, Translated from the Original Greek*. Boston: John P. Jewett and Company, 1858.

Schaff, Philip. *A Companion to the Greek Testament and English Version*. 4th rev. ed. New York: Harper & Brothers, 1892.

Schama, Simon. *Citizens: A Chronicle of the French Revolution*. New York: Alfred A. Knopf, 1992.

Schlenther, Boyd Stanley. *Charles Thomson: A Patriot's Pursuit*. Newark: University of Delaware Press, 1990.

Schudson, Michael. *Discovering the News: A Social History of American Newspapers*. New York: Basic Books, 1978.

Scott, Walter. *The Gospel Restored: A Discourse of the True Gospel of Jesus Christ*. Cincinnati, Ohio: O. H. Donogh, 1836.

Scudder, Horace E. *Noah Webster*. Boston: Houghton, Mifflin, 1897.

Seale, James M., ed. *Lectures in Honor of the Alexander Campbell Bicentennial, 1788–1988*. Nashville, Tenn.: Disciples of Christ Historical Society, 1988.

Sears Roebuck Catalogue (1897). Edited by Fred L. Israel. New York: Chelsea House, 1968.

The Second Report of the Bible Society Established at Philadelphia. Philadelphia: Fry and Kammerer, 1810.

Seelye, J. H. "The Bible in Schools." *Bibliotheca Sacra* 13:52 (Oct. 1856): 725–743.

Sellers, Charles. *The Market Revolution: Jacksonian America 1815–1846*. New York: Oxford University Press, 1991.

Shaftesbury, Anthony, Earl of. *Characteristics of Men, Manners, Opinions, Times*. 2 vols. Indianapolis, Ind.: Bobbs-Merrill Company, 1964.

Shaw, Richard. *Dagger John: The Unquiet Life and Times of Archbishop John Hughes of New York*. New York: Paulist Press, 1977.

Shea, John Gilmary. "The Bible in American History." *American Catholic Quarterly Review* 3 (1878): 131–150.

Sheehan, Donald. *This Was Publishing: A Chronicle of the Book Trade in the Gilded Age*. Bloomington: Indiana University Press, 1952.

Shepherd, Naomi. *Zealous Intruders: The Western Rediscovery of Palestine*. New York: Harper & Row, 1987.

Sher, Richard B., and Jeffrey R. Smitten, eds. *Scotland and America in the Age of Enlightenment*. Edinburgh, Scotland: Edinburgh University Press, 1990.

Shipps, Jan. *Mormonism: The Story of a New Religious Tradition*. Chicago: University of Illinois Press, 1985.

Shipton, Clifford K. *Isaiah Thomas: Printer, Patriot and Philanthropist, 1749–1831*. Rochester, N.Y.: The Printing House of Leo Hart, 1948.

247

Silver, Rollo G. *The American Printer: 1787–1825*. Charlottesville: University of Virginia, 1967.

Simms, Paris Marion. *The Bible in America: Versions That Have Played Their Part in the Making of the Republic*. New York: Wilson-Erickson, 1936.

The Sixth Report of the Bible Society Established at Philadelphia. Philadelphia: Fry and Kammerer, 1814.

Skeel, Smily Ellsworth Ford, ed. *Mason Locke Weems: Letters*, 3 vols. New York: Privately published by the author, 1929.

Slee, Jacquelynn. "A Summary of the English Editions of Illustrated Bibles Published in America between 1790 and 1825, with Indices of Subjects Illustrated and Engravers." Master's thesis, University of Michigan, 1973.

Smith, Adam. *Adam Smith's Moral and Political Philosophy*. Edited by Herbert W. Schneider. New York: Hafner, 1948.

Smith, Ethan. *View of the Hebrews: or, the Tribes of Israel in America*. 2nd ed. Poultney, Vt.: Smith & Shute, 1825.

Smith, Jeffrey A. *Printers and Press Freedom: The Ideology of Early American Journalism*. New York: Oxford University Press, 1988.

Smith, Joseph, Jr. *The Book of Mormon: An Account Written by the Hand of Mormon, Upon Plates Taken from the Plates of Nephi*. Palmyra, N.Y.: E. B. Grandin, 1830.

———. *History of the Church of Jesus Christ of Latter-Day Saints*, 7 vols. 2nd rev. ed. Salt Lake City, Utah: Deseret, 1963.

———, trans. *The Holy Scriptures*. N.p.: Church of Jesus Christ of Latter-Day Saints, 1867.

Smith, Nila Banton. *American Reading Instruction*. Newark, Del.: International Reading Association, 1965.

Smith, Timothy L. "Protestant Schooling and American Nationality, 1800–1850." *Journal of American History* 53:4 (March 1967): 679–695.

Smith, Wilson, ed. *Theories of Education in Early America 1655–1819*. Indianapolis: Bobbs-Merrill, 1973.

Smith-Rosenberg, Caroll. "The Female Animal: Medical and Biological Views of Woman and Her Role in Nineteenth-Century America." *Journal of American History* 60:2 (Sept. 1973): 332–356.

Soltow, Lee, and Edward Stevens. *The Rise of Literacy and the Common School in the United States*. Chicago: University of Chicago Press, 1981.

Spann, Edward K. *The New Metropolis: New York City, 1840–1857*. New York: Columbia University Press, 1981.

Starobinski, Jean, Philippe Duboy, Akiko Fukai, Jun I. Kanai, Toshio Horii, Janet Arnold, and Martin Kamer. *Revolution in Fashion: European Clothing 1715–1815*. New York: Abbeville, 1989.

Stein, Stephen J. "America's Bibles: Canon, Commentary, and Community." *Church History* 64:2 (June 1995): 169–184.

Steinberg, Sigfrid H. *Five Hundred Years of Printing*. London: Faber and Faber, 1959.

Stocks, Hugh Grant. "The Book of Mormon, 1830–1879: A Publishing History." Master's thesis, University of California, Los Angeles, 1979.

——. "The Book of Mormon in English, 1870–1920: A Publishing History and Analytical Bibliography." Diss., University of California, Los Angeles, 1986.

Stoddard, Roger E. "The Morphology and the Book from an American Perspective." *Printing History* 9:1 (1987): 2–14.

Stokes, Anson Phelps. *Church and State in the United States.* 3 vols. New York: Harper & Brothers, 1950.

Stout, Harry, ed. *Dictionary of Christianity in America.* Downers Grove, Ill.: InterVarsity Press, 1990.

——. *New England Soul: Preaching and Religious Culture in Colonial New England.* New York: Oxford University Press, 1986.

Stowe, Harriet Beecher. *Uncle Tom's Cabin; or, Life Among the Lowly.* 2 vols. Boston: John P. Jewett, 1852.

Strickland, William P. *History of the American Bible Society, from Its Organization to the Present Time.* New York: Harper & Brothers, 1849.

Stuart, Moses. *Sermon at the Ordination of the Rev. William G. Schauffler as Missionary to the Jews, Boston: Nov. 14, 1831.* 3rd ed. Boston: Crocker & Brewster, 1845.

Sweet, Leonard I., ed. *Communication & Change in American Religious History.* Grand Rapids, Mich.: William B. Eerdmans, 1993.

Taylor, Alan. "The Early Republic's Supernatural Economy: Treasure Seeking in the American Northeast, 1780–1830." *American Quarterly* 38 (Spring 1986): 6–34.

Taylor, Charles. *Sources of the Self: The Making of the Modern Identity.* Cambridge: Harvard University Press, 1989.

Taylor, Francis Henry. *Pierpont Morgan: As Collector and Patron, 1837–1913.* New York: The Pierpont Morgan Library, 1957.

Taylor, George Rogers. *The Transportation Revolution 1815–1860.* New York: Harper & Row, 1951.

Tebbel, John. *The American Magazine: A Compact History.* New York: Hawthorn, 1969.

——. *A History of Book Publishing in the United States.* 4 vols. New York: R. R. Bowker, 1972.

Theisen, Lee Scott. "'My God, Did I set all of this in Motion?' General Lew Wallace and *Ben-Hur*." *Journal of Popular Culture* 18:2 (Fall, 1984): 33–41.

The Third Report of the Bible Society Established at Philadelphia. Philadelphia: Fry and Kammerer, 1811.

Thomas, Benjamin Franklin. *Memoir of Isaiah Thomas.* Boston: Published privately, 1874.

Thomas, Cecil K. *Alexander Campbell and His New Version.* St. Louis, Mo.: The Bethany Press, 1958.

Thomas, George M. *Revivalism and Cultural Change: Christianity, Nation Building, and the Market in the Nineteenth-Century United States.* Chicago: University of Chicago Press, 1989.

Thomas, Isaiah. "The Diary of Isaiah Thomas 1805–1828." In *Transactions and Collections of the American Antiquarian Society.* Vols. 9–10. Worcester, Mass.: American Antiquarian Society, 1909.

———. *The History of Printing in America*. 2nd ed. Edited by Marcus McCorison. New York: Weathervane Books, 1970.

———. *Three Autobiographical Fragments*. Worcester, Mass.: American Antiquarian Society, 1812.

Thomson, Charles, trans. *The Holy Bible*. Philadelphia: Jane Aitken, 1808.

———, ed. *A Synopsis of the Four Evangelists*. Philadelphia: Wm. M'Culloch, 1815.

Thomson, William McClure. *The Land and the Book*. 3 vols. New York: Harper and Brothers, 1880.

Thuesen, Peter J. "Some Scripture Is Inspired by God: Late-Nineteenth-Century Protestants and the Demise of the Common Bible." *Church History* 65:4 (Dec. 1996): 609–623.

Todd, Janet. *Sensibility: An Introduction*. New York: Methuen, 1986.

Tompkins, Jane. *Sensational Designs: The Cultural Work of American Fiction, 1790–1860*. New York: Oxford University Press, 1986.

Trench, Richard Chenevix. *On the Authorized Version of the New Testament in Connection with some Recent Proposals for its Revision*. New York: Redfield, 1858.

Turner, James. *Without God, Without Creed: The Origins of Unbelief in America*. Baltimore, Md.: The Johns Hopkins University Press, 1985.

Underwood, Grant. "Book of Mormon Usage in Early LDS Theology." *Dialogue: A Journal of Mormon Thought* 17:3 (Aut. 1984): 35–74.

———. *The Millenarian World of Early Mormonism*. Chicago: University of Illinois Press, 1993.

Van Doren, Carl. *The American Novel: 1789–1939*. New York: Macmillan, 1940.

Vinovskis, Maris A., and Richard M. Bernard. "Beyond Catharine Beecher: Female Education in the Antebellum Period." *Signs* 3:4 (Summer 1978): 856–869.

Vogel, Dan. *Religious Seekers and the Advent of Mormonism*. Salt Lake City, Utah: Signature Books, 1988.

Vogel, Lester I. *To See a Promised Land: Americans and the Holy Land in the Nineteenth Century*. University Park: Pennsylvania State University Press, 1993.

Wakefield, Gilbert. *A Translation of the New Testament*. Cambridge, Mass.: The University Press, by Hilliard and Metcalf, 1820.

Wallace, Lew. *Ben-Hur: A Tale of the Christ*. New York: Harper & Brothers, 1899.

———. *Lew Wallace: An Autobiography*. New York: Harper & Brothers, 1906.

Walker, Edward. *The Art of Book-Binding: Its Rise and Progress*. New Castle: Oak Knoll Books, 1984.

Warner, Michael. *The Letters of the Republic: Publication and the Public Sphere in Eighteenth-Century America*. Cambridge: Harvard University Press, 1990.

Weathersby, Robert W., II. *J. H. Ingraham*. Boston: Twayne Publishers, 1980.

Webster, Noah, ed. *The Holy Bible*. New Haven, Conn.: Durrie & Peck, 1833.

Weitenkempf, Frank. "American Bible Illustration." *The Boston Public Library Quarterly* 3 (July 1958): 154–157.

Welter, Rush. *American Writings on Popular Education: The Nineteenth Century*. Indianapolis: Bobbs-Merrill, 1971.

Westcott, Brooke Foss, and Fenton John Anthony Hort. *The New Testament in the Original Greek*. New York: Harper & Brothers, 1882.

Where the Old and the New Versions Differ. New York: Anson D. F. Randolf, 1881.

Wilbur, Earl Morse Wilbur. *A History of Unitarianism*. 2 vols. Boston: Beacon, 1945.

Williams, Daniel Day. *The Andover Liberals: A Study in American Theology*. Morningside Heights, N.Y.: King's Crown, 1941.

Williams, E. F. "Recent Lives of Christ." *Bibliotheca Sacra* 63:170 (1886): 221–238.

Williams, George Huntston, ed. *The Harvard Divinity School: Its Place in Harvard University and in American Culture*. Boston: Beacon, 1954.

Williams, Henry T., and C. S. Jones. *Beautiful Homes*. New York: Henry T. Williams, 1878.

Wills, Gary. *Inventing America: Jefferson's Declaration of Independence*. New York: Vintage Books, 1978.

———. *Lincoln at Gettysburg: The Words That Remade America*. New York: Simon & Schuster, 1992.

———. "Mason Weems, Bibliopolist." *American Heritage* 32:2 (Feb./Mar. 1981): 66–69.

Wilson, Derek. *The People and the Book*. London: Barrie & Jenkins, 1976.

Wilson, John Albert. *Signs and Wonders upon Pharoah: A History of American Egyptology*. Chicago: University of Chicago Press, 1964.

Winter, J. Gould, and John Winter. *The Claims of the American & Foreign Bible Society, Maintained & Vindicated*. Warren, Ohio: William J. Tait, 1845.

Winthrop, Robert C., et al. "September Meeting." *Proceedings of the Massachusetts Historical Society* 8 (1864–1865): 442–462.

Winship, Michael. *Ticknor and Fields*. Chapel Hill, N.C.: Hanes Foundation, 1992.

Wishy, Bernard. *The Child and the Republic: The Dawn of Modern American Child Nurture*. Philadelphia: University of Pennsylvania Press, 1968.

Wolf, Edwin, II. *From Gothic Windows to Peacocks: American Embossed Leather Bindings, 1825–1855*. Philadelphia, Penn.: Library Company of Philadelphia, 1990.

Wood, Gordon S. *The Radicalism of the American Revolution*. New York: Alfred A. Knopf, 1992.

Wosh, Peter J. *Spreading the Word: The Bible Business in Nineteenth-Century America*. Ithaca, N.Y.: Cornell University Press, 1994.

Wright, Conrad Edick, ed. *American Unitarianism 1805–1865*. Boston: Massachusetts Historical Society and Northeastern University Press, 1989.

Wright, John. *Historic Bibles in America*. New York: Thomas Whittaker, 1905.

Wright, Paul. *The New and Complete Life of Our Blessed Lord and Savior Jesus Christ*. Philadelphia: Tertius Dunning and Walter W. Hyer, 1795.

———. *The New and Complete Life of Our Blessed Lord and Savior Jesus Christ*. New York: William Durell, 1803.

Wroth, Lawrence C. *The Colonial Printer*. Portland, Maine: Southworth-Anthoensen, 1938.

Wyckoff, William. H., and C. A. Buckbee, eds. *Documentary History of the American Bible Union*. 4 vols. New York: American Bible Union, 1857–66.

———. *A Sketch of the Origin and Some Particulars of the History of the Most Eminent Bible Societies*. New York: Lewis Colby, 1847.

Yalom, Marilyn. *A History of the Breast*. New York: Alfred A. Knopf, 1997.

Yeatman, Joseph Lawrence. "Literary Culture and the Role of Libraries in Democratic America: Baltimore, 1815–1840." *Journal of Library History* 20:4 (Fall 1985): 345–367.

Zafran, Eric M. *The Rococo Age: French Masterpieces of the Eighteenth Century*. Atlanta: High Museum of Art, 1983.

Zboray, Ronald J. *A Fictive People: Antebellum Economic Development and the American Reading Public*. New York: Oxford University Press, 1993.

Zboray, Ronald J., and Mary Saracino Zboray. "Books, Reading, and the World of Goods in Antebellum New England. *American Quarterly* 48:4 (Dec. 1996): 587–622.

Zerah: The Believing Jew. New York: New York Protestant Episcopal Press, 1837.

Index

In this index an "f" after a number indicates a separate reference on the next page, and an "ff" indicates separate references on the next two pages. A continuous discussion over two or more pages is indicated by a span of page numbers, e.g., "57–59." *Passim* is used for a cluster of references in close but not consecutive sequence.

Library of Congress Cataloging-in-Publication Data

Gutjahr, Paul C.
    An American Bible : a history of the Good Book
in the United States / Paul C. Gutjahr.
        p.   cm.
    Includes bibliographical references and index.
    ISBN 0-8047-3425-9 (alk. paper)
    1. Bible—United States—History—18th century.
2. Bible—United States—History—19th century.
3. Bible—Publication and distribution—United States—
History—18th century.   4. Bible—Publication and
distribution—United States—History—19th century.
I. Title.
BS447.5.U6G88   1999   98-37396
220'.0973—dc21   98-37396

⊚   This book is printed on acid-free, recycled paper.

Original printing 1999

Last figure below indicates year of this printing:
08   07   06   05   04   03   02   01   00